THE 21ST CENTURY TEACHERS' GUIDE TO RECOMMENDED INTERNET SITES

MARVIN DIGEORGIO AND SYLVIA LESAGE

NEAL-SCHUMAN NETGUIDE SERIES

NEAL-SCHUMAN PUBLISHERS, INC.
NEW YORK LONDON

Published by Neal-Schuman Publishers, Inc.
100 Varick Street
New York, NY 10013

Don't miss the companion Web site that accompanies this book! See preface for details!

The paper used in this publication meets the minimum requirements of American National Standard for Information Sciences—Permanence of Paper for Printed Library Materials, ANSI Z39, 48–1992.

Library of Congress Cataloging-in-Publication Data

DiGeorgio, Marvin.
The 21st century teachers' guide to recommended Internet sites / Marvin DiGeorgio, Sylvia Lesage.
p. cm. — (Neal-Schuman NetGuide series)
ISBN 1-55570-401-8 (alk. paper)
1. Computer network resources—Directories. 2. Web sites—Directories. 3. World Wide Web—Directories. I. Title: Twenty-first century teachers' guide to recommended Internet sites. II. Lesage, Sylvia. III. Title. IV. Neal-Schuman net-guide series.

ZA4201 .D54 2001
025.04—dc21 00-058412

DEDICATION

To Sandy and Rosalie
With love

Contents

List of Figures

Preface

Although the potential value of the Internet for promoting learning is indisputable, research shows that this tool is still not used nearly to its potential in our education systems. Most teachers are simply too busy to spend the many extra research hours needed to discover the most useful sites on the Internet; many are forced to give up long before they can utilize the true power of the Internet.

We designed this guide to help teachers reduce their workload while at the same time facilitate easier learning for their students. How is that possible? Through the power of the Internet, teachers can now access and share countless resources including thousands of pre-made lesson plans, excellent multimedia tools which promote independent learning, interactive lessons for students, and a wealth of other easily accessible resources for hundreds of different topics and subject areas. You only need to know where to look for them.

The 21st Century Teachers' Guide to Recommended Internet Sites is a practical Internet guide designed to help teachers and students discover an amazing selection of educational sites from around the world. More than four hundred sites are described and organized by academic discipline. These sites offer links to thousands of other educational sites on the Internet. By using the links provided in this guide and on the accompanying CD-ROM, teachers and learners at all levels and in all academic disciplines can navigate the Web effortlessly, without having to spend valuable time following links that too often lead to irrelevant or dead-end sites.

Each site has been carefully selected for usefulness of content, practical value for time spent, and, of course, ease of access. Many sites are classified according to academic levels as well, so teachers won't need to hunt around to match lessons with levels. All sites chosen were also selected for stability and reliability. They have been consistently updated.

Let's take a look at what you will find in this guide and more importantly what is available on the Internet. As a teacher or learner at any level, you can access the collective knowledge and shared resources of teachers, scientists, mathematicians, and countless other academics throughout the world who have generously contributed their work to be shared with others. You will find the latest facts and information on virtually any topic.

Each chapter of the guide shows the best available sites for teachers and students in each field of study. For example Chapter One, *Arts,* includes addresses for sites dealing with all standard areas of art such as drawing, painting, sculpting, photography and so forth. Teachers will find links to lesson plans, helpful tips for teaching, virtual tours of art museums, art dictionaries, interactive online lessons, and many other practical resources for teaching. There are similar resources in related areas of the arts, including dance, music, architecture, filmmaking, and even lesser known art forms such as origami.

Chapter Two is a treasure chest for teachers and students of business. It includes sites that contain excellent resources in the areas of accounting, general business, tax preparation, financial management, entrepreneurship, and many other areas of business. Teachers will find easy-to-use lesson plans, sample quizzes, business news, management tips, and even complete courses to model in any business classroom.

Succeeding chapters cover other disciplines: computing, education, English and ESL, foreign languages, health and physical education, math, sciences, social studies and social sciences. Each chapter is similarly organized so that hundreds of excellent resources are available in virtually all academic disciplines with a few clicks of a mouse. Teachers no longer have to spend valuable preparation time scanning expensive textbooks or searching the Web for useful educational resources. By using the resources referred to in this guide, teachers can often plan better lessons more easily and more efficiently than by using only conventional methods.

You can save even more time (and even have a little bit of fun) by following the links on the CD-ROM to access thousands of pre-made lesson plans, classroom tips, online exercises and sample tests, as well as the latest information and developments in your field available to print or to direct students to for study online.

Once you have looked over the descriptions given for each site, you will likely want to take a first-hand look at what is really waiting for you on the Internet.

Insert the accompanying CD-ROM into your drive, launch the Index HTML, and click on your favorite choices. For more information on using the CD-ROM, please refer to the next section entitled "How to Use This CD-ROM."

An outstanding addition to this guide is the follow-up feature. We are committed to providing the best possible service to users, and therefore will provide frequent updates of links on our Website well into the future. This feature will greatly increase the lifespan of this guide by continuously providing readers with up-do-date links whenever Websites included in the guide change their address. Just type in the following address and follow the links: *http://teachersguide.homepage.com.*

The authors would like to thank the creators, designers, and maintainers of all the educational Websites contained in this guide, firstly, for offering their educational resources in the public domain, and secondly for granting us permissions to use graphics from their pages. We would particularly like to thank Kathy Schrock and Patricia Carnabuci for their helpful and always prompt responses to our requests.

For questions, updates, recommendations, and reactions to this guide, or to report any bad links, please contact us by e-mail at the following address:

degeorgio_2000@yahoo.ca

We, the writers of this guide, along with the editors and staff at Neal-Schuman Publishers wish you many happy hours of learning and teaching.

Marvin DiGeorgio
Sylvia Lesage

How to Use This CD-ROM

The CD-ROM that accompanies the *21st Century Teachers' Guide to Recommended Internet Sites* has been included to help you navigate the Web easily and find resources even faster.

To use it, just follow the easy procedure below. Later we'll show you how to put all the sites in your own Bookmarks or Favorites, so you don't have to use the CD-ROM each time.

Follow these steps:

1) Insert the CD-ROM into your CD-drive.
2) Go to your "Start" menu and select the "run" feature.
3) Type in the letter for your CD-drive (normally "D") followed by a colon, (D:), and then click "OK."
4) Click on the "INDEX" icon. (This will launch your Internet Explorer or Netscape offline to read the index.)
5) Click on the academic section you want.
6) Click on the specific bookmark of the site you want. (This will signal your Internet Explorer or Netscape browser to go online and take you directly to the selected site on the Internet.)

To change sites, return to the CD-ROM and click on another selection. Return to the index file on the CD-ROM by clicking "Back to the Index" at the bottom of each page.

That's all there is to it!

HOW TO IMPORT FAVORITES FOR INTERNET EXPLORER

Here's a fairly easy way to copy all the educational sites into your Internet Explorer's Favorites. You'll only have to do this once, so don't panic if it looks difficult. It will save you a lot of time in the future.

Just follow the steps below.

1. Open the CD-ROM folder as explained above and double click on the "21st Century Teachers' Guide" folder to open it.
2. Next, right-click on the folder called "Internet Explorer Favorites" and click on "COPY."
3. Open the C-Drive on your computer, and select "Windows." (Don't worry about the warning shown in red. You won't be changing anything that will affect your computer's operation.)
4. Click on "Show Files" and you will see all your Windows files.
5. Select the "Favorites" folder, and then right-click with your mouse to "PASTE" the new bookmarks in the window's folder.
6. Close all the windows and open Internet Explorer to see your new favorites.

HOW TO IMPORT BOOKMARKS FOR NETSCAPE NAVIGATOR

(Not recommended unless you don't mind replacing the Bookmarks you have.) You may be better off to just add each bookmark individually as you visit the sites you like.

But, if Netscape is your browser of choice, and you want to import the Teachers' Guide bookmarks anyway, here is how to do it. Again this is a one-time-only procedure so don't despair if it seems a bit complicated.

Follow these steps.

1. Open Netscape.
2. Click on "Bookmarks."
3. Click on "Edit Bookmarks."

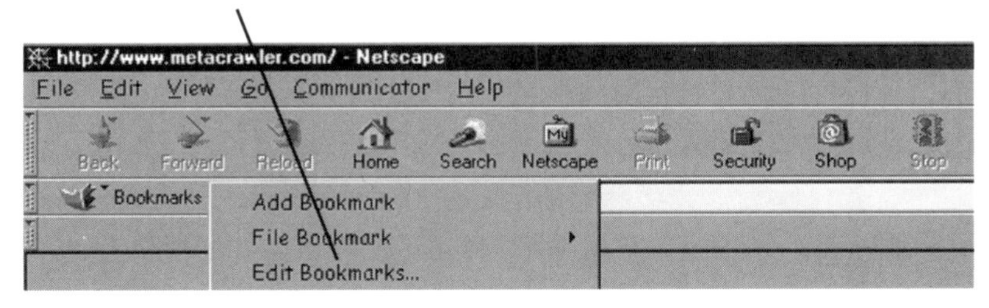

Once you are there:

4. At the top of your screen, click on "File."

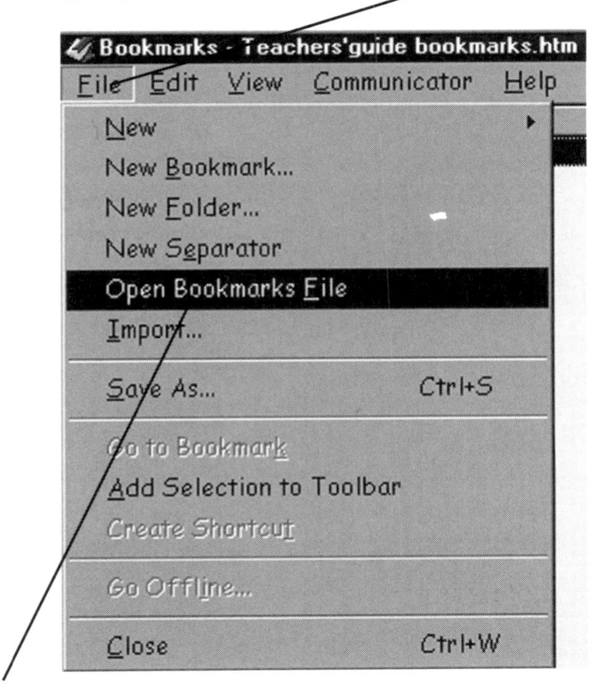

5. Select "Open Bookmarks File."

What you want now is to return to your CD-ROM drive. One easy way is to click a few times on the yellow folder shown here to go up several levels to find "My Computer." (It should be five or six clicks, depending on the setup in your computer.)

Once there, click on your CD-ROM folder to open it.

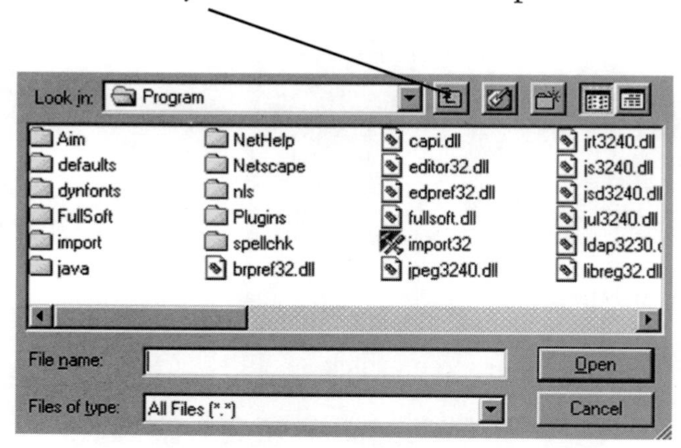

Okay, you've opened your CD-ROM drive.

1) Now double click on the "21st Century Teachers' Guide" folder.
2) Double click on "Favorites-Bookmarks."
3) Double click on "Netscape Bookmarks."
4) Double click on "Netscape Teachers' Guide Bookmarks."
5) Close the window to return to Netscape.

Voila, you should now have your bookmarks!

After you have imported all the bookmarks, you will have a menu like this one showing all the subject areas. Follow the arrows to specific sites in your subject area.

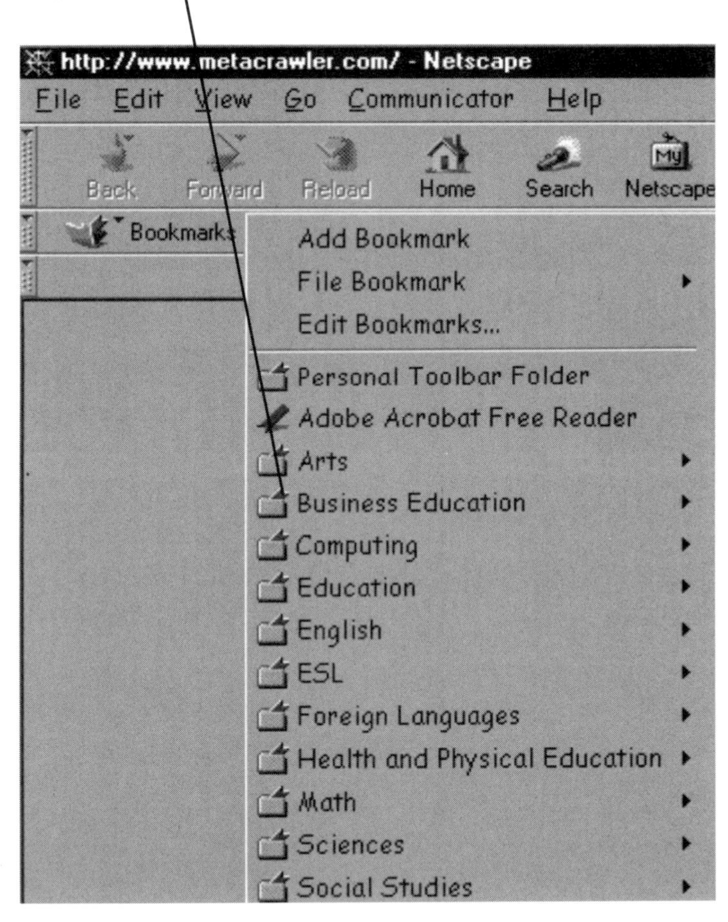

That's about all there is to it. Enjoy the sites.

Chapter 1

Arts

Since "Art" implies a wide range of subject areas from painting to music to dance to architecture, we have included sites with a good variety of resources, so that whatever your field in the arts, there should be something to help make your teaching or learning easier and more interesting. The sites selected in this section contain lesson plans, graphic illustrations, audio-visual materials, and a wealth of other resources for elementary to advanced level learning. Happy browsing!

CHAPTER OVERVIEW

ARTS

ArtLex—dictionary of visual art
www.artlex.com/

This is an excellent site (see Fig. 1.1) for artists, students, historians, critics, and educators in the field of art.

In this site, you will find definitions of more than 3,300 terms relating to visual arts, along with numerous images, pronunciation notes, great quotations, and links to other resources on the Web.
Advanced levels.

AskERIC Lesson Plans: Arts
http://ericir.syr.edu/Virtual/Lessons/Arts/index.html

This site is a gem for teachers and learners who are seeking information or answers to questions concerning almost any area of the arts. Teachers at any level will find pre-made lesson plans, which are sure to make teaching art, art history, music, or architecture easier and more fun. Levels K–12. Independent learners will be able to save hours of research by simply asking the art-related questions that they want answered. It's like having your own personal tutor.

Below is a summary of topics from the AskERIC Website.

- Architecture
- Art Activities
- Art History
- Music

Got an education question? If you are an educator, librarian, parent, or anyone interested in education, AskERIC's Q&A Service can help! Utilizing the diverse resources and expertise of the national ERIC System, AskERIC staff will respond to your question within two business days with ERIC database citations and publications, Internet resources, and referrals to other sources of information. AskERIC responds to *every* question with personalized resources relevant to *your* needs.

Also includes a SEARCH element, which allows users to search for lessons and resources on a specific topic.

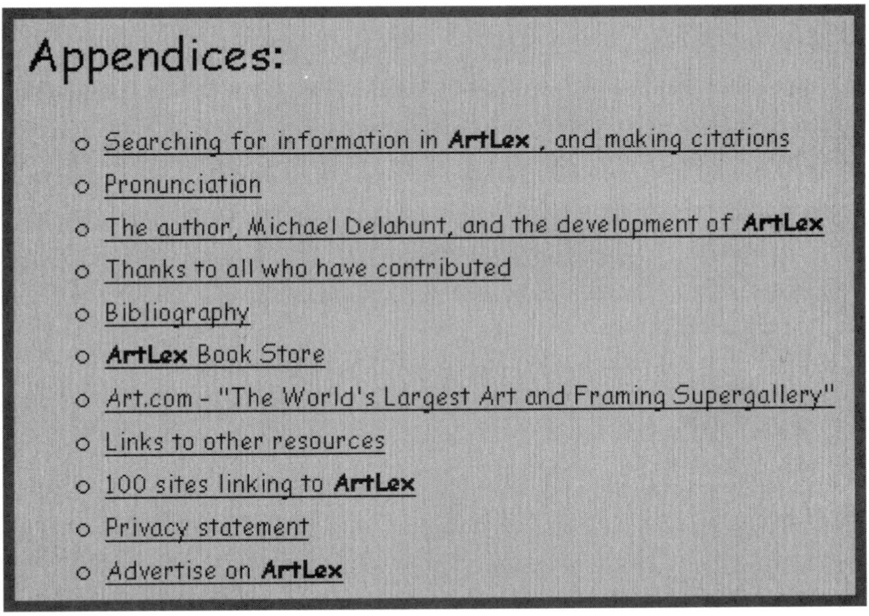

Appendices:

- Searching for information in **ArtLex**, and making citations
- Pronunciation
- The author, Michael Delahunt, and the development of **ArtLex**
- Thanks to all who have contributed
- Bibliography
- **ArtLex** Book Store
- Art.com - "The World's Largest Art and Framing Supergallery"
- Links to other resources
- 100 sites linking to **ArtLex**
- Privacy statement
- Advertise on **ArtLex**

Fig. 1.1 Follow the links shown in the image for information, pronunciation tips and links to more resources.

Canada's SchoolNet: Learning Resources

www.schoolnet.ca/home/e/resources/Links_Result_e.asp?SUBJECT=2

This site (see Fig. 1.2) contains resources and lesson plans in the areas listed below as well as links to many related sites. Many lesson plans indicate K–12 grade-level appropriateness and include pre-made tests.

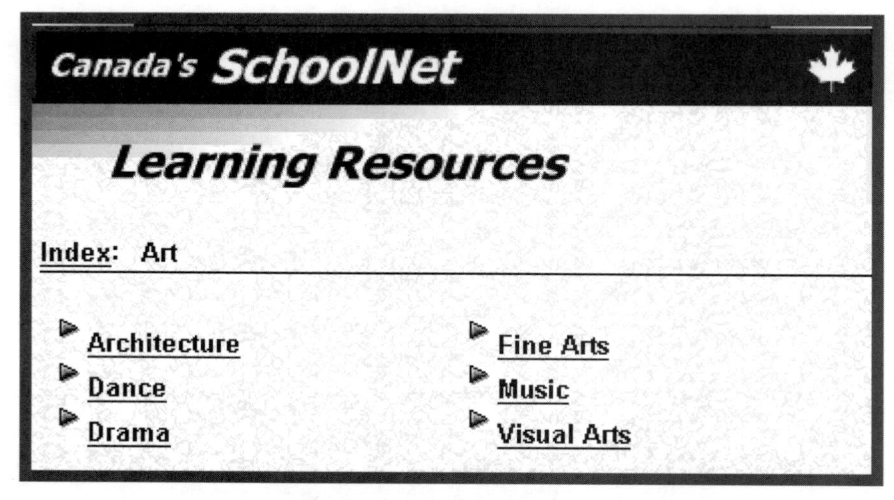

Fig. 1.2. Choose your academic area from the list shown in the image.
Used by permission

Included as well are biographies of famous artists, architects and musicians, and many links to exhibits and museums.

Bilingual, English and French.

CLN WWW Navigation Map
www.cln.org/map.html#FA

This is a wonderful site for teachers, students, and parents alike. It contains curriculum resources and instructional materials at the K–12 level. Subject areas include arts, crafts, dance, drama, theatre, and music. It also contains an easy to use index and loads of materials including somewhat less conventional art forms such as origami, puppetry, and cartoons.

Curricular Resources in:

- Art
- Arts and Crafts
- Dance
- Drama and Theatre
- Music

Instructional Materials in:

- Art

- Arts and Crafts
- Dance
- Drama
- Music

Theme Page:
- Art History
- Bubbles
- Careers in the Arts
- Celebrating Women
- Clip Art
- Drawing Cartoons
- Famous Canadians
- Hot Air Balloons
- Improv
- Kites
- Masks
- Origami
- Paper Airplanes
- Publish Your Creative Work On-Line
- Puppetry
- Simple Flying Machines
- Soaps and Soap Making
- Songs for Children
- Sound
- Stained Glass

Education World®—Arts & Humanities: Visual Arts: General Resources

http://db.education-world.com/perl/browse?cat_id=1135

Once again, here is truly a top-notch site for resources on visual and performance arts, art history and design. Many related activities and lessons, with excellent resources in conventional and non-conventional art forms.

The list below shows the categories from which you can choose. Levels K–12.

- Associations & Organizations
- Directories & Indices
- Teacher Resources
- Art & Technology

- Art Museums & Galleries
- Arts & Crafts
- Children's Art
- Companies
- Computer Generated
- Conferences
- Contemporary
- Digital Images
- Education Programs
- Film Making
- Illustration
- Magazines & Journals
- Newsgroups & Listservs
- Painting
- Photography
- Printmaking
- School Projects
- Sculpture
- Student Pages

Educational Resources in Fine Arts
www.cln.org/subjects/fine.html

As the site title indicates, this site is full of resources specifically designed for use within an educational setting, and containing a variety of well-thought-out lesson plans and teaching tips/ideas for Fine Arts teachers. As well, you will find some excellent galleries and theme pages. Levels K–12.

Choose your topic from the following curricular resources or instructional materials:

- Arts
- Arts & Crafts
- Dance
- Drama and Theatre
- Music

You can also choose from the many theme pages at the site.

Theme pages

- Art History
- Bubbles

- Careers in the Arts
- Celebrating Women
- Clip Art
- Drawing Cartoons
- Famous Canadians
- [Model] Hot Air Balloons
- Improv
- Kites
- Masks
- Origami
- Paper Airplanes
- Pictures
- Publish Your Creative Works On-Line
- Puppetry
- Soap Making
- Songs for Children
- Sound
- Stained Glass

Free Education: Art
www.free-ed.net/fr06/fr0601.htm

Free-Ed's exclusive online guides (see Fig. 1.3) are designed to help students get onto the right learning path and stay focused until they reach their goals. Designed primarily as an online virtual university, the resources are valuable for teachers as a resource for ideas and lessons as well as for students and independent learners to learn new skills or to reinforce those previously taught. The following list indicates the content areas. Some parts are still being developed, so at times you may have to be patient. Despite that, the site contains many useful resources, and is well worth visiting.
Advanced levels.

- Aesthetics: or, The Science of Beauty
- Art Recreations
- Art's True Mission in America
- Classics (not interactive)
- Course Outlines, Lecture
- Courses and Tutorials
- Elements of Art Criticism
- Helpful Study Materials
- Interactive Textbooks and References

Free Online Textbooks and Reference Works

Aesthetics: or, The Science of Beauty
John Bascom

Elements of Art Criticism
G. W. Samson

Lectures on Art, and Poems
Washington Allston

Art's True Mission in America
A. J. H. Duganne

The Retrospect of an Artist's Life
John Kelso Hunter

Knights of Art: Stories of the Italian Painters
Amy Steedman

Art Recreations
Levina Buoncuore Urbino

Fig. 1.3. Topics from the online textbook and reference works available at the Free-Ed site.

- Italian Painters
- Knights of Art
- Lectures on Art and Poems
- Notes, Quizzes, Etc.
- The Retrospect of an Artist's Life

K–12 Lesson Plans

http://teams.lacoe.edu/documentation/places/lessons.html#arts

Another gem filled with resources for teachers at the K–12 level. It contains excellent lesson plans for use in the classroom, many which are updated weekly. On a few of the linked sites, there are other subject areas included so you may need to scroll down a bit to find your specific interest, but it's well worth the few seconds of time it will take.

Check out the following resources and links on this site:

- Art and Music Lessons
- Art Lesson Plans
- Art Teacher Connections
- Encarta Fine Arts Lessons Plans
- Incredible Art Department Favorite Lessons
- Jarea Kinder Art
- Origami
- Teachnet.com Lesson Plans
- The Arts
- The Drama Teacher's Resource Room
- The Fine Arts Museum of San Francisco Teacher Guides

Kathy Schrock's Guide for Educators—Art & Architecture
http://discoveryschool.com/schrockguide/arts/artarch.html

We are not sure how she does it, but Kathy Schrock, at The Discovery Channel Site, consistently provides some of the best educational resources on the web. You will find this and the following section full of useful resources, from Kindergarten to advanced levels. You may want to tell your colleagues about the sites in other academic disciplines as well after checking out Kathy Schrock's home page.

- Art & Architecture

Kathy Schrock's Guide for Educators—Performing Arts
http://school.discovery.com/schrockguide/arts/artp.html

As the title suggests, this site will take you to resources in the performing arts and it also contains a good instrument encyclopedia, and Mojo's Magic Mouseum, a wonderful kid's resource site filled with songs, games, and activities for primary and elementary grades. And that's not all. How about American Sheet Music between 1870 and 1885 for a twist? Check out the top hits of the era and click near the top of the page to view actual images of the sheet music. There are also audio links for added realism.

Levels K–12.

- Music for the nation: American Sheet Music, 1870–1885 consists of over 47,000 pieces of sheet music registered for copyright during the years 1870 to 1885. Included are popular songs, piano music, sacred and secular choral music, solo instrumental music, method books and instructional materials, and music for band and orchestra.
- Performing Arts: Dance, Music and Drama

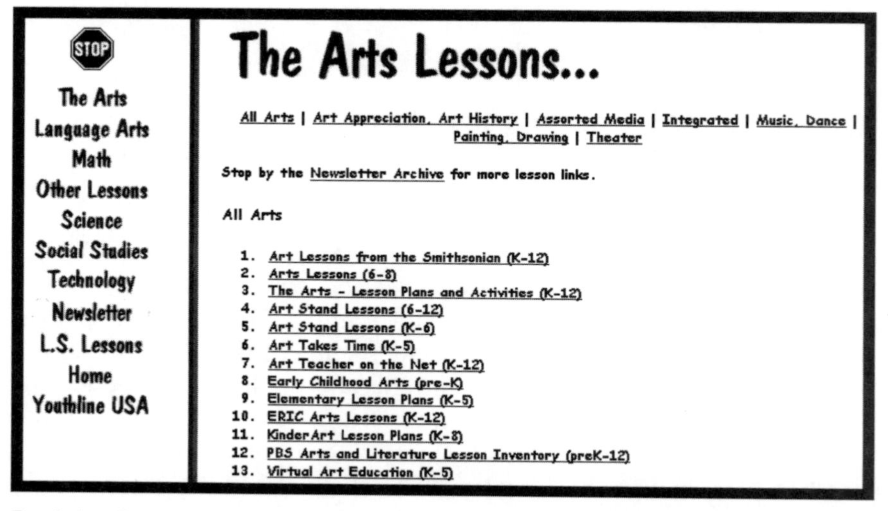

Fig. 1.4 Click on the topics shown near the top of the screen capture for specific areas, or go straight to the lessons and select your grade level and subject. *Copyright © 1998, 1999, 2000 Youthline USA. Used by permission*

Lesson Stop—The Arts

www.youthline-usa.com/lessonstop/art.html

Another excellent site (see Fig. 1.4) containing lessons classified by grade level appropriateness, K–12. Click on the section of your choice as shown in the menu below.

Educators are offered free and unrestricted use of the resources in this site for non-profit purposes.

- All Arts
- Art Appreciation
- Art History
- Assorted Media
- Integrated

- Music and Dance
- Painting and Drawing
- Theater

Online Schoolyard
www.onlineschoolyard.com/

Just click your mouse on the "Arts" button when you get to this site to open up a world of resources and references, at primary to advanced levels. There are two sections to scroll down on the main page, and they are a bit difficult to read, but particularly on the bottom section you'll find excellent resources available in the following areas:

- All About the Artists
- Architecture
- Art History
- Art Resources
- Cartooning
- Classical Music
- Dance
- Fashion
- Film & Video
- Museums
- Photography
- Sculpture
- Theatre
- Visual Arts

The Lesson Plans Page—Art Lesson Plans
www.lessonplanspage.com/Art.htm

Once again a click of your mouse lands you in a wonderland of art lessons classified by grade level. If they don't have what you are looking for, you don't need it.
Pre-K to 12.
Art Lesson Plans for:

- Grades PreK-1
- Grades 2-3
- Grades 4-5
- Grades 6-7
- Junior High & High School
- Multiple Grade Level Applications

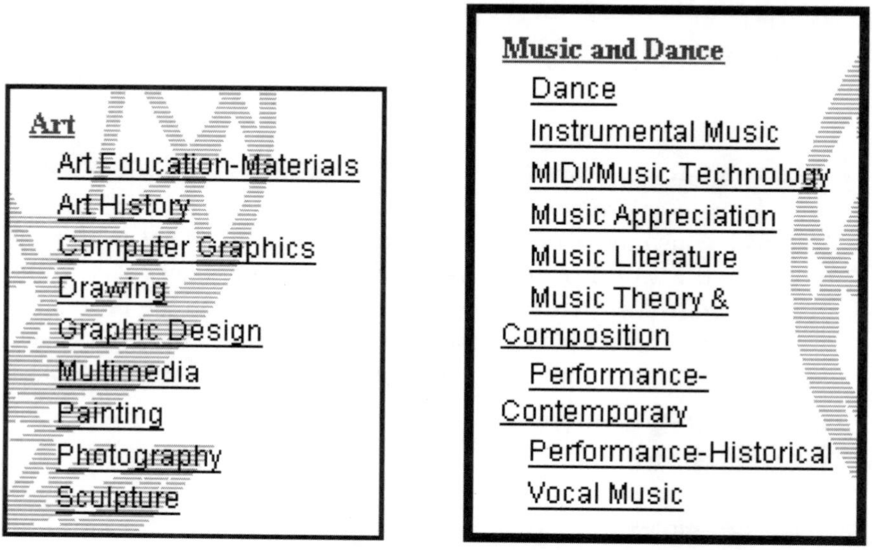

Art
- Art Education-Materials
- Art History
- Computer Graphics
- Drawing
- Graphic Design
- Multimedia
- Painting
- Photography
- Sculpture

Music and Dance
- Dance
- Instrumental Music
- MIDI/Music Technology
- Music Appreciation
- Music Literature
- Music Theory & Composition
- Performance-Contemporary
- Performance-Historical
- Vocal Music

Fig. 1.5–1.6. Click on the titles shown to take you straight to resources and lessons.
Used by permission

Vassar's CoolSchool/Go to Class!!
www.coolschool.edu/goart.htm

A couple of clicks here will land you in the Louvre in Paris or smack in the midst of any of the 15,000 artists listed according to period, medium, and style. More advanced levels here and some commercial art sites with art samples. Good references for students seeking information on specific post-secondary training in the arts, as well.

- Artists
- Exhibits
- Museums
- Music

Fig. 1.7 Follow the links to some very interesting and fun pages.
© Copyright Craig Roland 1996. Used by permission

Welcome to K–12 World!
www.K–12world.net/cy_pages/cy_static/index.htm

Two clicks again get you to another great site (see Fig. 1.5–1.6) filled with art lessons, resources, and links.

K to 12 levels, as the site title indicates.

Click on "ART" and then the area of your interest in the following areas:

- Art Education-Materials
- Art History
- Computer Graphics
- Drawing
- Graphic Design
- Multimedia
- Painting
- Photography
- Sculpture

Welcome to the @rtroom

www.arts.ufl.edu/art/rt_room/@rtroom_home.html

Making art an adventure of discovery for kids seems to be the dominant theme of this site (see Fig. 1.7) and the designers have done a great job of doing that. Visit the various activity rooms for stimulating and fun ideas, which are sure to stimulate all the future Rembrandts and Dalis in your classroom. Includes lots of games and quizzes.

Primary and elementary levels mainly, but also some higher level resources.

WWW Virtual Library: Art History

www.hart.bbk.ac.uk/VirtualLibrary.html

This field covers Art History and computer applications in Art History with a great list of collections and galleries, as well. The author's aim is to list sites relevant to people with a general interest in the subject as well as to students and scholars of Art History. You won't be disappointed with your visit here.

Advanced levels.

- Art History organizations
- Conferences, etc.
- Directories—museums listings, phone books, etc.
- Discussion lists (via email)
- Indexes and Large Collections of Art History Resources
- Interdisciplinary Collections
- Large Image Collections
- Libraries
- Online Publications

- Online Teaching Resources
- Other specialized connections
- Research Tools
- Specialist Suppliers (books, slides, etc.)
- University departments
- Virtual Library Specialized Fields

WWW Virtual Library Museums in the USA
www.museumca.org/usa/index.html

If you live in the U.S. and want some information on what's showing at a nearby museum, this is the place to go.

But if you happen to live far away from the museum showing the kind of exhibits you want, you can always take a virtual tour of some great online exhibits.

Chapter 2

Business Education

The following sites offer mostly free resources that will assist both teachers and individuals who wish to improve their knowledge of business. By just clicking once or twice on your mouse, you can access a wealth of resources including lesson plans, simulations, online entrepreneurial advice, accounting resources, research aids, and many other useful tools for teaching and learning. The sites selected are those that consistently offer practical and easy-to-access information so you don't have to spend hours sorting through hundreds of links.

CHAPTER OVERVIEW

ENTREPRENEURSHIP STUDIES pages 27–29

GENERAL BUSINESS EDUCATION pages 30–33

ACCOUNTING

Accounting Lesson Plans and Links

www.angelfire.com/ks/tonyaskinner/acctg.html

This site (see Fig. 2.1) is an excellent place to find primary or supplementary teaching resources and links that are sure to liven up any Business Education classroom. Follow the links to a variety of lesson plans and resources.

All levels.

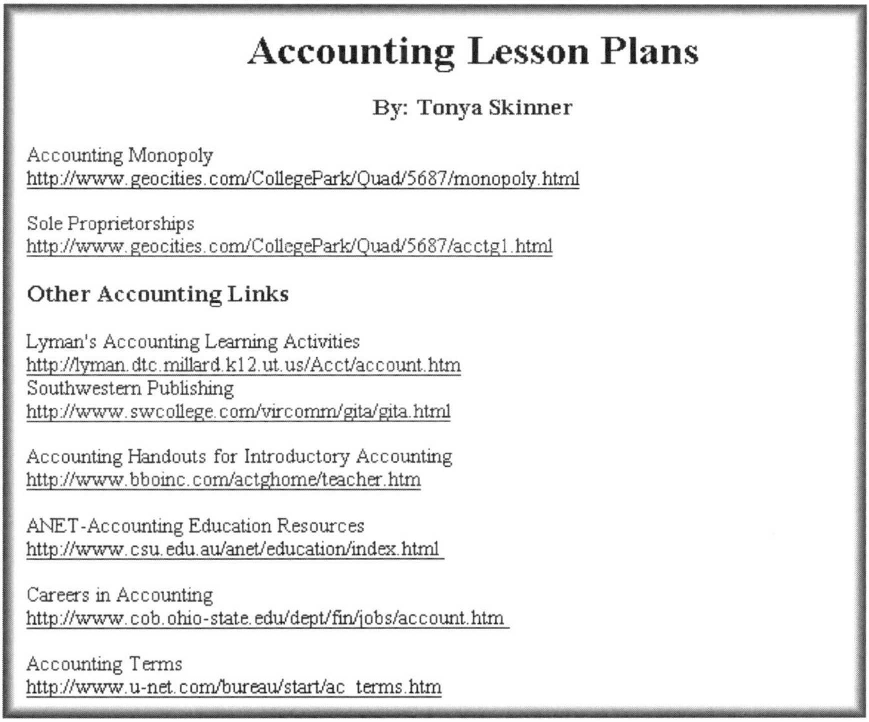

Accounting Lesson Plans

By: Tonya Skinner

Accounting Monopoly
http://www.geocities.com/CollegePark/Quad/5687/monopoly.html

Sole Proprietorships
http://www.geocities.com/CollegePark/Quad/5687/acctg1.html

Other Accounting Links

Lyman's Accounting Learning Activities
http://lyman.dtc.millard.k12.ut.us/Acct/account.htm
Southwestern Publishing
http://www.swcollege.com/vircomm/gita/gita.html

Accounting Handouts for Introductory Accounting
http://www.bboinc.com/actghome/teacher.htm

ANET-Accounting Education Resources
http://www.csu.edu.au/anet/education/index.html

Careers in Accounting
http://www.cob.ohio-state.edu/dept/fin/jobs/account.htm

Accounting Terms
http://www.u-net.com/bureau/start/ac_terms.htm

Fig. 2.1. This image from the Accounting Lesson Plans and Links site shows some of the many available resources.
Used by permission

AICPA

www.aicpa.org/

This site is chalk-full (pun intended) of good resources for teachers, students and practitioners in the field of accounting. The screen capture below (Fig. 2.2) gives you an indication of some of the contents of this frequently updated site. (In fact it updates too fast for our

News for CPAs

- Exposure Draft: Accounting for and Reporting of Certain Health and Welfare Benefit Plan Transactions
- AICPA Views on the IRS Electronic Filing Debt Indicator Program
- Download Exposure Draft for Statement Standards for Continuing Professional Education (CPE)
- NEW! Group of 100 Task Force — Members Urgently Needed
- Form 5500 Package Released
- Apply to Committees—New Volunteer Skills Web Site
- Download the Exposure Draft of the WebTrust Principles and Criteria for Certification Authorities
- Journal of Accountancy: Current Issue
- Exposure Draft: Financial Statements Included in Written Business Valuations
- Section 536 of HR 1180 Poses Trap for Tax Practitioners
- Download the WebTrust-ISP Principles and Criteria for Internet Service Providers in Electronic Commerce.

AICPA News/Products

- AICPA's Tax Season Special!
- Register for Spring 2000 Tax Division Meeting
- Save 50% on CPE
- New! CPA Performance View PLUS
- Ballot on Proposed Revisions to AICPA Code of Conduct and Bylaws
- AICPA Forms New Industry Expert Panels
- New AICPA Affinity Partner - Paymentech
- CapitolWiz: AICPA's Online Grassroots Tool
- New Online Service! IncAdvantage.com
- Tax Section Members: Download 1999 Tax Practice Guides and Checklists
- Compensation Practices in Public Accounting: Survey Report
- New AICPA International Category
- Five Top-Selling CPE Courses On Sale!
- AICPA Strikes Alliance With Fidelity

Fig. 2.2. Click on the links shown here to access the site's many resources. *Used by permission*

screen captures to completely keep up with it, so the topics are always current.) Check the site out frequently for the latest topics. The site also contains a good link for educators and students that may be a bit hard to navigate at first because of its format, but it is well worth it if you have a bit of extra time.
All levels.

Canada's SchoolNet: Learning Resources
www.schoolnet.ca/home/e/resources/browse_results.asp?SECTION=0&SUBJECT=9&LANGID=1&SEARCHINGEX.asp.
No lesson plans here but good links to associations and societies, to accompany some useful resources for budding accountants and their teachers. Note: We found it difficult to access the site some evenings and weekends particularly, but the site is worth visiting so don't give up if you can't get there on your first attempts. Listed below are available links.
Advanced levels.

- Assessment of Science and Technology Achievement Project (ASAP)
- Certified General Accountants
- Society of Management Accountants
- The Canadian Institute of Chartered Accountants

Free Education: Accounting & Bookkeeping
www.free-ed.net/fr01/fr0101.htm
You will need to scroll down the page a bit to see the wide range of free online tutorials designed by the wonderful people at Free-ed.net. Check out the variety of topics. Certainly one of the best sites available anywhere for learning about accounting or bookkeeping.
All levels.

Courses and Tutorials
- Bookkeeping and Accounting: From Start to Finish
- Introduction to bookkeeping & accounting
- Map of the territory—what you will learn
- Why keep good records?
- Where's the beginning?
- Setting up your chart of accounts
- Basic bookkeeping—A tutorial

- Monthly accounting—A guide
- Owners' review checklist
- Accounting software

Accounting Tutorial
Management Accounting
Helpful Study Materials

- Accounting Students.com
- Business 1013 Online Quiz

Great Ideas for Teaching Accounting
www.swcollege.com/vircomm/gita/gita.html#contents

Another very good higher level site, where accounting professors can access the shared resources of accounting professors. The site, prepared by the folks at Southwestern College, is appropriately named. The ideas are great! Be sure to scroll down the page to access the full menu where you will find a great selection of classroom management tips.

Hot Links!
www.southlight-group.com/hotlinks.htm

The operative word here is "Links," and there are a good number of useful ones for anyone currently in the field or learning the essentials of accounting and tax preparation (USA). Current links are outlined below.
All levels.

National Association of Computerized Tax Processors

- The NACTP has a super page for quick links to all the Departments of Revenue for individual states. This is a very fast way to get downloads of state tax forms in Adobe PDF format.

Inc. Magazine Online

- Visit for a great source of information for large and small growing companies.

Home Office and Small Business Computing Magazines online site

- Great stuff for small and home offices.

Pro2Net (ex Accounting Net)

- Your Internet Link to the Accounting World. Tons of great information!

North American Industry Classification System (NAICS)

- The North American Industry Classification System (NAICS) provides common industry definitions for Canada, Mexico, and the United States. The NAICS will replace the Standard Industrial Classification system. Good information here . . .

Don't forget to check out the section "Tried and true favorites" for even more government-related sites.

Ms. Goodyear Accounting 1

www.cobb.k12.ga.us/~techquest/demos/colleng/page1.htm

This site, which was carefully constructed by an accounting instructor, contains some good ideas for teaching a high school accounting course.

High school level.

Pro2Net

http://accounting.pro2net.com/

This site (see Fig. 2.3) has a membership requirement for some features, but educators and students will have access to a lot of good free accounting news and resources. This site seems to be updated fre-

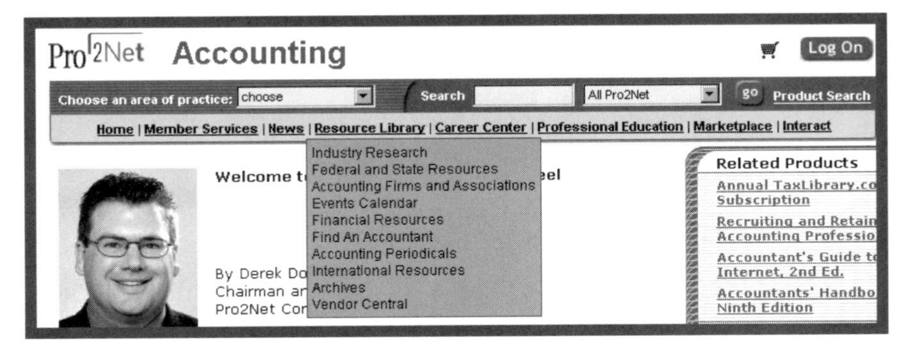

Fig. 2.3. Click on the "Resource Library" link to access the drop-down menu shown.

quently so the news should never be stale. The links to such sites as Accounting Students.Com are worth the time to explore as well. There is plenty of stuff to keep students' interests high as they learn about the world of accounting.
All levels.

Rutgers Accounting Web
www.rutgers.edu/Accounting/
You have to navigate your way around here since it is a site built for registered students at Rutgers University. However, if you are patient, you'll find some useful ideas and links for teaching or studying accounting.
Advanced levels.

- International Accounting Network Sites
- Online Accounting Faculty Directory

Small Business Corner—IRS
www.irs.ustreas.gov/plain/bus_info/sm_bus/index.html
Accounting is only one facet of this site's well set up guide to small business needs. It provides links to government sites dealing with the needs of small business. Lots of information on taxes. (USA).
All levels.

- Before Starting Your Business
- Operating Your Business
- Employment Taxes
- IRS Modernization
- Small Business News
- The Taxpayer Advocate Service
- Tax Stats, Tax Info For You, Tax Info For Business, Electronic Services, Taxpayer Help & Ed, Tax Regs In English, IRS Newsstand, Forms & Pubs, What's Hot, Meet The Commissioner, Comments & Help, Site Tree

StudyWeb: Business and Finance: Accounting

www.studyweb.com/

This is one of the best and most complete sites for learning or teaching accounting using the web. Once you get to the Studyweb main page, just type "accounting" in the search box, or else click on the "Business and Finance" section down the page. You will find a lot of well-presented information here on general accounting and US taxes. All appropriate levels.

Teacher Page 1

www.bboinc.com/actghome/teacher.htm

You need to scroll down the page to find these ready-made handouts. Click on the numbers at the left of the page to access the lessons. Teachers can also access other handouts by e-mail. Below (see Fig. 2.4) is a list of topics available at the time of writing but you are likely to find even more as the site is updated.
All levels.

~~ List of Handouts ~~~~	
1.1	Account Classifications & Normal Balances
1.2	Analyzing Transactions
2.1	Effects of Debits and Credits in Transactions
2.2	Account Analysis and Identification
3.1	Classification of Accounts & Normal Balances
3.2	Debiting and Crediting Accounts
4.1	Adjustments
4.2	Adjusting Entries
5.1	The Steps in the Accounting Cycle
5.2	Steps in the Closing Process
6.1	Quick Quiz
6.2	Closing Entries & Temporary Accounts

Fig. 2.4. This illustration shows some sample handouts at the Teacher Resource Page.
Used by permission

Welcome to K–12 World!

www.k-12world.net/cy_pages/cy_static/index.htm

Scroll down the page to the Business education section and click on "Accounting". You may find some useful stuff in the "Economics" section as well. Below (Fig. 2.5) are a couple of sample links from the page. Click on them to find the resources that you want for your particular area of interest.

Upper-elementary to high school level.

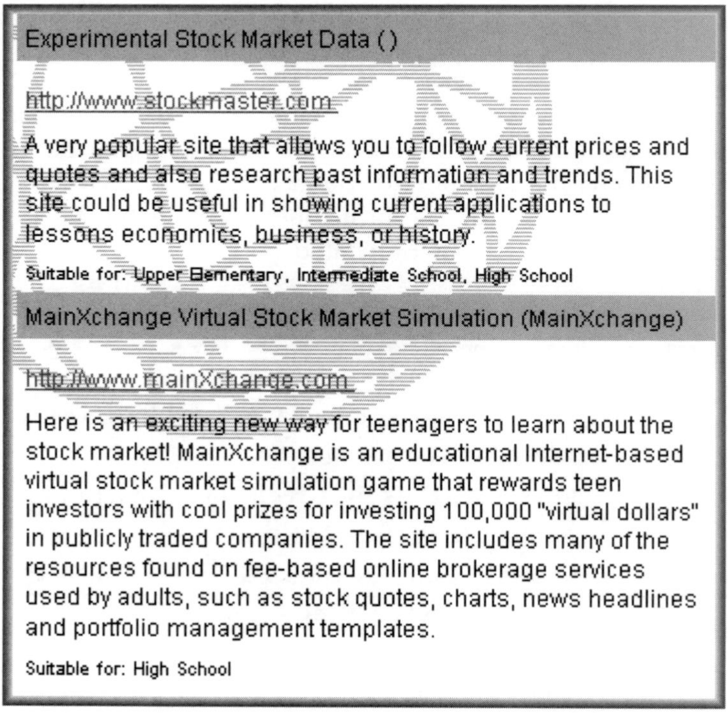

Experimental Stock Market Data ()

http://www.stockmaster.com

A very popular site that allows you to follow current prices and quotes and also research past information and trends. This site could be useful in showing current applications to lessons economics, business, or history.

Suitable for: Upper Elementary, Intermediate School, High School

MainXchange Virtual Stock Market Simulation (MainXchange)

http://www.mainXchange.com

Here is an exciting new way for teenagers to learn about the stock market! MainXchange is an educational Internet-based virtual stock market simulation game that rewards teen investors with cool prizes for investing 100,000 "virtual dollars" in publicly traded companies. The site includes many of the resources found on fee-based online brokerage services used by adults, such as stock quotes, charts, news headlines and portfolio management templates.

Suitable for: High School

Fig. 2.5. This illustration shows recent sample topics from the K–12 World site. *©1998 JDL Technologies, Inc. Used by permission*

ENTREPRENEURSHIP EDUCATION

Canada/British Columbia Business Service Centre
www.sb.gov.bc.ca/smallbus/sbhome.html

This site (see Fig. 2.6) is a treasure house of information for teaching or learning the essentials of entrepreneurship, presented in an intelligent and user-friendly manner.

It contains, in fact, a whole course online.

You'll even find a link to an interactive business planner if you click on the yellow button at the top of the page. It's bilingual as well, in English and French.

Online Small Business Workshop
Designed to provide you with techniques for developing your idea, starting a new venture and improving your existing small business.

Popular Requests
Our most requested business activities are available as Small Business Sourcing Guides The Guides contain trade shows, associations, books, magazines, videos, government services and more.

Web Sites for Small Business
Our favourite links for Business Start Up, Export Import, Directories of Companies, Market information, Selling to Government and BC's communities.

Interactive Business Planner
A step by step business planning tool. Prepare your own professional plan on line, then down load it to your computer

Fig. 2.6. Click on any of the topics shown here to access great resources and practical information.
Used by permission

Canada's SchoolNet: Learning Resources
www.schoolnet.ca/home/e/resources/Links_Result_e.asp?SUBJECT =11

When you get to this site, you'll find an impressive list of education and curriculum support materials such as the following at levels 7–13.

Here is what the site creators have to say about their site.

Junior Achievement of Canada

- The purpose of this site is to educate and inspire young people to value free enterprise, to understand business and economics, and to be workforce ready.

National Institute for Consumer Education

- This site contains mini-lessons on credit, financial management, children and money, cars and housing, and frauds and scams. The mission of the National Institute for Consumer Education is to empower people to become informed consumers, reasoned decision-makers and participating citizens in a global marketplace.

Network for Entrepreneurs with Disabilities

- This site is of interest to entrepreneurs. It includes links to some really good resources on the Internet and is ideally suited for small and/or home-based businesses, those considering entrepreneurship and especially persons with disabilities involved in or interested in entrepreneurship.

Office of International Partnerships

- The purpose of this site is to provide a single point of access to the best of Canada's information communication technology skills and products for any country or foreign organization seeking to build their own electronic learning network.

Spirit of Aboriginal Enterprise

http://strategis.ic.gs.ca/engdoc/sitemap.html

Go to this site and you will be rewarded with a lot of good business-related information and resources, some specific to aboriginal enterprise, and much applicable to any business venture.

Aboriginal Digital Collections

- Your gateway to outstanding web sites of Canadian Aboriginal images and information, created by Aboriginal youth with funding from Industry Canada.

Aboriginal Business Map

- The Aboriginal Business Canada pathfinder to provincial and municipal information for Aboriginal business.

Aboriginal Entrepreneurs in Canada: Progress and Prospects

- This special supplement of Industry Canada's Micro-Economic Monitor provides information focusing exclusively on Aboriginal businesses, demonstrating their role in Canada's economy. The report highlights a flourishing entrepreneurial spirit among Aboriginal enterprises that is increasingly contributing to the growth and prosperity of the wider Canadian economy, through business start-ups, job creation, capital investment, and trade.

SAE Business Forum

- A fully interactive and searchable message center about and for Aboriginal business. The Forum is organized around six areas of Aboriginal business activity: cultural products, innovation, youth, tourism, trade, and expanding your markets.

GENERAL BUSINESS EDUCATION

Business Majors—Home Page

http://businessmajors.about.com/education/businessmajors/

This site (see Fig. 2.7–2.8) is an excellent place for teachers and students of business to access a lot of good resources on the topics shown in the screen captures below. You'll find some great case studies, tutorials, and many more related resources. The screen captures below show the topics that are listed at the site. Click on any of them to access the information and resources you are seeking.

All levels.

Related sites
on About
Accounting
Adult/Continuing Education
College Admissions
Financial Aid/Scholarships
Grad School Admissions
Job Searching: College Grads
Management
Management Consulting
Marketing

Accounting
Economics
Entrepreneurship
Finance
Human Resources
Int'l Business
Labor Studies
Logistics

Fig. 2.7–2.8. The images show the wide variety of available resources at the Business Majors site.

Business Resource Center

www.morebusiness.com/

This site (see Fig. 2.9) contains a lot of current articles and news from the world of business, as well as a very good selection of practical resources for teaching or learning about business. Check out the "Templates" button at the left of the screen to find Sample Business and Marketing Plans, Business Agreements, and Business Checklists. Some topics from the site are listed below.
All levels.

- Ask the Expert
- Business Plans
- Interactive Quiz

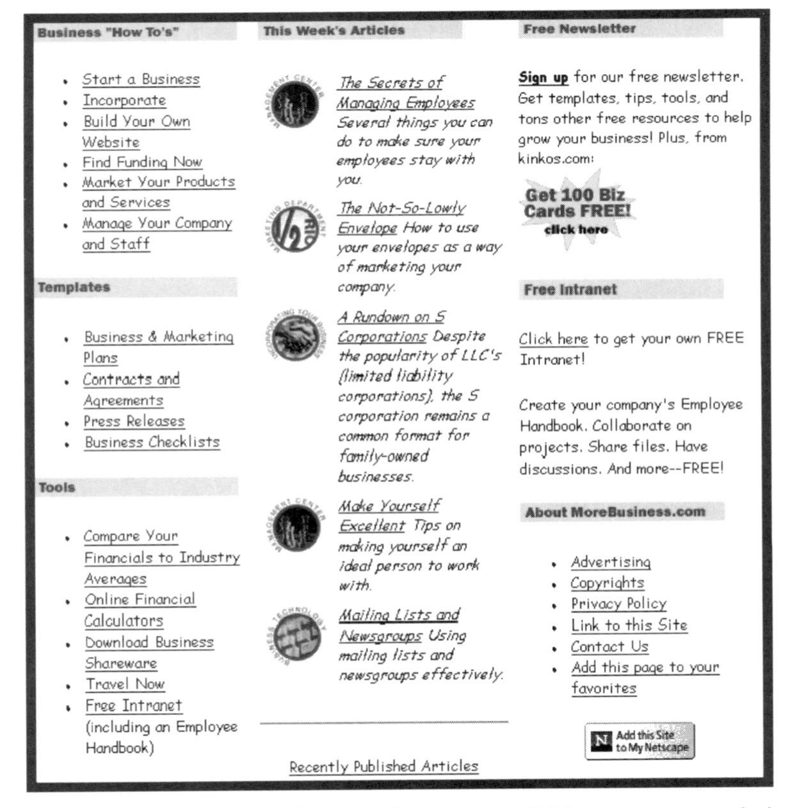

Fig. 2.9. Above is an image showing the many available resources to help any teacher or student of business.

- Market place
- Perspectives
- Running your own business
- Stocks
- Templates for agreements
- Tools
- Top Business News

Financial Dictionary and Financial Glossary

www.ventureline.com/glossary.htm

This financial dictionary and glossary offers an extensive list of defined financial terms in an easy-to-use format. Just click on a letter of the alphabet for concise and clear definitions.

Management Articles

www.ee.ed.ac.uk/~gerard/Management/index.html

This site (see Fig. 2.10) contains various articles on Basic Management Skills including good links to articles specifically on teaching these skills. A lot of the information is designed to educate people in Engineering Management, but there are clearly applications in all fields of management including a good exercise on Group Work.

Higher levels mainly.

1. Teams and Groups.
2. Presentation Skills.
3. Time Management.
4. Quality in the Team.
5. Writing Skills (expanded here).
6. Delegation.
7. Managing People.
8. Oral Communication.
9. Project Planning.
10. Becoming a Great Manager.

Fig. 2.10. This picture shows some available topics and resources at the site. *Used by permission*

The American Success Institute

http://success.org/

This site states that it offers "A Free Business Education on the Web." You'll find lots of good articles giving practical advice on business plus inspirational quotations by business leaders. Trilingual in English, French, and Spanish. The list below shows some of the available topics.

All levels.

- Legendary Advice: Words of Wisdom
- Motivation
- Positive Mental Attitudes
- Real Estate
- Small Business Advisor
- Small Business Course
- Stock Market

Chapter 3

Computing

The following sites contain many excellent resources available for use in computer classes. All have been selected for their practical applications in education, as well as for their reliability and ease of use. We are confident that teachers will find them helpful for course development and day-to-day teaching of computing skills. You will find a wide variety of topics and levels ranging from elementary to advanced. There are many lesson plans, activities, ideas, exercises, quizzes, and multimedia learning aids to make your teaching and/or learning a lot easier, consistently up to date, and always more fun. Happy clicking!

CHAPTER OVERVIEW

- ➢ Programming, pages 39, 52
- ➢ Search tools, pages 37, 61
- ➢ Tips & tricks, pages 48, 52, 54, 56
- ➢ Word processing, spreadsheets, etc., page 40

COMPUTING

A Complete Illustrated Guide to the PC Hardware

www.mkdata.dk/click/

Here is an illustrated, easy-to-read, and complete online guide to the personal computer, its hardware and internal architecture (see Fig. 3.1). The site also has an excellent online dictionary of computer terms. All levels.

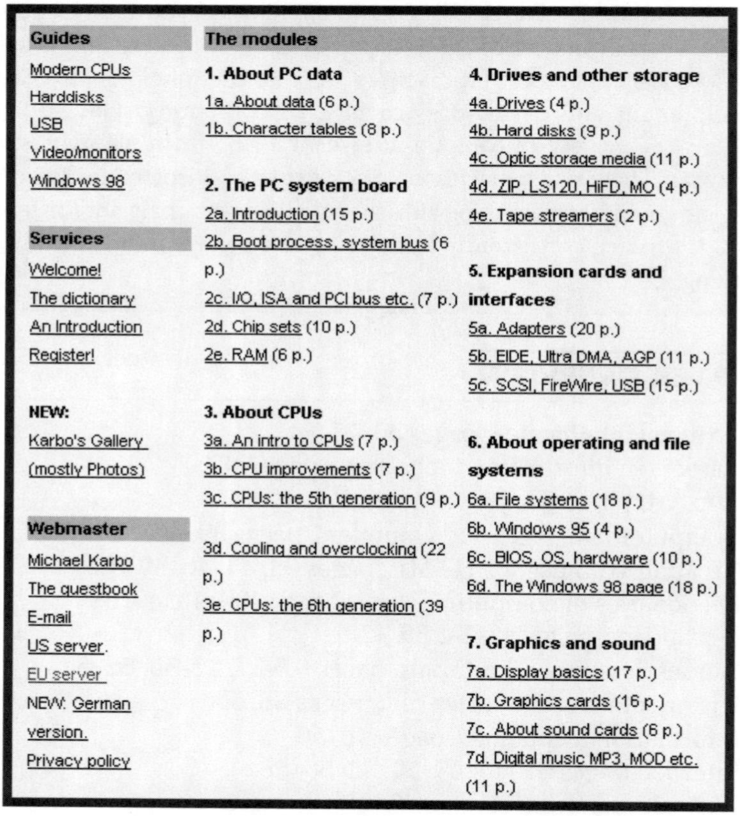

Guides

Modern CPUs
Harddisks
USB
Video/monitors
Windows 98

Services

Welcome!
The dictionary
An Introduction
Register!

NEW:
Karbo's Gallery (mostly Photos)

Webmaster

Michael Karbo
The guestbook
E-mail
US server.
EU server
NEW: German version.
Privacy policy

The modules

1. About PC data
1a. About data (6 p.)
1b. Character tables (8 p.)

2. The PC system board
2a. Introduction (15 p.)
2b. Boot process, system bus (6 p.)
2c. I/O, ISA and PCI bus etc. (7 p.)
2d. Chip sets (10 p.)
2e. RAM (6 p.)

3. About CPUs
3a. An intro to CPUs (7 p.)
3b. CPU improvements (7 p.)
3c. CPUs: the 5th generation (9 p.)
3d. Cooling and overclocking (22 p.)
3e. CPUs: the 6th generation (39 p.)

4. Drives and other storage
4a. Drives (4 p.)
4b. Hard disks (9 p.)
4c. Optic storage media (11 p.)
4d. ZIP, LS120, HiFD, MO (4 p.)
4e. Tape streamers (2 p.)

5. Expansion cards and interfaces
5a. Adapters (20 p.)
5b. EIDE, Ultra DMA, AGP (11 p.)
5c. SCSI, FireWire, USB (15 p.)

6. About operating and file systems
6a. File systems (18 p.)
6b. Windows 95 (4 p.)
6c. BIOS, OS, hardware (10 p.)
6d. The Windows 98 page (18 p.)

7. Graphics and sound
7a. Display basics (17 p.)
7b. Graphics cards (16 p.)
7c. About sound cards (6 p.)
7d. Digital music MP3, MOD etc. (11 p.)

Fig. 3.1. As the illustration shows, there are many excellent resources to explore and employ at this site.

Note: Although we normally only provide links to free sites, this site called "Click & Learn" is a worthwhile exception because of its thoroughness of content and ease of use. The provider requests a minimal payment for using this site in educational institutions. Please comply with this request if you decide to use it in your classroom.

AskERIC Lesson Plans: Educational Technology
http://ericir.syr.edu/Virtual/Lessons/Ed_Tech/index.html

This link (see Fig. 3.2) takes you directly to a list of technology-related lesson plans for use in classrooms from Preschool to grade 12.

Samples of topics are listed below. You can also use the "AskERIC" service to ask specific questions as stated below.

- Advertising Project, Grade: 7–8
- Computer Writing Lesson, Grade: 7–8
- Computer Olympics, Grade: any level
- "Let Me Tell You About My State!" Grade: 4–6
- Technology Centers for the Integrated Technology Classroom, Grade: any level

- Got an education question? If you are an educator, librarian, parent, or anyone interested in education, AskERIC's Q&A Service

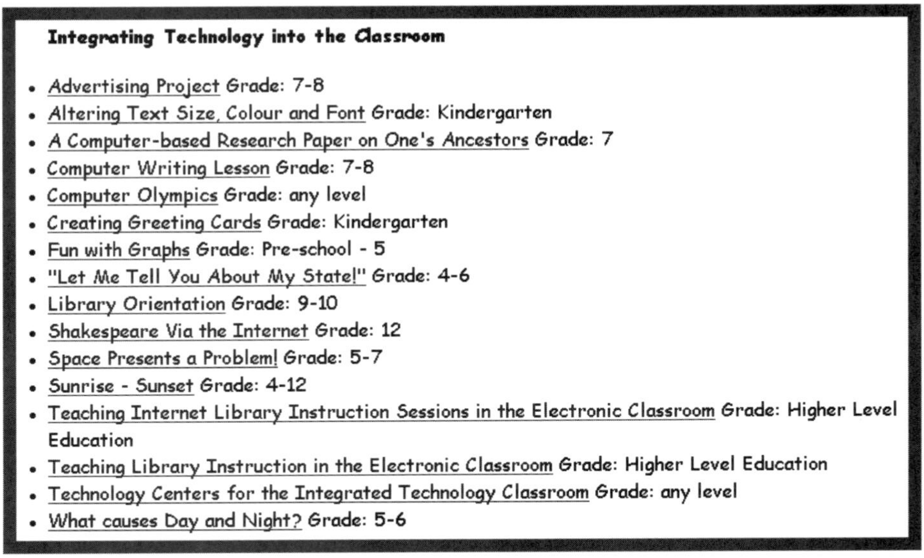

Integrating Technology into the Classroom

- Advertising Project Grade: 7-8
- Altering Text Size, Colour and Font Grade: Kindergarten
- A Computer-based Research Paper on One's Ancestors Grade: 7
- Computer Writing Lesson Grade: 7-8
- Computer Olympics Grade: any level
- Creating Greeting Cards Grade: Kindergarten
- Fun with Graphs Grade: Pre-school - 5
- "Let Me Tell You About My State!" Grade: 4-6
- Library Orientation Grade: 9-10
- Shakespeare Via the Internet Grade: 12
- Space Presents a Problem! Grade: 5-7
- Sunrise - Sunset Grade: 4-12
- Teaching Internet Library Instruction Sessions in the Electronic Classroom Grade: Higher Level Education
- Teaching Library Instruction in the Electronic Classroom Grade: Higher Level Education
- Technology Centers for the Integrated Technology Classroom Grade: any level
- What causes Day and Night? Grade: 5-6

Fig. 3.2. Choose your subject and grade level as shown in the menu above.
Used by permission

can help! Utilizing the diverse resources and expertise of the national ERIC System, AskERIC staff will respond to your question within two business days with ERIC database citations and publications, Internet resources, and referrals to other sources of information. AskERIC responds to *every* question with personalized resources relevant to *your* needs.

- Also includes a SEARCH element, which allows users to search for lessons and resources on a specific topic.

Beginners' Central, a Users Guide to the Internet
http://northernwebs.com/bc/index.html

We found this site particularly easy to use and very thorough in providing new users with the essentials of the Internet. Contains a good Glossary of Net Terms and Chapter Quizzes, as well.
Beginners level.

Here's what the people there had to say about their own site:

- This site is dedicated to helping people learn to use the Internet in a coherent manner. Divided into several chapters, the tutorial guides users through the basic concepts and practical details of using the Internet. Topics include file downloading, email and newsreader configuration and operation (on the two major browsers), FTP and Telnet basics, and Internet myths. A summary and brief quiz conclude each chapter.

CLN—Information Technologies
www.cln.org/map.html#IT

Another good site mainly for more advanced users, this site is part of the excellent multicurricular resources provided by CLN. Click on any of the theme pages listed below for many great resources, links, and lessons.

- Theme Page: Clip Art
- Theme Page: Creating Web Pages (Advanced Level)
- Theme Page: Creating Web Pages (Introductory Level)
- Theme Page: History of Computers/Internet
- Theme Page: Learning How to Search the Internet
- Theme Page: Multimedia
- Theme Page: Networks

- Theme Page: Privacy and Technology
- Theme Page: Programming

CTC Math/Science Gateway: Computers
www.tc.cornell.edu/Edu/MathSciGateway/computing.html

The people at Cornell Theory Center Math and Science Gateway provide this site which contains too many good things to mention. Click on the links at the top of the page to find tutorials, computer languages or online courses. There are good links to online dictionaries, directions for setting up a classroom server, and a modular course designed to assist teachers in setting up a program to teach the World Wide Web.

Lots more.

All levels.

- Computer Languages, Tutorials & Online Courses
- Computer Modeling Software
- Computer Companies
- The Internet and the World Wide Web
- Searching the Web

Epeople Helpdesk Online
www.epeople.com/helpdesk.jsp

You need to register at this site but it is free, and it permits you to ask technology-related questions which will be answered online or by E-mail. We tried it and they were very friendly and prompt at answering a couple of questions that we asked, and more importantly, their answers worked to solve our problems.

Free Education: Computer Science
www.free-ed.net/fr03/index.html

The free education site lives up to its billing by providing free online courses in a great variety of topics. Many of the courses do not offer online certification, but the information is there to help learners hone their skills, or to use as resources for teachers.

Some of the topics are listed below:

Computer Information Systems

- Database Management
- Desktop Publishing
- Graphics
- Integrated Packages
- Internet
- Management Information Systems
- Multimedia
- Networking & Intranet
- Operating Systems
- Spreadsheets
- Word Processing

Computer Languages & Compilers

- Assemblers
- Basic & Visual Basic
- C & C++
- COBOL
- Java
- Pascal
- Perl & CGI

Free Education: Computer Technology

www.free-ed.net/fr02/fr0212.htm

This site (see Fig. 3.3) is similar to the one mentioned before, but with the focus shifted to the technology side of computing.

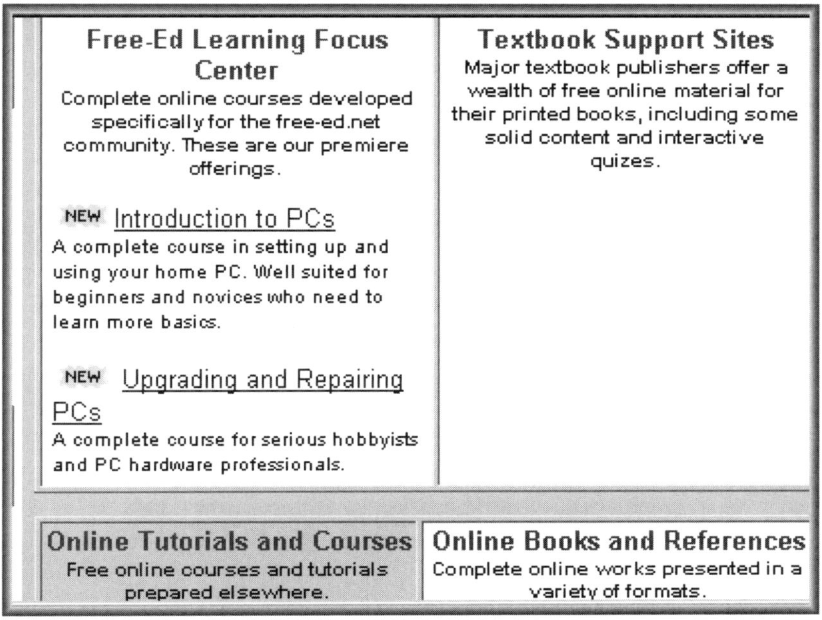

Free-Ed Learning Focus Center
Complete online courses developed specifically for the free-ed.net community. These are our premiere offerings.

NEW Introduction to PCs
A complete course in setting up and using your home PC. Well suited for beginners and novices who need to learn more basics.

NEW Upgrading and Repairing PCs
A complete course for serious hobbyists and PC hardware professionals.

Textbook Support Sites
Major textbook publishers offer a wealth of free online material for their printed books, including some solid content and interactive quizes.

Online Tutorials and Courses
Free online courses and tutorials prepared elsewhere.

Online Books and References
Complete online works presented in a variety of formats.

Fig. 3.3. Topics shown in this figure were those available at the time of writing. Check back for updates as the site is developed further.

Free Education: Networking
www.free-ed.net/fr03/fr030108.htm

The third site in this excellent series again shifts its focus to Networking and Intranets with a variety of resources for the teacher or independent learner.

The topics are listed in Figures 3.4 and 3.5.

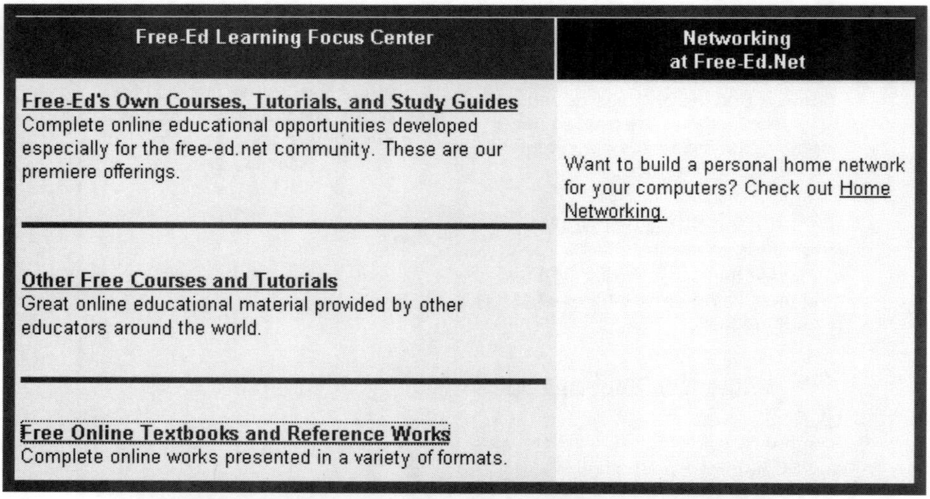

Free-Ed Learning Focus Center	Networking at Free-Ed.Net
Free-Ed's Own Courses, Tutorials, and Study Guides Complete online educational opportunities developed especially for the free-ed.net community. These are our premiere offerings. **Other Free Courses and Tutorials** Great online educational material provided by other educators around the world. **Free Online Textbooks and Reference Works** Complete online works presented in a variety of formats.	Want to build a personal home network for your computers? Check out Home Networking.

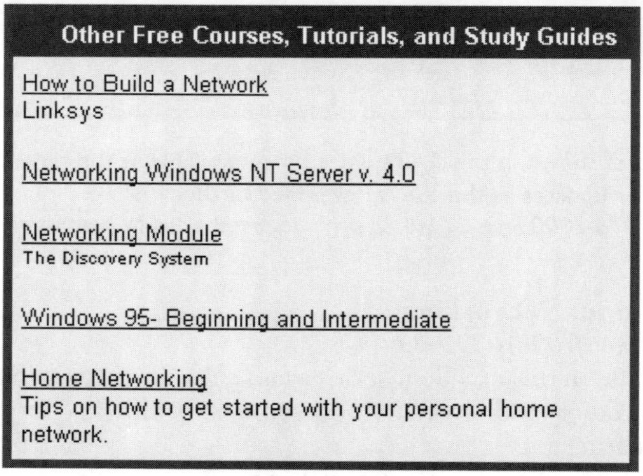

Other Free Courses, Tutorials, and Study Guides

How to Build a Network
Linksys

Networking Windows NT Server v. 4.0

Networking Module
The Discovery System

Windows 95- Beginning and Intermediate

Home Networking
Tips on how to get started with your personal home network.

Fig. 3.4–3.5. These illustrations show the networking topics at the Free Ed Center plus tips and study guides.

Free Online Dictionary of Computing

www.instantweb.com/foldoc/foldoc.cgi?Free+On-line+Dictionary

This online dictionary of computing contains over 12,000 entries in searchable format plus links to online computer guides and tutorials from beginner to advanced levels. If you just want to browse in the dictionary, you can just click on the "random" button for a page of computer-related definitions at a time.

Generation www. Y—Partners

http://genwhy.wednet.edu/curriculum/index.html

The description below, taken directly from this site (see Fig. 3.6), accurately describes its contents. The twelve units, which teach both technical and educational skills, are well presented and easy to follow, even for those students and teachers with limited computer skills. Secondary School level.

- Y model is an 18–week course for secondary school students. This course contains 12 Units of Study.
- Eight units teach students the technical skills they need to help their teachers infuse technology into the curriculum. The final four units teach students some educational skills such as the components of a lesson plan and state and local academic standards.

Unit 1: Introduction
Unit 2: Electronic Mail
Unit 3: Netiquette, Copyright, and Citing Internet Resources
Unit 4: Researching on the Internet
Unit 5: The Collaboration Process
Unit 6: Digital Imagery
Unit 7: Project Planning
Unit 8: Publishing on the Web
Unit 9: Forums, Newsgroups, and Mailing Lists
Unit 10: Presentation Tools
Unit 11: Real-Time Communications
Unit 12: Writing the Project Final Report

Fig. 3.6. The easy menu makes it a snap to navigate this site.
Used by permission

HTML for Educators

www.learningspace.org/tech/HTML/HTML.html

Here's a nice site (see Fig. 3.7) specifically designed for teachers who are looking for help in designing home pages, and of use to anyone wanting to learn about HTML and other home-page creation tools. Just click on the topic or tutorial of your choice for resources and tutorials at the beginner to advanced levels.

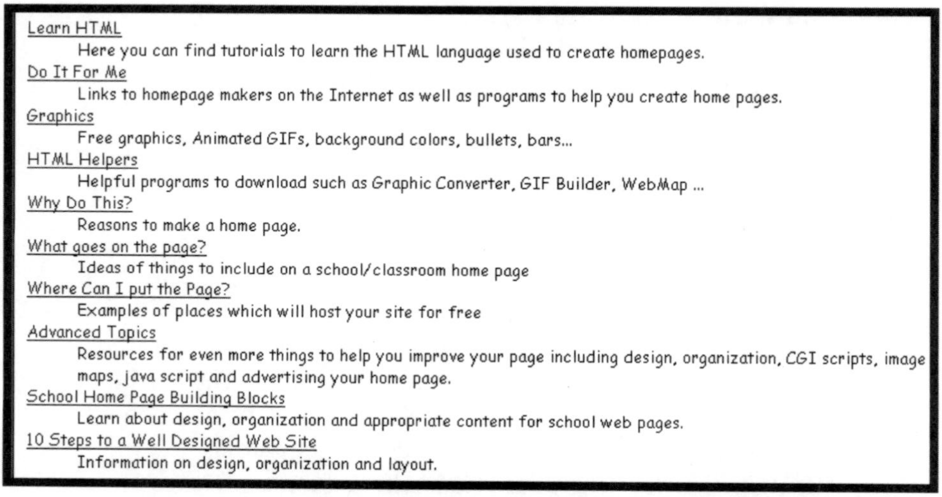

Learn HTML
Here you can find tutorials to learn the HTML language used to create homepages.
Do It For Me
Links to homepage makers on the Internet as well as programs to help you create home pages.
Graphics
Free graphics, Animated GIFs, background colors, bullets, bars...
HTML Helpers
Helpful programs to download such as Graphic Converter, GIF Builder, WebMap ...
Why Do This?
Reasons to make a home page.
What goes on the page?
Ideas of things to include on a school/classroom home page
Where Can I put the Page?
Examples of places which will host your site for free
Advanced Topics
Resources for even more things to help you improve your page including design, organization, CGI scripts, image maps, java script and advertising your home page.
School Home Page Building Blocks
Learn about design, organization and appropriate content for school web pages.
10 Steps to a Well Designed Web Site
Information on design, organization and layout.

Fig. 3.7. As you can see in the illustration above, there are topics for every level of user.
Used by permission

Kathy Schrock's Guide for Educators—Computing & Technology

http://discoveryschool.com/schrockguide/sci-tech/scicom.html

The "Acceptable Use" policy guidelines will be useful to administrators and educators who want to establish a framework for what is or is not appropriate for use in the classroom.

There are many other practical resources for teachers and learners as well, so take a few minutes to peruse the many links at this site (see Fig. 3.8).

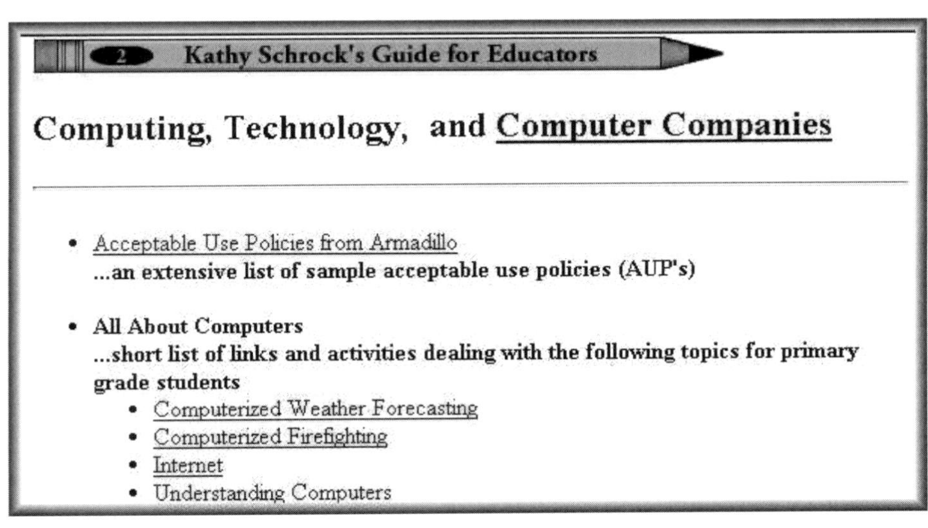

Fig. 3.8. This screen capture shows only a small sampling of what this site has to offer. You will also find links to Macintosh and ClarisWorks tutorial.

Learning HTML

www8.bev.net/civic/htmlhelp/

This is a good site to begin learning the skills and finding the tools to help you write your own web page. It's not nearly as tough as you might think once you find the right HTML editor, so don't give up before you start.

Lesson Stop | Technology

www.youthline-usa.org/lessonstop/technology.html

There are a lot of excellent lessons and teaching resources here classified according to subject matter and grade level, K–12. The list was extensive and growing at last check.

Learning about Technology

- Ainsworth Computer Seminar—QBasic (6–12)
- Ainsworth Keyboard Training Demo (6–12)
- Computer Skills Lesson Plans (K–12)
- Curriculum and Lesson Plans for Information Literacy (K–12)
- Internet Lesson Plans (K–12)
- Lesson Plans for Computer Literacy in Education (9–12+)
- Lesson Plan for Evaluating Web Sites (K–12)
- Mr. Cassuto's Computer Application Lesson Plans (K–12 educators)
- Teaching Media Literacy (K–12)
- Technology Lessons (K–12)
- Using Audio Cassettes in a Foreign Language Course (K–12)
- WebTeacher Tutorial (K–12)

Teaching with Technology

- Computer and Internet Lesson Plans (3–12)
- The Computer as Learning Partner Project (9–12)
- Cyber English: An Internet Project (9–12)
- ERIC Technology Lessons (K–12)
- The Great Satellite Search (9–12)
- Healthy Computer Home Page (K–12)
- High School Thematic Units (K–12)
- Integrated Technology Lessons (K–5)
- Integrating the Internet into the Classroom (K–12)
- Integrating Technology Lesson Plans (K–12)
- Intel Computer Education Resources (K–12)
- Judi Harris' Network-Based Educational Activity Structures (K–12)

- Learning Exchange for Teachers and Students through the Internet (K–12)
- LION: Lesson Plans & Teaching Activities for Information/Library/ Media Skills (K–12)
- Multimedia Teaching Strategies (K–12)
- Networthy Lessons (K–12)
- Organizing and Facilitating Telecommunications Projects (K–12)
- PBS TechKnow Lesson Inventory (preK–12)
- School Projects that Connect with the Internet (K–3)
- Software Integrated Lesson Plans (K–12)
- Technology Integration Lessons
- The Tele-Garden—A Tele-Robotic Installation on the WWW (K–12)
- T'NT Lesson Plans for Technology (K–12)

Lessons & Activities: Integrate Technology into K–12 Classrooms and Schools

www.microsoft.com/education/k12/integrate.htm

This site has links to Microsoft products, but you will also find a lot of free resources if you click on the Instructional Resources button. Here you will be able to access tutorials, lesson plans, information on putting classes online, and a whole lot more.
K–12 level.

Productivity in the Classroom is a curriculum workbook jam-packed with ideas for integrating computer applications into the intermediate, middle school, or high school classroom.
- Language Arts & Social Studies Lessons
- Math, Economics, & Science Lessons
- Geography & History Lessons

Search for Lesson Plans Created By Teachers
- Search the lesson plan database by school subject and grade level.

Macintosh Tips and Tutorials

http://users.supernet.com/ohora/index.html

Here's the site to go to when you want to get your Mac running like a Mercedes. You will find tips and tutorials on Macintosh computers as well as Claris Works and Apple Works, plus a problem-oriented index, software reviews, a teacher's resources page, Macintosh links and more.

Higher levels.

MacIntosh Tips

- ClarisWorks / AppleWorks Tutorials

Internet scavenger hunts

- Problem oriented index

Macintosh links

- Software reviews / Freeware/shareware for kids

Search the site

- On Inspiration / Gaelic Blessing

Site Map / Purchasing advice

- Habitat Garden / Conestoga, Pa / Author

School Computer Volunteering

- Article about the web site

NONAGS

http://ded.com/nonags/

Here is another great site which is "upgraded daily except Sundays." You can find freeware here and shareware downloads that you may find useful.

Parents Guide to the Internet

www.ed.gov/pubs/parents/internet/

Published by the U.S. Department of Education, this site has useful basic information for teachers and students about the Internet despite the fact that it was designed for parents.

This Parents Guide to the Internet is intended to help parents—regardless of their level of technological know-how—make use of the online world as an important educational tool. The guide cuts through the overwhelming amount of consumer information to give parents an introduction to the Internet and how to navigate it.

Resources—Info Source—Glossary—Index
www.cnet.com/Resources/Info/Glossary/index.html

This site contains a huge glossary of computer terms where you can 'Netify' your vocabulary and impress your friends (assuming that you still have some since you are spending so much time at your computer).

Internet terminology from A to Z.

SchoolNet's Web Page Tutorial (Index)
www.schoolnet.ca/vp-pv/html_tut/e/

This site (see Fig. 3.9) is sometimes hard to access, but worth it once you get there. Try on different days or times. There is a very good tutorial for basic web authoring here. Here's what the people there have to say about their site:

- The CPHO Web Page Tutorial is intended to act as a resource for students and teachers who wish to learn the basics of Web

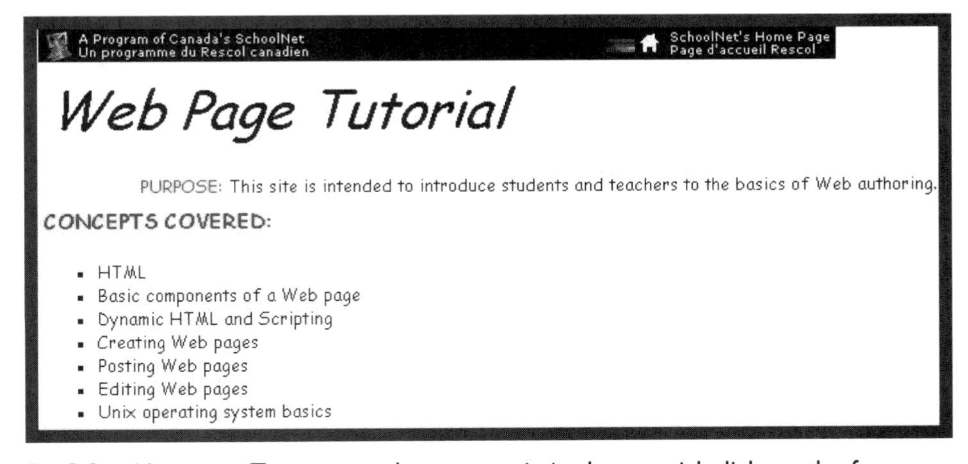

Fig. 3.9. *Navigation:* To move to the next topic in the tutorial, click on the forward arrow. Clicking on the back arrow will return you to the previous topic. *Used by permission*

authoring. It covers a variety of concepts, including HTML; basic components of a web page, dynamic HTML and scripting; creating, posting, and editing Web pages; and Unix operating system . . .

Scientific American: Ask the Experts: Computers
www.sciam.com/askexpert/computers/index.html

Check out the latest technologies such as artificial noses or browse the back issues of this popular magazine.

Or, if you have a question concerning computers, just ask the experts. Check out their archives of questions as well by clicking on the "Ask the Experts" button as shown in the screen capture below and then on "Computers." Can they really make computers out of DNA? Find out here.

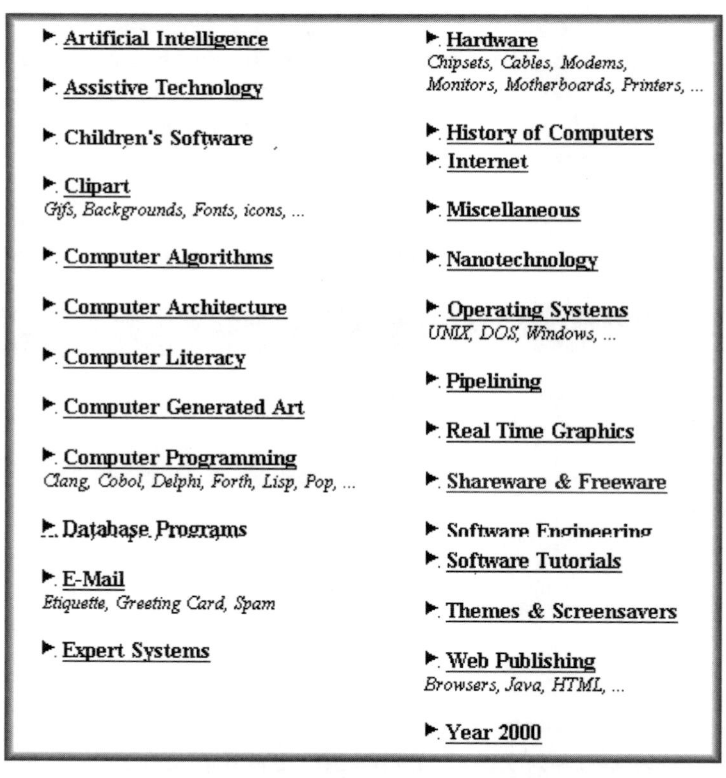

Fig. 3.10. As you can see from the illustration, the list of resources is extensive. *(c) Copyright 1996-2000, Lightspan Inc. All rights reserved. Used by permission*

StudyWeb®

www.studyweb.com/index2.htm

The screen-capture (Fig. 3.10) shows some of the topics from this comprehensive site. The resources they have are very good so don't skip this one.

Virtual Library: Computer Science

http://vlib.org/Computing.html

This site contains information and resources on everything from Artificial Intelligence to World Wide Web Development. See the list of topics in Figure 3.11.

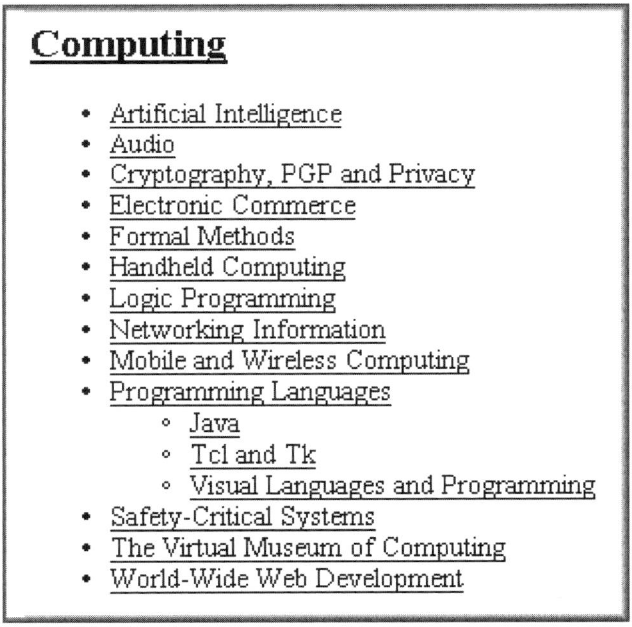

Computing

- Artificial Intelligence
- Audio
- Cryptography, PGP and Privacy
- Electronic Commerce
- Formal Methods
- Handheld Computing
- Logic Programming
- Networking Information
- Mobile and Wireless Computing
- Programming Languages
    - Java
    - Tcl and Tk
    - Visual Languages and Programming
- Safety-Critical Systems
- The Virtual Museum of Computing
- World-Wide Web Development

Fig. 3.11. Check out some of the many interesting topics available from the extensive list.

Walt Howe's Internet Learning Center

http://people.ne.mediaone.net/walthowe/ilrntree.html

Here is a good place to learn about the Web and the Internet and to find resources for both students and teachers. Lessons start at the beginners level and provide information on such topics as what the Internet is and how to use it, how to use mail and newsgroups, and so forth. As well, there is a very good glossary and a brief Internet history.

As you can see in Figure 3.12, there are a lot of good resources for learning the basics about the Internet, and related subjects.

Easy question and answer format for beginners.

Welcome to K–12 World!

www.k–12world.net/cy_pages/cy_static/index.htm

This site has a very good section on Computer Science along with a whole lot of other subjects you may want to refer your colleagues to if they aren't computer people. The topics shown below were available on our last visit.

- HTML
- Information Technology
- Internet/Web
- Networking
- Programming

Windows 95 Tips and Tricks

www.geocities.com/SiliconValley/Heights/6348/tips.html

There are several categories here to help you more efficiently use Windows 95 with some application to later versions such as Windows 98 as well. Categories range from "Usefull" (who says computer people have to be able to spell?), to "Regedit" (whatever that is) to "Just for fun."

Some of the topics from the site are shown below.

- **Usefull:** Close several windows at once, make bitmaps show their picture as the icon, easy Restart, find fast, change default program, speed up your computer.
- **Regedit:** Speed up the start menu, stop animation, customize the start menu button.

The Internet Learning Tree

About the Learning Center

Internet Learning Tree

Find-It Search Guide

Training Resources

Each main "trunk" question below branches to another set of questions and answers

Below the "trunk" questions are links to the "roots"--an Internet Glossary and a brief Internet History

The Main Branches...

1. What is the Internet?
2. What is the World Wide Web?
3. How do I use the Internet?
4. How do I search the Internet?
5. How do I find Internet Addresses?
6. How do I use Mail?
7. What is telnet?
8. How do I find and join listservs and other Email discussion lists?
9. How do I use Usenet Newsgroups?
10. What is a gopher?
11. How do I use FTP and search engines to find and get files on the Internet?
12. What is Internet Relay Chat (IRC) and how do I use it?
13. How do I listen to audio files
14. Should I be concerned about privacy on the web?
15. Are there any training resources to help me and others to learn?

...and the roots...

Internet Glossary. Look up those terms you don't understand.

Internet History. A brief background on the development of the Internet and the World Wide Web.

Fig. 3.12. Click on the question of your choice as shown in the sample illustration of topics.

- **Misc:** Change the startup & shutdown screens, my icons, teach windows to not put "shortcut to," put the control panel on the desktop, get rid of shortcut arrows.
- **Software:** Magic folders and magic files, powertools and a tip.
- **Just for fun:** Move the start button, change the icons on hard disks, win 95 easter egg.

ZDNet Help and How To

www.zdnet.com/zdhelp/

Get expert help to fix the computer glitches that pop up from time to time, and learn new tips and tricks for customizing your computer while keeping things running smoothly in the future.

You will also find virus alerts, performance boosters, and more. Information is available for both PCs and Macintosh systems.

Getting Started

- Fix It Now
  Expert help, solutions, repairs.
- Alerts & Solutions
  Bug alerts, fixes, viruses, security, protection.
- How-To
  Step-by-step tutorials, helpful know-how.
- Beginner Guides
  Getting started with hardware, software, and more.
- PC Check-Up
  Software updates, utilities, anti-virus, downloads.
- Performance Boosters
  Diagnostics, utilities, benchmarks.

Find help with these topics

- Windows
  Windows 95, 98, NT, 2000, CE . . .
- Hardware
  Desktops, DVD, digital cameras . . .
- Macintosh
  Hardware, OS, scripts, TCP/IP . . .
- Software
  Office, graphics, operating systems . . .
- Linux
  HOWTOs, utilities, GUI . . .

- HealthyPC
  Anti-virus, tools, ergonomics . . .
- Internet
  E-mail, browsers, chat, MP3s . . .
- Games
  Demos, cheats, strategy guides . . .

Online Classes
- Databases
- Hardware
- Software Applications
- Web Design & Graphics
- Webmaster
- Web User
- All classes . . .

ZDWindows.com: Windows 95
www.zdnet.com/windows/95/index.html

Although Windows 95 users are likely to be moving on sooner or later to the newer versions of Windows, there are a lot of good computing tips in this site which are also applicable to newer windows versions, as well as downloads, freebees, tips, resources, and reviews.

Windows Guide
- Windows 98 Windows NT
- Windows 95 Windows 2000
- Windows 3.1 Windows CE
- Windows News Windows Downloads

Resources
- Windows News
- Win 95 Help
- Win 95 Tips
- Windows 95 Forum

Tips
Downloads
Reviews

Chapter 4

Education

Welcome to the Education section of this guide. Each of the following sites contains educational resources on a wide variety of subjects which can be of great help to both teachers and independent learners. Like all the sites in this guide, they were selected to help you easily find materials, resources such as lesson plans, and will save you many hours of searching the Internet on your own. Some sites contain hundreds of individual subjects, so whatever your area of interest, there is likely to be something for you here. Some of the sites listed here have been included in other chapters in this guide when they direct users to more specific topics. Several sites contain alphabetical listings. Simply click on the letter that begins your topic to access the information. Happy teaching and learning!

CHAPTER OVERVIEW

English, pages 60–66, 70–74, 76, 81–90, 93

- Communications and the media, pages 66, 84
- Dictionaries, page 84
- Encyclopedias, pages 66, 72, 82
- Literature, pages 66, 70, 72–73, 82, 84, 88
- Reading, page 64
- Writing and writers, pages 6, 84

ESL, pages 60, 70, 84, 86

Foreign languages, pages 61, 66, 70, 72–73, 75, 81–82, 84, 90

- Classical languages, page 70
- Modern languages, pages 66, 70

Health and Physical Education, pages 61, 63–64, 66–67, 73, 81–82, 84–86, 90, 93

Math, pages 60–61, 63–67, 70–76, 79, 81–82, 84–90

Sciences, pages 60–61, 63–64, 66–67, 70–72, 74, 76, 78–79, 81–82, 84–91, 93

- Animals and zoology, page 66
- Astronomy, pages 66, 70
- Biology, pages 64, 70, 72, 82, 89
- Chemistry, pages 64, 70, 72, 82, 89
- Climate change, pages 78, 93
- Earth science, pages 64, 69–70, 72–73, 78, 81–82, 89, 91
- Engineering, pages 64, 93
- Geology, pages 66, 70, 82, 89
- Human ecology, page 66
- Meteorology, pages 64, 70
- Physics, pages 60, 64, 72, 82, 89

Social Studies, pages 61, 63–64, 72, 74–76, 79, 81, 84–90, 93

- Aboriginal studies, page 84
- Anthropology, page 70
- Geography, pages 64, 66, 70, 72–73, 75, 85, 88, 93
- History, pages 60–61, 64, 66, 71–74, 82, 84–85, 87
- Humanities, page 70
- Law & criminology, page 71
- Philosophy, pages 60, 70, 81–82, 84–87
- Political science, pages 67, 71, 75, 82, 84
- Psychology, pages 69, 71
- Religion, pages 60, 70, 81, 84, 90

- ➢ Sociology, pages 71, 93
- ➢ World & culture, pages 70, 91

Miscellaneous Education

- ➢ Administration & leadership, pages 67, 69
- ➢ Adult Education / Special Needs Education, pages 60, 63, 66, 71
- ➢ Aeronautics, page 78
- ➢ Agriculture, pages 63–64, 66, 78, 84, 90, 93
- ➢ Aquatics, page 78
- ➢ Archeology, page 66
- ➢ Associations, pages 67, 71, 80, 90
- ➢ Canadian studies, page 63
- ➢ Career and technology, pages 60, 63, 67, 73
- ➢ Career and vocational, pages 60, 63, 67
- ➢ Classroom management, pages 67
- ➢ Curriculum and instruction training, pages 69, 71
- ➢ Dictionaries, pages 72, 84
- ➢ Distance education, page 60
- ➢ Early childhood education, pages 60, 67, 71
- ➢ Education and technology, pages 60, 66–69, 76, 81, 90
- ➢ Education standards and testing, pages 67, 69
- ➢ Educational methods, pages 67, 69
- ➢ Encyclopedias, pages 72, 84
- ➢ Financial aid, pages 60, 67–68, 90
- ➢ Gardening and landscape, page 84
- ➢ General Resources, pages 60–93
- ➢ Guidance, pages 63, 69, 71
- ➢ Homeschooling, pages 69, 84
- ➢ Libraries, pages 63, 67–68, 74, 80, 85, 90, 92–93
- ➢ Maps, pages 66, 82
- ➢ Multi-age classrooms, page 67
- ➢ Multi-culture education, page 67
- ➢ Museums, pages 78, 80
- ➢ News sources / magazines, pages 61, 83, 93
- ➢ Professional development, pages 67, 90
- ➢ Search Tools, page 66
- ➢ Student motivation, pages 67, 71
- ➢ Substitute teaching, page 67
- ➢ Technology education, pages 67, 90–91
- ➢ Travel, pages 64, 78
- ➢ Universities / Colleges, pages 60, 63

EDUCATION

About.com—Education

http://home.about.com/education/index.htm?PM=59_0204_T

Here is a good place (see Fig. 4.1) to begin if you are looking for educational resources on a number of topics or different subject areas and levels. You can find resources and lessons in areas such as adult/continuing education, primary/secondary education, or college/university. Topics include arts, history, languages, literature, philosophy/religion, sciences and social sciences. There are also featured articles, and reference materials such as dictionaries, encyclopedias, maps and factbooks.

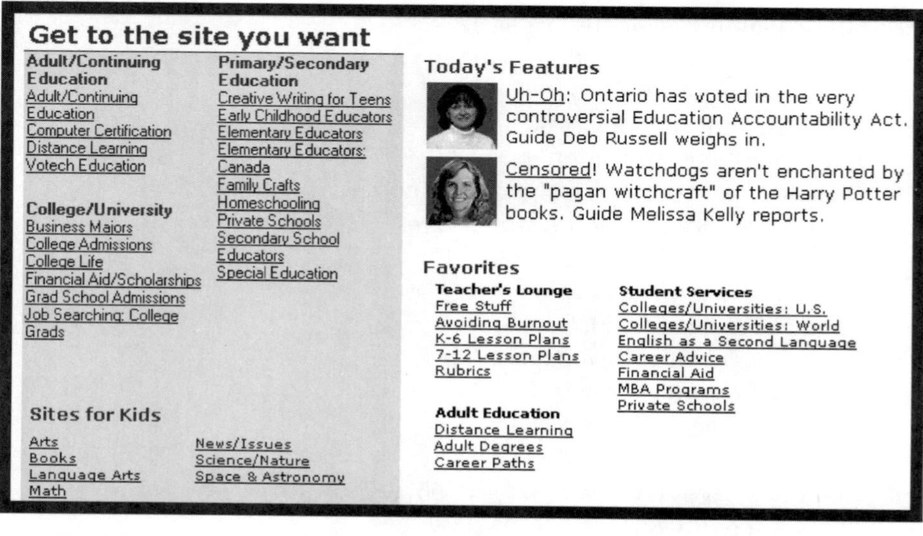

Fig. 4.1. Choose your subject and click away. Features will change daily so check back frequently for educational updates.

Ask Magpie Magazines

www.askmagpie.com/

This site includes hard-to-find titles, trades magazines, and even obscure and unusual interests. Click on the topic area or type in the search box. Here is what the site's creators have to say:

The bigger the web gets the harder it gets to find what you want. AskMagpie makes it easy with over 7,000 magazines and journals on one easy to use magazine directory.

BJ Pinchbeck—Homework Help—Discovery Channel School

http://school.discovery.com/homeworkhelp/bjpinchbeck/

This page is courtesy of the youthful BJ Pinchbeck, who began this page with the help of his father in 1996, at the tender age of nine. You will be very pleasantly surprised at the quality and professionalism of this resource-rich site if you haven't visited here before. There is also a homework question section for students suffering the slings and arrows of outrageous assignments. It's free, but you need to sign up as a member for this service.

Topics are shown in the screen capture below.

- Art
- Computer Science and Internet
- Current Events
- English
- Foreign Languages
- Health and P.E.
- History
- Math
- Music
- Reference
- Science
- Search Engines
- Social Studies

Canada's Digital Collections

http://collections.ic.gc.ca/E/index_e.asp

This site is accessible in English or in French. It contains a huge index of Canadian Educational resources. Check out the menu on the left of the page to find an alphabetical listing, subject listing, and teacher's resources.

There are also featured sites on various themes which are updated regularly, and a search feature.

Canada's SchoolNet

www.schoolnet.ca/home/e/resources

Containing over 1,000 learning resources and counting, this is an excellent site for teachers of any school discipline at the K–12 level. It is available in both English and French. You can also connect from here to the provincial sites where you will find even more resources. Although this site is designed primarily for Canadian educators, teachers from all countries will find the resources useful. Some of the topics from this Website are listed in Figures 4.2 and 4.3.

Classroom Connect's Connected Teacher

www.connectedteacher.com/library/bestofweb.asp

Here's another site loaded with resources, and it's also a good way to stay in touch with other educators on the Web. You can just peruse and use the many resources, or you can easily sign up for free membership, which will entitle you to participate in community bulletin boards.

Besides the "Teachers' Resources" section which is filled with lesson plans, don't miss the educator-submitted Web site section called "Bookmark it." There is also a good "Weekly Web picks" section and a good collection of K–12 school sites from around the U.S.

All levels.

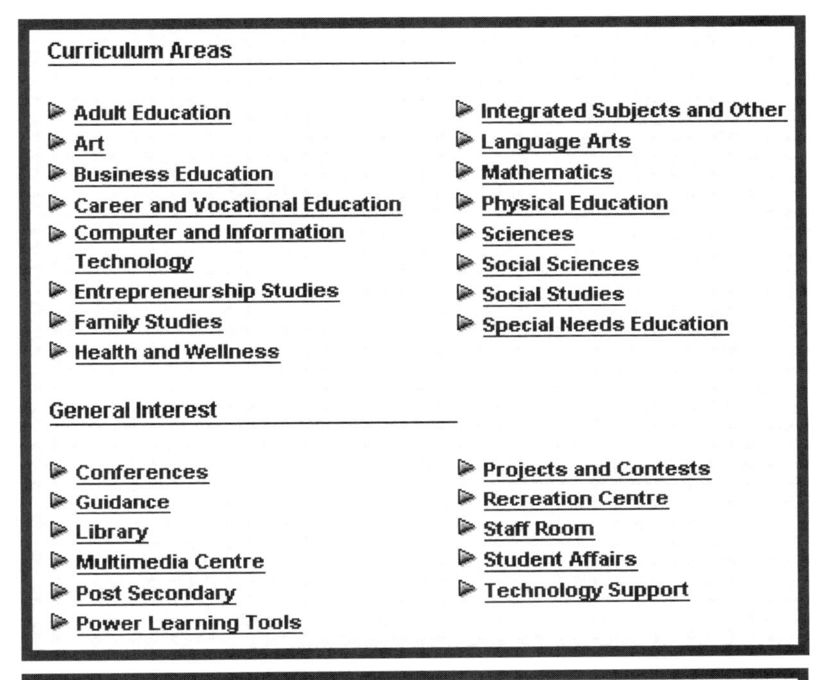

Fig. 4.2–4.3. These images show the wide range of educational resources at the SchoolNet site.
Used by permission

Collaborative Lesson Archive

http://faldo.atmos.uiuc.edu/CLA/

Join the more than ten thousand educators who visit this site every week to access the huge volume of educational resources here.

Resources for Preschool to Undergraduate levels. Simply click on the grade level and subject from the selection listed below.

- Art
- Drama
- Geography
- History
- Math
- Music
- Physical Education
- Reading
- Science
- Social Studies
- Trips
- Writing

Cornell Theory Center Math and Science Gateway

www.tc.cornell.edu/Edu/MathSciGateway/

You will find K–12 resources at this site maintained by the Cornell Department of Education. Some of the topics are shown in the screen capture (Fig. 4.4), but there are many more in the "resources" section. Just scroll down the page and click on the topics illustrated below.

Astronomy	Agriculture
Biology	Chemistry
Computers	Earth & Environmental Science
Engineering	Health and Medicine
Mathematics	Meteorology
Physics	Monthly Sci/Math Topic

Fig. 4.4. Choose your topic and click away. Shown here are some sample subjects from the site.

Used by permission

CurriculumWeb

www.curriculumweb.org/ercntr/spiceislands/sivoyage/sivhome.html

There are a lot of good resources here for teachers and learners in a variety of subject areas. The "Spice Island Voyage" is a bit outdated since it was completed in the mid-1990s, but the site contains a good record of the voyage of discovery to fascinating tropical islands.

Resources in the listed subject areas are related to the voyage adding interest and "spice" to any classroom. For example in the "math" section students can learn to calculate sea-wave heights, wavelengths, and wave periods during a storm at sea. Lots of fun.

Elementary to Senior-high level.

Education Index

www.educationindex.com/education_resources.html

Here is another very good site to begin your search for resources in a wide variety of subject areas. Topics range from conventional school subjects to more specific areas such as agriculture, construction trades, ethnic/cultural studies, law, military technologies, public administration, statistics, women's studies and many others.

All levels.

Education Planet—The Education Web Guide

www.educationplanet.com/

You can browse through the over 300,000 quality educational resources here to find what you are looking for. There are curriculum tools in the "Teacher's Section," and a lot of Lesson Plans. Click near the top of the page on the appropriate blue button or choose from the list shown in the screen capture (Fig. 4.5).

Arts & Music
Music, Arts Resources, Visual Arts ...

Communications and the Media
Journalism, Radio, Television ...

Computers & the Internet
Computers, Fun Web Resources for Kids, Internet ...

Economics & Business
Business, Economics, Finance ...

Education
Higher Ed, K-12 Resources, Teacher Resources ...

Environment
Agriculture, Animals, Gardening ...

Geography & Countries
Geography, Maps, Regional Resources ...

Government & Law
Government, Law, Military Science ...

Health, Nutrition & Sports
Family Health, Medical Ailments, Sports ...

History
Resources, U.S. History, World History ...

Linguistics & Language Arts
Grammar, Foreign Languages, Writing Technique ...

Literature
Authors & Poets, Poetry, Mythology ...

Math
Resources, Tables & Tools, Activities ...

People & Society
Culture, Food & Eating, People ...

Research Tools
Encyclopedias/Almanacs, Libraries, Reference Sources ...

Science & Technology
Science Themes and Topics, Social Science, Technology ...

Fig. 4.5. Here is a list of available topics at the Education Planet site.

Education World®: Education Topics

http://db.education-world.com/perl/browse

This site is loaded with resources for educators, and includes sections for counselors, administrators, parents, and students. Besides the many resources for standard school curricula, K–12, there are also resources for Vocational Education, Gifted Education, Disabilities, and University and College levels.

- Administration Resources; Grants, Reform, School Counselors
- Adult & Continuing Ed; Institutes, Courses, Workshops
- Arts & Humanities; Art History, Language, Art
- Distance Education; K12, Internet, Vocational
- Education Organizations; Africa, Asia, Europe, US
- History; Regional, US, World
- Internet Resources; Forums, Internet Safety, Web Quests
- K12 Schools: Primary, Secondary, School Districts

- Math; Primary, Secondary
- Parent Resources: Children's Health, College Ed
- Physical Education; Exercise, Nutrition, Sports
- Regional Resources: Africa, Asia, Europe, US
- Research Resources: Government, Libraries, Newspapers
- Science; Life, Physical, Space
- Social Sciences; Archaeology, Area Studies, Law
- Special Education: Disabilities, Gifted Ed
- Student Resources: School Life, College Prep
- Teacher Resources: Lesson Plans, Professional Development
- Universities: Asia, Canada, Europe, US
- University Departments: A&H, Science, Social Science
- Vocational Resources: Auto, Culinary, Tech Schools

Education World®—Teacher Resources

http://db.education-world.com/perl/browse?cat_id=1844

This is the "Resources" page of the Education World site (see Fig. 4.6), and resources are what you will find. Click on the "Lesson Plans" link on the left of the page or scroll down to browse the lesson plans or any of the many other categories.

Other resources at this site:

- Teachers' Home Pages
- Teaching Methods
- Teaching Strategies

*Associations & Organizations
*Directories & Indices
Brainstorming
By Grade Level
Classroom Management
Companies
Concept Mapping & Graphic Organizers
Developmental Learning
Education & Technology
Education Employment Opportunities
Education Grants
Education Standards & Testing
Lesson Plans
Magazines & Journals
Multi-Age Classrooms
Multicultural Education
Professional Development
School Projects
Student Motivation
Substitute Teaching

Fig. 4.6. Click on the "Lesson Plans" section as shown here to access great resources.
Used by permission

Electronic Journals Library Online

www.lib.utexas.edu/ejour/

This site, from the University of Texas at Austin, contains an extensive list of journals in areas from arts and humanities to education, engineering, nursing, science, social sciences, and many more. Reference for advanced levels.

FinAid | Scholarships

www.finaid.org/scholarships/

If you or your students are looking for the best sources for financial aid in the U.S., you may not have to look any further than the pages of this very thorough and well-organized site. There is even a link to many Canadian resources for financial aid as well.

- Loans
- Scholarships
- Military Aid (The information on this page is intended primarily for US citizens)
- Other Types of Aid

Free-ed.net: Free Education on the Internet

www.free-ed.net/

If this is your first visit to Free-ed.net, you are in for a real treat. This site is dedicated to providing free academic, career, and vocational education for all people everywhere. Great job guys! Just look in the General Course Catalog at the selection of online courses that are continually growing.

Business & Economics

- Accounting & Bookkeeping
- Business
- Economics
- Finance
- Marketing & Sales
- Legal Studies
- Personal Finance

Career & Technology

- Automotive

- Computer Technology
- Construction
- Electronics
- Environment
- Fashion & Textiles
- Health Occupations
- HVAC
- Hospitality
- Legal Assisting & Court Reporting
- Manufacturing
- Welding

Information Technology
Computer Information Systems
- Database Management—Desktop Publishing—Graphics—Integrated Packages—Internet—Management Information— Multimedia—Networking—Operating Systems—Spreadsheets—Word Processing

Computer Languages & Scripts
- Assemblers—Basic & Visual Basic—C & C++—COBOL—HTML—Java—Pascal—Perl & CGI

Education
- Administration & Leadership
- Counseling
- Early Childhood Education
- Educational Methods
- Psychology, Tests & Measurement
- Special Education
- Homeschooling

Engineering
- Chemical Engineering
- Civil & Construction Engineering
- Electrical Engineering
- Industrial Engineering
- Mechanical Engineering

GED Preparation

Humanities

- Art
- English
- English as a Second Language
- Journalism
- Modern Languages
- Arabic—Chinese—Dutch—French—German—Modern Greek—Hebrew—Italian—Japanese—Portuguese—Russian—Spanish
- Classical Languages
- Performing Arts
- Philosophy
- Religion
- Literature

Mathematics

- Arithmetic
- Algebra
- Trigonometry
- Geometry
- Calculus
- Statistics & Probability

Science

- Agriculture
- Astronomy
- Biology
- Anatomy & Physiology—Botany—Biochemistry—Biophysics—Ecology—Evolution—Genetics & Cell Biology—Microbiology—Zoology
- Chemistry
- Analytical Chemistry—Biochemistry—Inorganic Chemistry—Organic Chemistry—Physical Chemistry
- Geography
- Human & Cultural Geography—Physical Geography—Regional Geography
- Earth Sciences
- Geology—Meteorology—Oceanography
- Physics

Social Science

- Anthropology

- Criminal Justice
- History
- Human Ecology
- Political Science
- Psychology
- Sociology

Galaxy Education

http://galaxy.com/galaxy/Social-Sciences/Education.html

This is a very good site (see Fig. 4.7) to find resources in some of the less common areas such as Adult Education, Special Education, Education for Gifted Students, and Guidance and Counseling information, but it also has a lot of general K–12 resources.

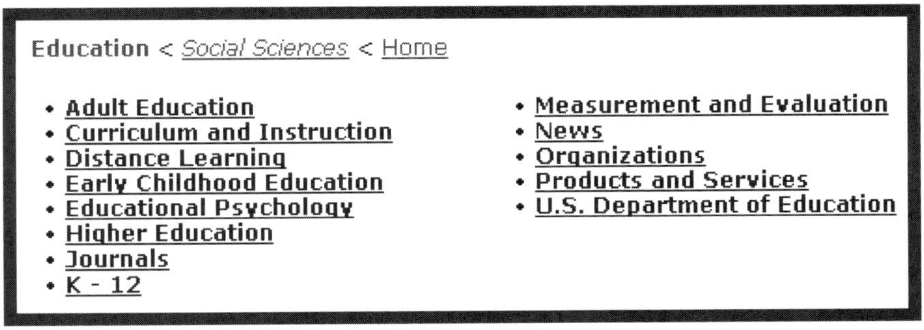

Education < Social Sciences < Home

- Adult Education
- Curriculum and Instruction
- Distance Learning
- Early Childhood Education
- Educational Psychology
- Higher Education
- Journals
- K - 12
- Measurement and Evaluation
- News
- Organizations
- Products and Services
- U.S. Department of Education

Fig. 4.7. The links shown in the image lead to some excellent resources for educators in a variety of specialized areas.

Gopher Menu

gopher://bvsd.k12.co.us:70/11/Educational_Resources/Lesson_Plans/Big%20Sky

We picked this one out because of the superior quality, and easy-to-access lesson plans in the subject areas listed below. The "Miscellaneous" section contains some good lessons on developing self-esteem as well as lessons in other academic and non-academic areas.

- Language Arts Lesson Plans
- Mathematics Lesson Plans
- Miscellaneous Lesson Plans

- Science Lesson Plans
- Social Studies

Homework Help—Home Page

www.homeworkhelp.about.com/teens/homeworkhelp/

There are so many topics at this resource-rich site (see Fig. 4.8–4.9) that it is hard to know where to begin to tell you about them. Students will benefit from the articles on writing exams, study tips, dealing with school issues, and many more topics. There are also articles and links for specific topics including art and music, English (grammar and literature), math (general, fractions, geometry, math for kids, etc.), all the sciences, plus geography, history, computer help, and much, much more.

All levels.

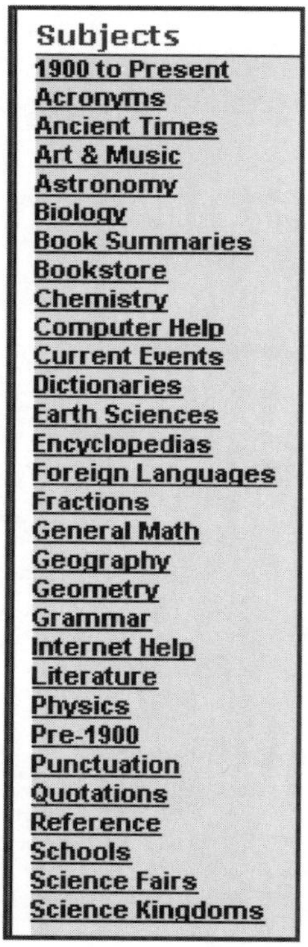

Subjects
1900 to Present
Acronyms
Ancient Times
Art & Music
Astronomy
Biology
Book Summaries
Bookstore
Chemistry
Computer Help
Current Events
Dictionaries
Earth Sciences
Encyclopedias
Foreign Languages
Fractions
General Math
Geography
Geometry
Grammar
Internet Help
Literature
Physics
Pre-1900
Punctuation
Quotations
Reference
Schools
Science Fairs
Science Kingdoms

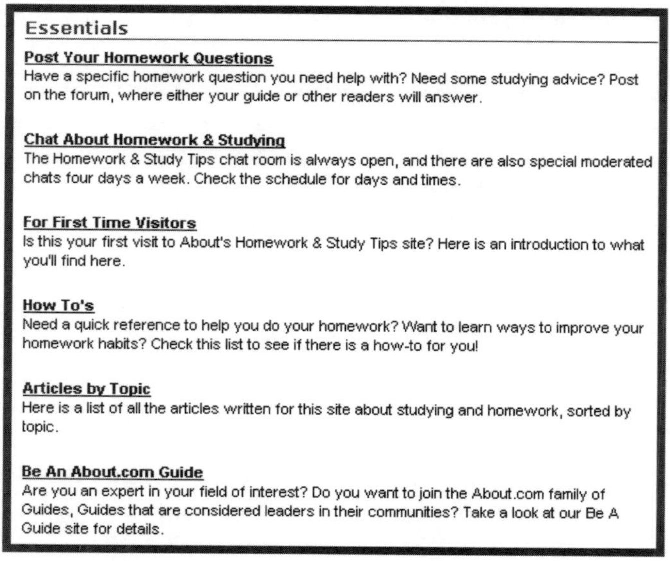

Essentials

Post Your Homework Questions
Have a specific homework question you need help with? Need some studying advice? Post on the forum, where either your guide or other readers will answer.

Chat About Homework & Studying
The Homework & Study Tips chat room is always open, and there are also special moderated chats four days a week. Check the schedule for days and times.

For First Time Visitors
Is this your first visit to About's Homework & Study Tips site? Here is an introduction to what you'll find here.

How To's
Need a quick reference to help you do your homework? Want to learn ways to improve your homework habits? Check this list to see if there is a how-to for you!

Articles by Topic
Here is a list of all the articles written for this site about studying and homework, sorted by topic.

Be An About.com Guide
Are you an expert in your field of interest? Do you want to join the About.com family of Guides, Guides that are considered leaders in their communities? Take a look at our Be A Guide site for details.

Fig. 4.8–4.9. The two images above show the great range of topics that you will find in addition to homework help, chat, and helpful articles for students.

Homeworkcentral Knowledge

www.bigchalk.com/cgi-bin.webobjects/WOPortal.woa/wa/HWCDA/sections?

Here is another site that is absolutely loaded with educational resources for all levels. You can select the subject and level from the drop-down menu or go directly to the curriculum design or lesson plans page. The menu is far too extensive to begin to list but you can be reasonably sure that the resources or lesson plans that you want will be here. (There are even lesson-plan templates, information on completing lesson plans and other handy stuff to help teachers).

Besides resources for conventional school subjects, you will also find some for special education, life skills, consumer education, and vocational and industrial arts education.

K–12 level.

- Arts
- English language arts
- Literature
- Communications
- Languages
- United States history
- World history
- Geography
- Economics & business
- Civics & government
- Cultural studies
- Regional studies
- General history topics
- Basic math
- Algebra
- Geometry
- Life sciences
- Physical sciences
- Earth sciences
- Computer science
- Social sciences
- Special education
- Life skills & consumer education
- Vocational & industrial arts
- Health, physical education & personal development
- Lesson plan aids

K–12 Lesson Plans

http://teams.lacoe.edu/documentation/places/lessons.html

This site is full of links to lesson plans in the following subject areas.

- Mathematics
- Science
- History/Social Science
- Language Arts
- The Arts
- Multi-Subject Lesson Plans

Kathy Schrock's Guide for Educators

http://school.discovery.com/schrockguide/

From the Discovery Channel School, Kathy Schrock's Guide (see Fig. 4.10) contains one of the most complete collections of educational resources on the web. It is updated daily to include the best new sites to support teaching and learning.

Lesson Plans for Teachers

www.externalharddrive.com/education/teacher/lessonplans.html

This site contains excellent links to all kinds of educational resources in English, math, sciences, social studies, Spanish, and more. There are many pre-made lesson plans, so don't miss this one if you want to save yourself some work while making your classes more interesting and exciting.
K–12 level.

- Blue Web'n Learning Application
- English Lesson Plans, Ray Saitz
- Galileo Science Lessons
- Human Languages Page
- Index of Resources for K12, Armadillo, lesson plans by subject
- ILTweb:LiveText, Lesson Plans
- Israeli English Teachers Network
- K–12 Lesson Plans, Teams Distance Learning
- K–12 Math Lesson Plans, The Awesome Library
- Lesson Plans, ASU
- Lesson Plans, K–12 Sources
- Lesson Plans, U Virginia

- Mathematics Lesson Plans, CSUN,
- Newton's Apple Lesson Plans
- Online Educator, Weekly Educational Hot Lists
- Put the Internet into your Lesson Plans
- Social Studies Lesson Plans, CSUN
- Spanish Lessons
- Volcano Lesson Plans

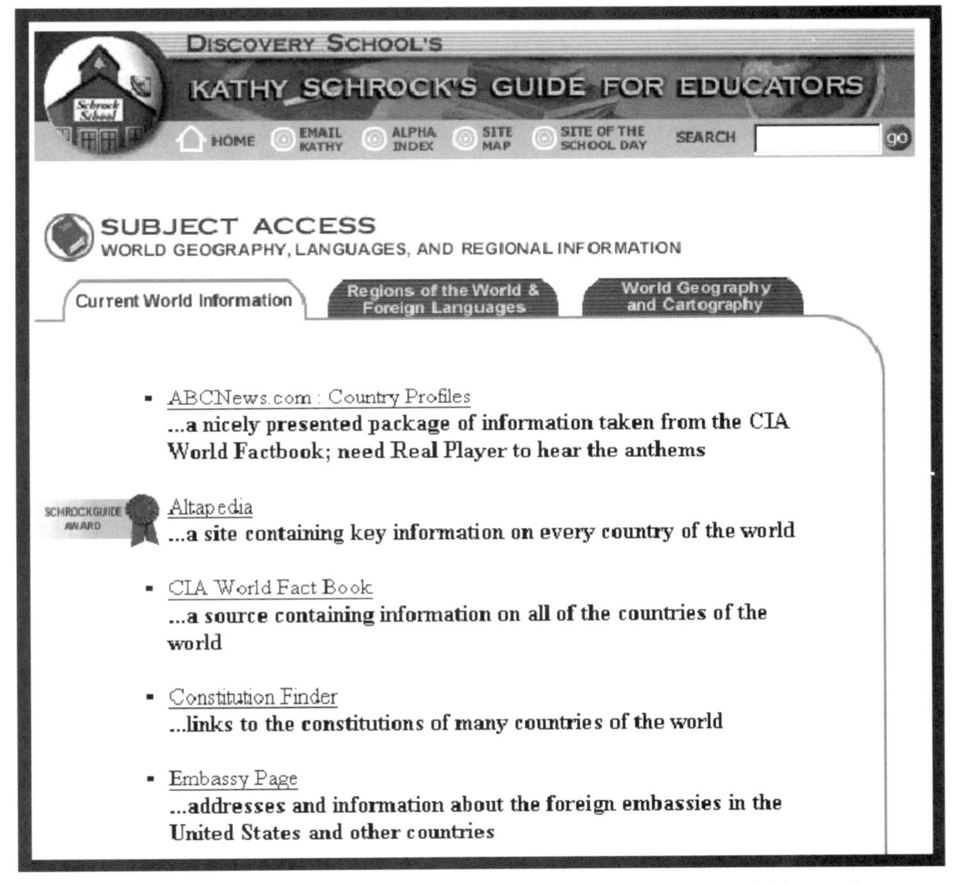

Fig. 4.10. The image illustrates some of the many resources available at this excellent site.

Fig. 4.11. You'll have arrived at the right site once you see the traffic light.
Copyright © 1998, 1999, 2000 Youthline USA. Used by permission

Lesson Stop
www.youthline-usa.com/lessonstop/

Here is another great site (see Fig. 4.11) where you will find about 500 links to educational web sites, organized by topic and grade level in the following seven subject areas, and providing thousands of lesson plans:

- L.S. Lessons
- Language Arts
- Math
- Other Lessons
- Science
- Social Studies
- Technology
- The Arts

Links 2
www.ccph.com/links/page6.html

We particularly liked the variety of resources on this site including some unusual ones, particularly in the areas of international and cultural education. Refer to the screen capture (Fig. 4.12–4.13) for a list of available topics.

All levels and many subject areas.

Resource and Research Links for Teachers and Parents

Web 66 - International schools registry and lots more.
Skewl Sites - The Best of Educational Web Sites: 'A current Internet educational site review newsletter by teachers for teachers'
Integrating the Internet - Internet Travel Guide, curriculum resources, project ideas, etc.
Multicultural Pavilion - An excellent resource for all who teach about different cultures.
Berit's Best Sites: World Travel -Links to the best global exploration sites for kids.
UNICEF USA - Kids Helping Kids - Activities and resources for teaching peace.
Reber's Resources for K-6 Teachers - Comprehensive, well organized list, with links to other great lists. See SS page for global links.
Blue Web'n - Library of 'Blue Ribbon' learning sites on the Web.
Gander Academy's Theme-Related Resources on the WWW - Extensive resource organized by themes.
West Loogootee Elementary West's Educational Resource Links - Award-winning elementary school site with tips for creating Web pages, online projects, & annotated list of educational resource links.
K-5 Cyber Trail - A well organized and entertaining Web guide for teachers and students.
Web Teacher - Extensive online tutorial for learning about the Web.
Education World - 'Where educators go to learn.'

Global Schoolnet Foundation - 'Linking Kids Around the World.' Links to 'The Global Schoolhouse: Internet Resources for Educators.'
The Global Schoolhouse Projects and Programs - GSN projects and registry for lots of others.
The GLOBE Program - Network of students, teachers and scientists working together to understand the global environment.
Scholastic.com - Lots of excellent teacher and student resources.
Scholastic Network - Comprehensive, high quality curriculum resource for K-6. Available by subscription, w/ free trial.
Scholastic Instructor - Online version of popular teacher magazine.
KIDPROJ - Variety of projects centered around using the Internet to connect kids to their world and others in it.
ETC: Educational Technology Center - Among other things, list 1550+ educational sites by theme and by subject.
The Mining Co. Guide to Parenting of K-6 Kids - Excellent resource for parents and educators dealing with range of issues.
Technological Horizons in Education Journal - Includes thorough and well organized 'Road Map to the Web for Educators II.'
From Now On: The Educational Technology Journal - Provides links for schools/classrooms interested in creating their own Web sites.
Cyber Schools - Among other projects, provides blueprint for student-created school Web site.
Safe Surf - Lists monitoring and filtering software.
Phil's Place - Page on 'Child and Internet Safety.'

Fig. 4.12–4.13. Note the wide variety of excellent resources available.
© 1999 Paul Hurteau/Creative Connections. Used by permission

Looksmart Encyclopedias and references online
www.looksmart.com/eus1/eus53706/eus53709/eus53741/r?l

Look here to find a good list of online encyclopedias such as Encarta, Worldbook, Britannica, and others, many of which have free trial periods. Others are free. There are also links to almanacs, information on countries of the world, and other fascinating links.

Good reference material for all levels.

NASA's LTP—Topic by Topic
http://learn.arc.nasa.gov/education/topics.html

This site is maintained by NASA's Learning Technologies Project. It is resource-rich and easy to navigate. The general categories available at the site are shown in Figure 4.14.

Kindergarten to advanced levels.

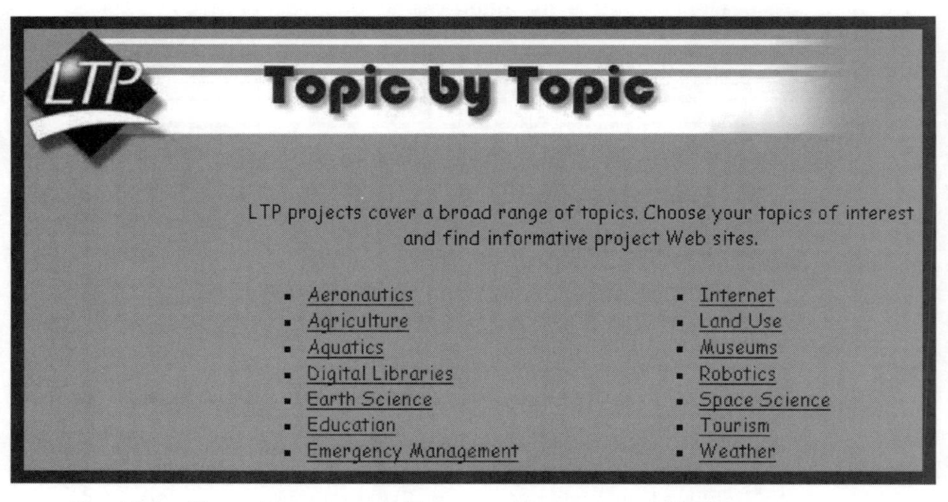

Fig. 4.14. Everything you would expect from a great NASA site.

NickNacks Telecollaborate! Site Index

http://home.talkcity.com:80/academydr/nicknacks/NNindex.html

You are going to get a pop-up window each time you click on a page here, but it is worth it to access the many resources.

You can start by clicking on the "How NickNacks Can Help You" link or check around on the menu for such options as "Participate in a Telecollaboration," "Exchange Files," "Find Tools," or "Find Projects" in the main menu. If you want specific lessons and ideas, click on "Resources" in the left frame. There you will find the following list:

- Lessons
- MultiResource
- Language Arts
- Math/Science
- Social Studies
- Reference
- Other Subjects
- Searches

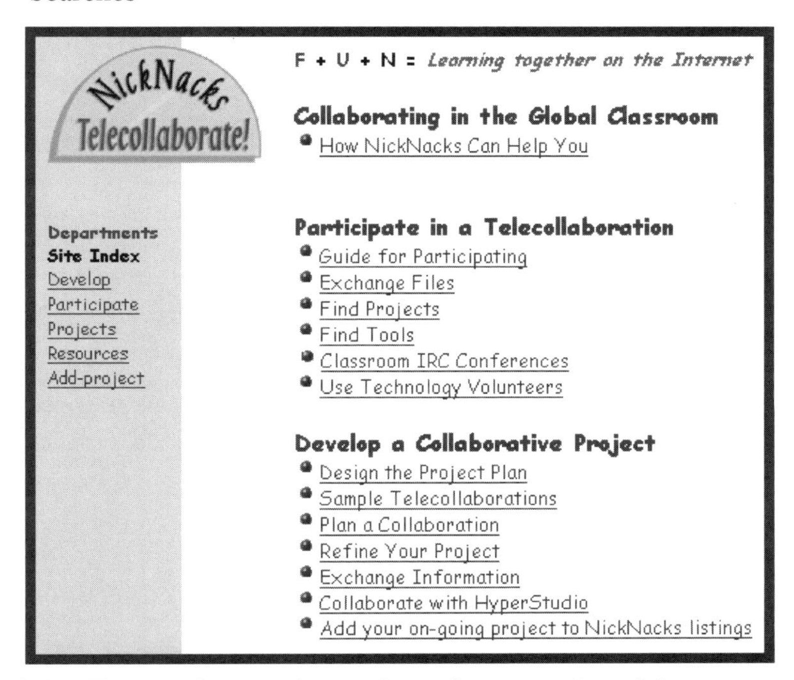

Fig. 4.15. The main frame in the site shows the options for collaborative projects with other educators around the world.

©1996-2000 NickNacks. Used by permission

Online Educational Resources

http://quest.arc.nasa.gov/OER/edures.html

There are a lot of good resources here at this alternate NASA site. Click on the Resources Lists and Subject Trees on Education, if you can't find what you want in the screen capture (see Fig. 4.16). There are resources for high school as well as university-and-college-level resources.

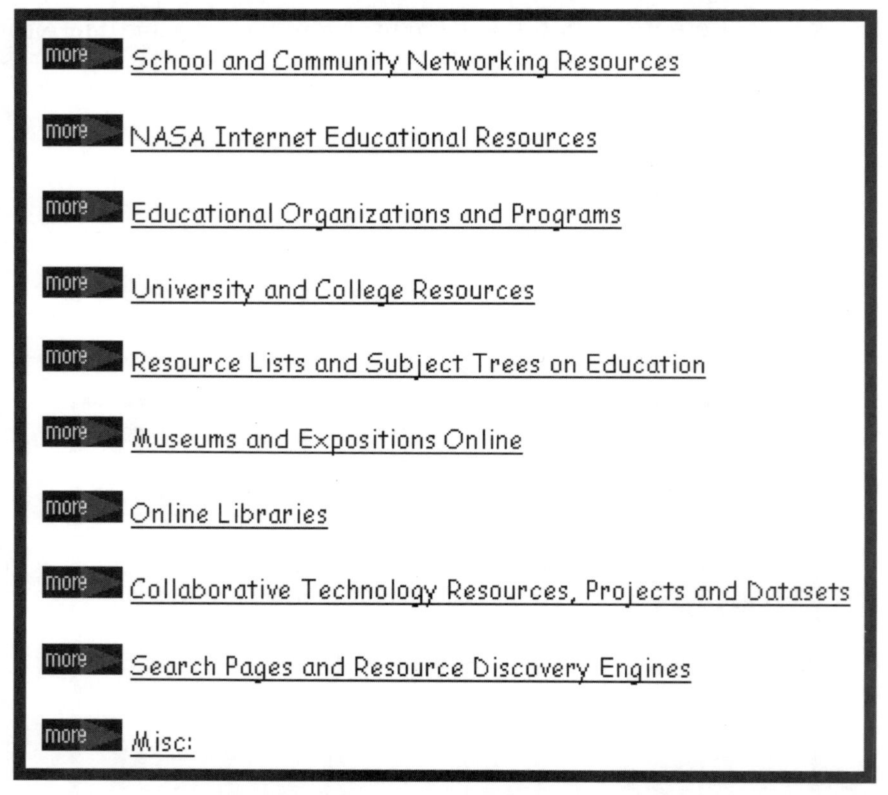

Fig. 4.16. Navigating this site is easier than flying a space shuttle. Just click away on your choice of resources.
Used by permission

Online Schoolyard

www.onlineschoolyard.com/

Click on the menu at the left to choose your subject area, then follow the links to your specific area and level of interest. The "Miscellaneous Subjects" category provides some interesting resources in addition to the regular subjects in the categories listed below.
Many K–12 level resources.

- Arts
- Computers
- English
- Languages
- Math
- PE/Health
- Science
- Social Sciences
- Misc. Subj.

Schoolhouse

http://encarta.msn.com/schoolhouse/default.asp

From the people at Encarta, of encyclopedia fame, this site has wonderfully developed lesson plans in many subject areas and at all grade levels.

- Arts
- Foreign Language
- Health
- Information Technology
- Language Arts
- Mathematics
- Philosophy
- Physical Education
- Religion
- Science
- Social Studies
- Vocational Education
- Special Collections

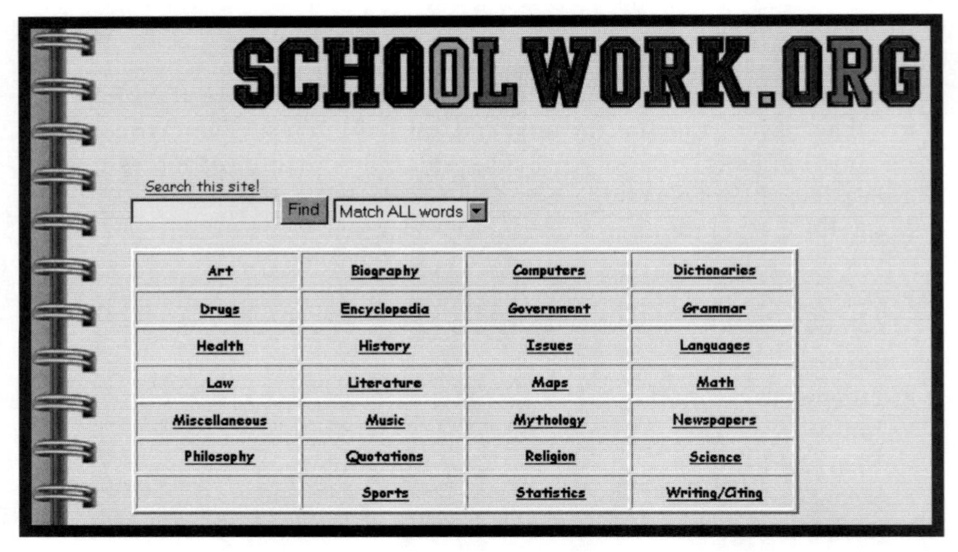

Fig. 4.17. Just look at the range of topics in the easy-to-use format. Search the site for specific topics using the "Search" feature shown at the top of the image. *Graphics and Text Copyrighted © 1996-2000. Used by permission*

Schoolwork. Ugh!
www.schoolwork.org/

Lots of great links to information here to help students from grades 7 to 12 with homework assignments. Teachers will find links to many resources including lesson ideas and lesson plans. There is a wide range of links to sites with conventional school subjects and topics including most in the list above (Fig. 4.17) plus biographies, drug and drug abuse information, maps, quotations, and much more. There is also a link to resources for kids.

Scientific American: Ask the Experts
www.sciam.com/askexpert/

You can check out the current questions posted, or ask the experts yourself if you have a question in any of the areas of Astronomy, Biology, Chemistry, Computers, Environment, Geology, Mathematics, Medicine, or Physics.

Skewl Sites

www.skewlsites.com/siteind.htm

This link takes you directly to the site index where you will find a list of subject areas and links to teacher's resources, lesson plans, or Web-based projects. You can also subscribe to a monthly educational newsletter. Topics include the following with a caution that all links may not work due to "the dynamic nature of the Internet."

StudentAwards.com

www.studentawards.com/

Here is another good awards site, this one specifically for Canadian students. You will have to take a minute or two to sign up, but the service is free, and very efficient in matching students to available funding.

- This Canadian web site gives you immediate access to our database of thousands of scholarships, bursaries, fellowships, grants, and other financial awards.

StudyWeb: General Resources

www.studyweb.com/

This site (see Fig. 4.18) has links to over 118,000 Research Quality URLs.

Agriculture
Cooperatives, Organic, Crops,...

Animals & Pets
Veterinary Medicine, Endangered,...

Architecture
History, Landscaping, Urban Planning,...

Business & Finance
& Kids, Telecommute Personal Finance,...

Communications
Public Service Broadcasting, Radio,...

Computer Science
Children's SW, Web Publishing, Shareware,...

Criminology

Grammar & Composition
Literacy, Languages, Composition,...

Government & Politics
Military Science, World Gov, U.S....

Health & Nutrition
Athletics, Nutrition, History of Sports...

History
Modern, Ancient, American...

Home & Garden
Cooking, Crafts, Home Improve...

Literature
Children's Literature , Biographies, E- Text ...

Math
Puzzles & Problems, Study Skills,

Music
Instruments, Songwriting...

Philosophy
Critical Thinking, Ethics,...

Reference
Dictionaries, OnLine Libraries, Museums...

Religion
Cults, Native American Religions,...

Science
Ecology, Engineering, Weather,...

Social Studies & Culture
Current Events, Genealogy, US Studies,...

Teaching Resources
Administration, Homeschooling, Curriculum...

Fig. 4.18. Use the drop-down menu at the top of the page for a subject list, or you can type in your preference in the search area or click on topics indicated in the sample screen capture shown above.

Teacher Talk Forum Lesson Plans

http://education.indiana.edu/cas/ttforum/lesson.html

Once again only superlatives come to mind for this exceptional site which contains all sorts of lesson plans on many different topics, from Arts to English, Computers, Math, Science, Social Studies, you name it. There are also sections for interdisciplinary and thematic units, ice-breakers, home economics, and tools for your classes such as links to sites on human anatomy, or automotive learning online.

Many lessons are in the middle school to high school range.

- Art
- Computers and Internet
- Conflict Resolution
- English as a Second Language
- Foreign Language
- Health Education
- Home Economics

- Icebreakers
- Interdisciplinary & Thematic Units
- Language Arts
- Logic, Reasoning, and Problem Solving
- Mathematics
- Miscellaneous
- Music
- Physical Education
- Science
- Social Studies
- Students With Disabilities
- Tools for Your Classes
- Other Lesson Plan Databases

Teachers' Guild Lesson Plan Library TOC
www.EDsOasis.org/TGuild/Lessons/TGuildTOC.html
There are some excellent and unusual lesson plans here at all school levels. At the K–3 level, check out lessons like "Spiders" where teachers and students search the net to read multicultural literature, research facts, and produce factual and fictional reports about spiders. At the high-school level you might try out The Periodic Table Project in science, take a multimedia look at "The Crucible" and the McCarthy era, or try "Cooking with Geography" to involve students in online projects for social studies classes.
Grades K–3, 4–6, 7–9, 9–12.

- Arts
- History/Geography
- Language Arts
- Math
- Science
- Social Science

Teachers Page of Lesson Plans
www.library.ualberta.ca/library_html/libraries/coutts/lessons.html
This site, from the University of Alberta's H.T. Coutts Library, contains a great variety of lesson plans and teaching tips for teachers at all levels and in nearly all academic disciplines.

- From Canada's SchoolNet: Staff Room/Lesson Plans and Classroom Activites: Lesson Plans from CanaDisk
- From P.I.G.S. Space: Co-op Lesson plans related to the New Brunswick curriculum.
- From The Media Awareness Network (Canada): Teaching Media, classroom ideas, teaching units, student handouts and background, information on child related media topics.
- From ERIC: AskERIC Lesson Plans, Newton's Apple
- From Statistics Canada: Lesson Plans and Classroom Activities
- Lesson Plans & WebQuests: the process
- Other Lesson Plan Pages on the Web:
  - Art
  - ESL
  - Social Studies
  - Multiculturalism
  - Math & Science
  - Environmental Education
  - Multidisciplinary or Thematic Approach Lesson Plans
  - Utilizing the Internet or other Technologies
- Other Lesson Plan Archives

Teachers.Net

http://teachers.net/

Choose your lessons here by grade level or by subject simply by clicking on the "lessons" section at the top of the page. There are also chatboards and live chatrooms, curriculum resources, webtools, and even a place to look for a new job if you feel like you need a change of scenery. Lots of good stuff here.

K–12 and advanced.

Teachnet.com

www.teachnet.com/lesson/

Here is another site full of lesson plans in Art, Music, Language Arts, Math, Science, Social Studies, and more. Check out the "How To" section for many great tips on classroom decor (some fun and interesting stuff to brighten any classroom), classroom management tips, ideas on getting organized, fundraising, and so much more.

Elementary to high school levels.

Ten simple secrets for a paper

www.talion.com/sachi-3.htm

If you are a student looking for ways to improve your writing marks on papers in any subject area, or a teacher looking for ways to help students write better, check out this site.

They also offer a pay-for-use editing service.

Higher levels.

The English Server

http://eserver.org/

The English Server's primary function is to publish texts online in the arts and humanities. Their collections include art, architecture, drama, fiction, poetry, history, political theory, cultural studies, philosophy, women's studies and music. Teachers can use this site to direct students to online research assignments or to any of the more than 20,000 texts in a range of humanities topics.

High school through university level.

The Lesson Plans Page

www.lessonplanspage.com/javaframe.htm

Here you can choose your subject with the click of a button from the color coded selection, then choose the grade level you wish to access,

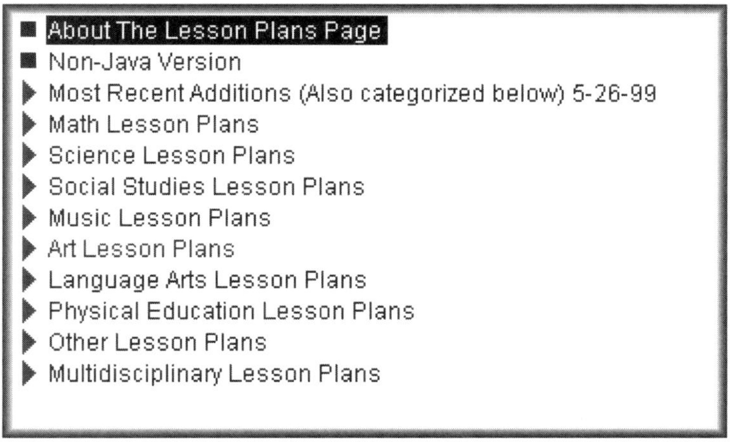
About The Lesson Plans Page
Non-Java Version
Most Recent Additions (Also categorized below) 5-26-99
Math Lesson Plans
Science Lesson Plans
Social Studies Lesson Plans
Music Lesson Plans
Art Lesson Plans
Language Arts Lesson Plans
Physical Education Lesson Plans
Other Lesson Plans
Multidisciplinary Lesson Plans

Fig. 4.19. Begin by clicking on your subject area as shown here, then choose your grade level at the next link.

The Lesson Plans Page is owned and operated by EduScope, L.L.C. All rights reserved. Used by permission

and poof, you are knee-deep in lesson plan heaven. Lots of topics in the hundreds of lesson plans here.
Pre–K to 12 level.

The Mental Edge®—The Mental Edge Reviews
www.learningshortcuts.com/new1Reviews.html
Students can click onto sites here and practice skills independently through the interactive exercises on a good variety of topics as shown below. The exercises teach as they correct wrong answers.
Mainly high school level.
Lessons from Elementary to Proficiencies:

- English
- General Science
- Life Science
- Mathematics
- Standardized Test Preparation
- Vocabulary
- World Geography

Vassar's CoolSchool/Mainly Text
http://coolschool.edu/startlow.htm
Here is another route to a lot of pre-made lesson plans and other resources for teachers and students brought to you by Vassar College. Besides the standard academic curricula, this interesting site has a good "Silly Stuff" selection that can brighten up most learning environments. The site also has several other good academic and non-academic links such as College and University Home pages, teen talk, and much more. Two of the categories are shown in the lists below.

Go to Class
- Art
- Music
- Literature
- Language and cultures
- Social studies
- People in mathematics and the sciences
- Mathematics
- Astronomy

- Biology
- Physics
- Chemistry
- Geology—Earth science
- References and resources

Teachers' lounge
- General Resources for Teachers
- Science Teaching Aids
- Math Teaching Aids
- Language Arts Teaching Aids
- Social Studies Teaching Aids
- Music Teaching Aids
- Art Teaching Aids

Welcome to How Stuff Works!

http://howthingswork.com/

We really like this site because it answers a lot of interesting questions about the way many things work. Students will explore such phenomena as the workings of air bags, computers, electronics, engines, and even their bodies, along with a lot of other topics which are sure to inspire learners to learn. You can even ask your own question if you can't find the answer you want in the extensive archives. Recommended for motivating students to learn, particularly in the areas of Math, Science, Computer Studies, Vocational Training and other school subjects.

Welcome to K–12 World!

www.k–12world.net:80/cy_curr_res.cfm

Choose from the "curriculum resources" listed below (see Fig. 4.20–4.21) to find many good lessons and other resources at all academic levels.

Don't miss the "Teacher's Resources" section which connects you to good resources for curriculum planning and puts you in touch with other educators.

K–12 level.

Agriculture
Art
Business Education
Computer Science
Drama/Forensics
Family Consumer Services
Home Economics
Industrial Technology
Language Arts
Libraries, Research, Reference
Mathematics
Music and Dance
News, Current Events
Physical/Health Education
Religion
Science
Social Studies
Special Education
World Languages

Award Winning School Sites
Curriculum Planning
Technology Planning
Professional Devolopment
Educational Associations
Grants

Fig. 4.20–4.21. As you can see from the images, the list of resources is extensive.

Welcome to the Alphabet Superhighway

www.ash.udel.edu/ash/

Here is a colorful and interesting site (see Fig. 4.22 and 4.23) full of resources particularly in the areas of Sciences and Social Sciences. K–12 levels.

Fig. 4.22. On the main page, click on "Exhibit Hall" to access the resources shown here.
Used by permission

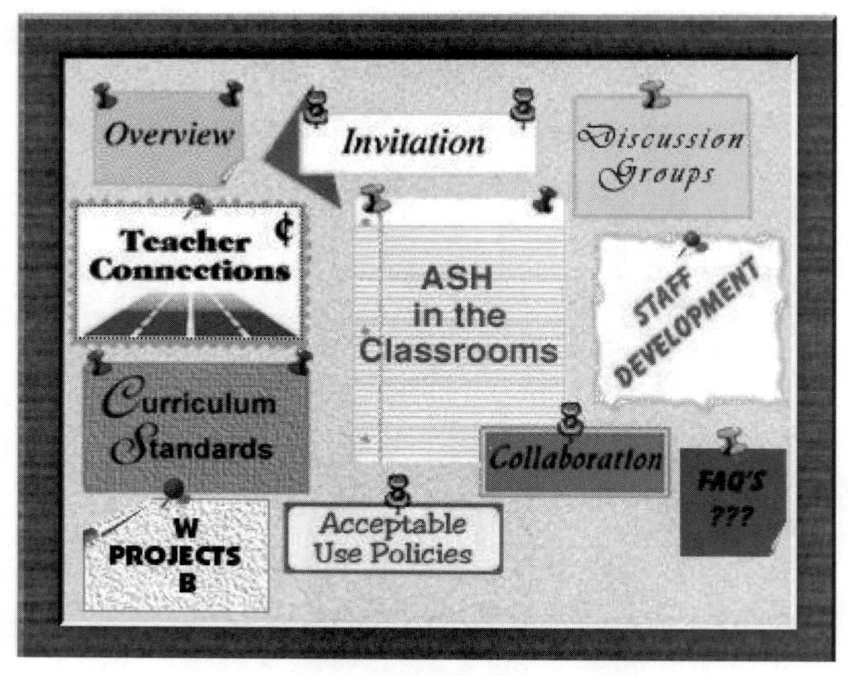

Fig. 4.23. Visit the "Teacher Connections" page shown on the bulletin board to learn about web projects or to collaborate with other teachers online.
Used by permission

WWW Virtual Library

http://vlib.org/

This site (see Fig. 4.24) is loaded with resources for mainly higher-level classes in a wide variety of subject areas. Everything from brewing beer to astrophysics. Check out the "Education" section for an even wider range of topics classified alphabetically, by Education level, Kindergarten to Post-Graduate, by resources provided, by type of site, or by country. Also links to other virtual libraries and educational newsgroups.

High school and up.

The WWW Virtual Library

- **Agriculture**
  Agriculture, Beer and Brewing, Gardening...
- **Business and Economics**
  Economics, Finance, Transportation...
- **Computer Science**
  Computing, Languages, Web...
- **Communications and Media**
  Communications, Telecommunications, Journalism...
- **Education**
  Education, Cognitive Science, Libraries, Linguistics...
- **Engineering**
  Civil, Chemical, Electrical, Mechanical, Software...
- **Humanities**
  Anthropology, Art, Dance, History, Museums, Philosophy...
- **Information Management**
  Information Sciences, Knowledge Management...
- **International Affairs**
  International Security, Sustainable Development, UN...
- **Law**
  Law, Environmental Law...
- **Recreation**
  Recreation and Games, Gardening, Sport...
- **Regional Studies**
  Asian, Latin American, West European...
- **Science**
  Biosciences, Health, Earth Science, Physics, Chemistry...
- **Society**
  Political Science, Religion, Social Sciences...

Fig. 4.24. Take your pick of topics as shown in the image to find the many resources available in each section.

Chapter 5

English

Welcome to the English Section of this Guide! Here you will find hundreds of lesson plans and other resources to assist in teaching and learning from the very basics to the most advanced levels. All sites have been chosen for their ease of use, practical application, and time-saving opportunities. Teachers can use many of the lesson plans for daily classroom preparation or they can direct students to interactive exercises that will allow them to work independently at their own pace while freeing up teachers' time to work with other students.

CHAPTER OVERVIEW

ENGLISH

Alberta Education Website

http://ednet.edc.gov.ab.ca/studentprograms/

You will need Adobe Acrobat Reader to access the information on this excellent site. You can download Acrobat Reader for free directly from the Alberta Education site by clicking on the blue Adobe link. Once you have Acrobat Reader, you will be able to download complete curriculum information, and many useful resources for language arts classrooms including a complete description of expected learning outcomes. Although some of the information is specific to the curriculum in Alberta, Canada, most is applicable in any school system.
Levels K–12.

Alphabet Superhighway

www.ash.udel.edu/ash/tutor/tutorframe.html

We are very impressed with this site, particularly the "Reading" section, where you will find online books for grades K–12, some with audio-visual accompaniment. For higher level learners, there is a link to The American Literary Classics Library where students can choose from a wide selection of books. Click on the gray icon in the library to find the books.

Students can also check out the homework helper, while teachers will find a helpful section on training read/write tutors.

The writing section is good as well, but mainly focuses on higher levels. Below is a list of topics from the site.

Writing Center

Explore the Writing Center to:

- Write better, write more often, and be more aware of what you are writing.
- View classroom pre-writing, writing, and editing activities.
- Access other online writing and reference tools.

Reading Center

Take a break and read a good book. Here are some links to online books for students in grades:

- K–4
- 5–8
- 9–12

Homework Helper

Here you will find links to sites geared towards helping students with their homework. Help for most subjects is available, while several sites focus primarily on helping students with the following core subjects:

- Math
- Science
- Social Studies
- Literature
- Foreign Languages

APA-Style Documentation

http://webster.commnet.edu/apa/apa_index.htm

The complete guide found here provides a very handy reference for documenting research papers. The description below is taken from the site.

A Guide for Writing Research Papers based on Styles Recommended by the American Psychological Association.

- The APA Manual contains a great deal of material on the art of writing itself, which this guide cannot go into. We do recommend, however, the CCTC's GUIDE TO GRAMMAR AND WRITING, which provides numerous digital handouts about grammar and style, 99 computer-graded quizzes, guidance on essay writing, and a place to ask questions about grammar and writing.

AskERIC Lesson Plans: Language Arts

http://ericir.syr.edu/Virtual/Lessons/Lang_arts/index.html

This link takes you directly to the Language Arts page where you will find many well written lesson plans and resources mostly at the K–6 level but some higher. Click on the following subjects at the site, check the question archives or ask a question yourself. A description taken from the site is shown below.

- Debate
- Handwriting
- Journalism
- Listening
- Literature
- Reading
- Spelling
- Story telling
- Vocabulary
- Whole language
- Writing composition
- Got an education question? If you are an educator, librarian, parent, or anyone interested in education, AskERIC's Q&A Service can help! Utilizing the diverse resources and expertise of the national ERIC System, AskERIC staff will respond to your question within 2 business days with ERIC database citations and publications, Internet resources, and referrals to other sources of information. AskERIC responds to every question with personalized resources relevant to your needs.
- Also includes a SEARCH element, which allows users to search for lessons and resources on a specific topic.

Bartleby.com Great Books Online

www.bartleby.com/

If you are familiar with Herman Melville's short story masterpiece, the name "Bartleby" will likely stir up some fine memories. Bartleby.com contains great works of fiction, nonfiction and classic poetry as well as reference works such as the Columbia Encyclopedia, Roget's II Thesaurus, Bartlett's and Simpson's quotations, English Usage and even the Farmer's Cookbook for those home economics classes.

High school and up, reference and reading.

Business English grammar, vocabulary, listening and reading exercises

www.better-english.com/exerciselist.html

Despite the title's emphasis on business English, this site (see Fig. 5.1) has a lot to offer for teachers wanting to provide supplementary exercises for students who need to improve their general English skills. The interactive exercises begin at an elementary level and progress from there.

Try out the Business English Crosswords and Business English Hangman.

Grammar Exercises	Spelling exercises
Vocabulary Exercises	Sentence Construction exercises
Find the Pairs Exercises	Business English Crosswords
Missing Words Exercise	Business English Hangman
Matching Exercises	Text Exercises
Grammar by e-mail every week.	*Multi Word Verbs* by e-mail every week
Sign our Guest Book	Read our Guest Book
Books we like	Links to other sites of interest

Fig. 5.1. The image taken from the site shows the variety of exercises available.

California State Board of Education

www.sdcoe.k12.ca.us/score/stand/sbestd.html

Somewhat similar in focus to the Alberta Education Website previously mentioned, this site outlines the California standards and curriculum content for language arts programs at K to 12 levels. Teachers and administrators can use the contents as a model for curriculum development and setting academic standards.

The list below is selected from the site.

Introduction to Language Arts Standards (Kindergarten, Grades 1 to 12)

Reading
- Word Analysis and Systematic Vocabulary Development
- Reading Comprehension
- Literary Response and Analysis

Writing
- Writing Strategies
- Writing Applications (Genres and their Characteristics)

Listening and Speaking
- Listening and Speaking Strategies
- Speaking Applications (Genres and their Characteristics)

Oral and Written English Language Conventions
Language Arts Standards Glossary

Canada's SchoolNet / Learning Resources

www.schoolnet.ca/home/e/resources/

There are some good resources here for teachers in the areas shown in Fig. 5.2. Lots of stuff for primary and elementary levels. Higher-level and independent learners can find a lot of good resources as well, including links to a complete online English 30 (Grade 12) course, and an excellent Online Literature Library, with many classic titles.

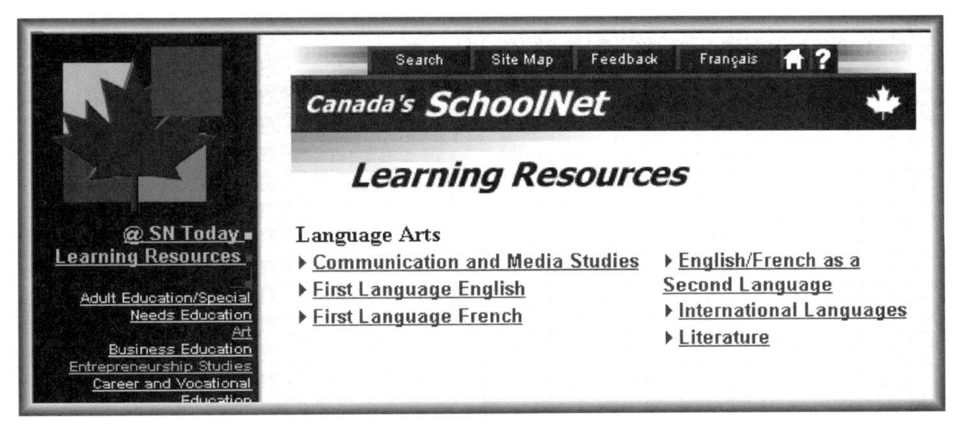

Fig. 5.2. Choose from the menu shown in the image, or scroll down the page for more resources.
Used by permission

Classic Short Stories

www.bnl.com/shorts/

English teachers take heart. Literature is alive and well and represented admirably by the collection shortstory classics chosen in this excellent site.

The works of Guy de Maupassant, Charles Dickens, Joyce, Kipling, Hawthorne, Poe, H.G. Wells, and many more of the greats are here to read online. Reluctant readers might find online reading more attractive than books, so give it a try with them.

High school level and up.

CLN WWW Language Arts

www.cln.org/map.html#LA

Scroll down the page to the English/Language Arts section (see Fig. 5.3), and one click will get you to a ton of resources on English-related topics from puppetry to poetry.

- English/Language Arts
  - Curricular Resources in General English
  - Curricular Resources in Literature and Books
  - Curricular Resources in Poetry
  - Curricular Resources in Writing
  -
  - Instructional Materials in Engish
  -
  - Theme Page: Celebrating Women
  - Theme Page: Clip Art
  - Theme Page: English Grammar and Style
  - Theme Page: Mythology
  - Theme Page: Publish Your Poetry
  - Theme Page: Puppetry
  - Theme Page: Shakespeare
  - Theme Page: Stories, Folklore, and Fairy Tales
  - Theme Page: W. O. Mitchell

Fig. 5.3. Here is a recent list of available topics from the site.
© 2000 Open School. Used by permission

Dave's ESL Cafe
www.eslcafe.com/

We have included this site (see Fig. 5.4) in the English section as well as the ESL section of this guide because many of the resources here can be used for elementary learners of any linguistic background including English. The interactive quizzes and other resources are good ways to get reluctant learners to practice and review. Be sure to check out the Idea Cookbook for lots of great teaching/learning ideas and activities.

Elementary level.

ESL Cafe News
Address Book | Announcements
Bookstore | Chat Central | Discussion Forums
FAQs | Help Center | Hint-of-the-Day | Idea Cookbook | Idioms
Job Center | Mailing List | Message Exchange | Phrasal Verbs | Photo Gallery
Quizzes | Quotes | Search the Web | Slang | Student Email | Teacher Email | Today in History | Web Guide Links

Fig. 5.4. The image shows the menu of available resources and topics.
Copyright © 1995-2000 Dave's ESL Cafe. All rights reserved. Used by permission

Education World®: Lesson Planning Center: Archives: Language Arts

www.education-world.com/a_lesson/archives/lang.shtml

Scroll down the page and you will find an impressive Language Arts resource list including Lit to Fit: Literature Lessons for every grade.

Other topics from the site are shown below:

- A Quotation a Day: Just What the Language Doctor Ordered!
- Priceless Works of Language Arts: Invaluable Activities!
- Kids Can W.R.I.T.E. (Write, Revise, Inform, Think, and Edit)—Activities for Every Grade!
- Vocabulary and Spelling: Do Your Students Say "Boring"?
- "Every Day" Activities: Language
- Taking the "Pain" out of Lesson Planning: Children's Book Resources on the Web
- ABC Books Aren't for Babies!
- Reading Activities for Read-In Day!
- 25 Ideas to Motivate Young Readers!
- Seventh Graders Writing Italian Sonnets? You Bet!

English Zone—Welcome! EZ Main Page

http://english-zone.com

This fast and easy-to-navigate site (see Fig. 5.5) is filled with resources such as interactive exercises and quizzes. Don't miss this one. Be sure to click on the Teacher Zone for practical resources like printable worksheets. Check out the FunStuff page as well.

All levels, including lots of elementary stuff.

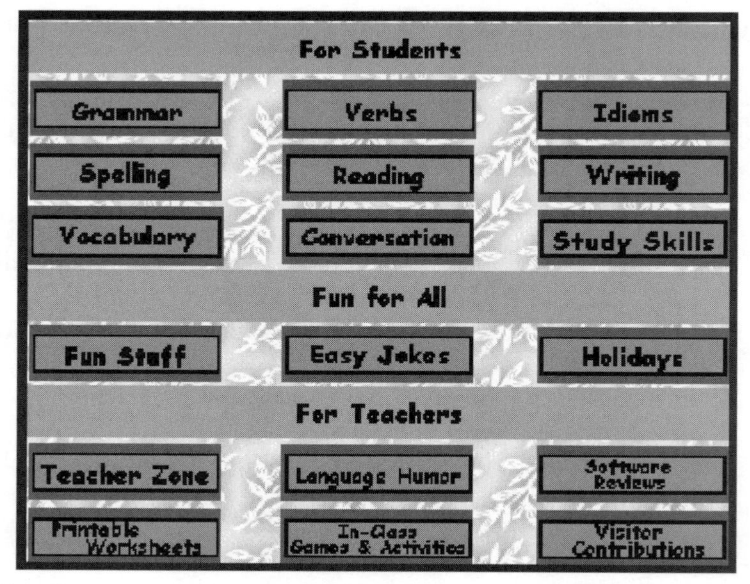

Fig. 5.5. Once you are here, just click on the words to bring you to the many great resources at this site.
English-Zone.Com Copyright © 2000 Kaye Mastin Mallory. Used by permission

Free Education: English
www.free-ed.net/fr06/fr0602.htm

This site offered by free-ed.net has online courses and tutorials as well as interactive texts and references. The interactive guide to writing a term paper will be helpful for students learning to write. Topics and resources available at the time of writing are listed below.
Higher levels.

Courses and Tutorials
- Learn How to Write
- Teach Me Spelling
- Guide to Grammar and Writing
- Online English Grammar
- Step by Step Interactive Guide to Writing a Term Paper

Interactive Textbooks and References
- Bartlett's Familiar Quotations
- Roget's Internet Thesaurus
- Webster's Dictionary

Classics
- Elements of Style, William Strunk, Jr
- Course Outlines, Lecture, Notes, Quizzes, Etc.

Helpful Study Materials
- AP English Language & Literature
- AP Studies at free-ed.net

Gopher Menu

gopher://bvsd.k12.co.us:70/11/Educational_Resources/Lesson_Plans/Big%20Sky/language_arts

This site has a good variety of links to lesson plans and resources. Topics range from basic vocabulary to more advanced writing and literature. For ease of use, grade-level applicability is shown beside each title.
K–12 levels.

Grammar Links

www.gl.umbc.edu/~kpokoy1/grammar1.htm

This site has some good links to resources for lower-level English students as well as ESL. Scroll down to access online quizzes and a teacher's section. Other contents are indicated in the following list taken directly from the site.
Elementary level.

References
- An On-Line English Grammar: This link will take you to the Table of Contents of a grammar reference from Edunet. From this page, you can follow links to explanations and examples of specific elements of grammar.
- Grammar Resources for English Language Learners: This is a list of links to many grammar-related resources on the Web.

Exercises
- Animal Idioms: If you are an advanced ESL student, this exercise can help test your knowledge of idiomatic expressions that contain animal names, like "taking the bull by the horns."

- CNN Newsroom and Worldview for ESL students: This site contains grammar, vocabulary and discussion questions based on real news stories.
- Interactive English Language Exercises: Four grammar exercises are offered here. These exercises are relatively advanced. When you finish each exercise, you can submit your answers and receive your score and explanations for the more difficult questions right away.

Note: These exercises are only available during the school year, but you can look at previous exercises at any time!

Quizzes

- Test Your English. Also from Edunet, this quiz contains 80 questions. When you've completed the quiz, you can submit your answers with the click of a button, and you will receive the results by email!
- The ESL Quiz Center: Part of Dave Sperling's ESL Cafe, this page contains a Grammar section where there are 17 quizzes for all levels of ESL. You can submit your answers at the end of each quiz and receive the results immediately!
- Grammar Quiz: This quiz page is for advanced ESL students. Just click on an answer—you will be told whether you are right or wrong.
- Self-Study Quizzes for ESL Students: From the Internet TESL Journal, this page contains 23 quizzes especially for students of ESL.

For Teachers

- Grammar Grammar Grammar: Download Mastery Learning Grammar 4.0 for Win95 (or 3.0 for DOS) from this site. This is shareware that includes tutorials and drills which teach English grammar including:
  —recognizing subjects and verbs;
  —parts of speech;
  —recognizing simple, complex, compound, and compound/complex sentences; clause types (adverb, adjective, noun);
  —sentence patterns (subject-verb-direct object, etc.);
  —verbals;
  —capitalization;
  —punctuation;
  —pronoun/case.

Exam Writer

- This site allows you to create your own multiple choice and true/false quizzes online, without the need for your own web server.

Grammar Quizzes

This is a part of The Internet TESL Journal's Self-Study Quizzes for ESL Students

Page Contents

Articles | Cloze | Conjunctions | Dialogs | Plurals | Prepositions | Pronouns | Sentence Structure | Tag Questions | Verbs | What's the Correct Sequence | Word Choice | Other Quizzes

Fig. 5.6. See the topics as outlined in the image above. Elementary and ESL levels.
Copyright (C) 1995-1999 by The Internet TESL Journal. Used by permission

Grammar Quizzes (Self-Study Quizzes for ESL Students)
www.aitech.ac.jp/~iteslj/quizzes/grammar.html

Once again this site (see Fig. 5.6) is intended primarily for ESL students, but the interactive quizzes are very good practice for any lower-level student of English.

Guide to Grammar and Writing
http://webster.commnet.edu/HP/pages/darling/original.htm

From basic grammar to developed writing, this site offers many easy-to-access resources, including quizzes, exercises, and grammar rules. Higher levels. Topics are shown in the following images (see Figs. 5.7 and 5.8).

Paragraph Level

- Sentence Variety
- Consistency of Tense and Pronoun Reference
- Avoiding Primer Language
- Sentence-Combining Skills
- Coherence and Transitions
- Paragraph Development

Essay Level

- PRINCIPLES OF COMPOSITION

A whole section for writers in Composition courses—featuring handouts on Getting Started, Structure, Tone, Transitions, Editing, Logic, Formats, Rhetorical Patterns, Research, and more—along with plenty of sample essays.

Forms of Communication

Samples (in .pdf format) for business letters, memos, application letters, thank-you letters, resumes, meeting minutes and agendas, and the research paper.

Fig. 5.7. As you can see from the image, there are many helpful topics to choose from.
Copyright 2000; Hartford, Connecticut. Used by permission

Hakan's ESL (English as a Second Language) Pages

http://members.tripod.com/~hakancan/index2.html#COM

There are more quizzes and other resources here (see Fig. 5.9) for ESL and elementary practice. You have to put up with pop-up windows at each new page, but it's worth it. Close pop-up windows by clicking on the cross in the right corner.

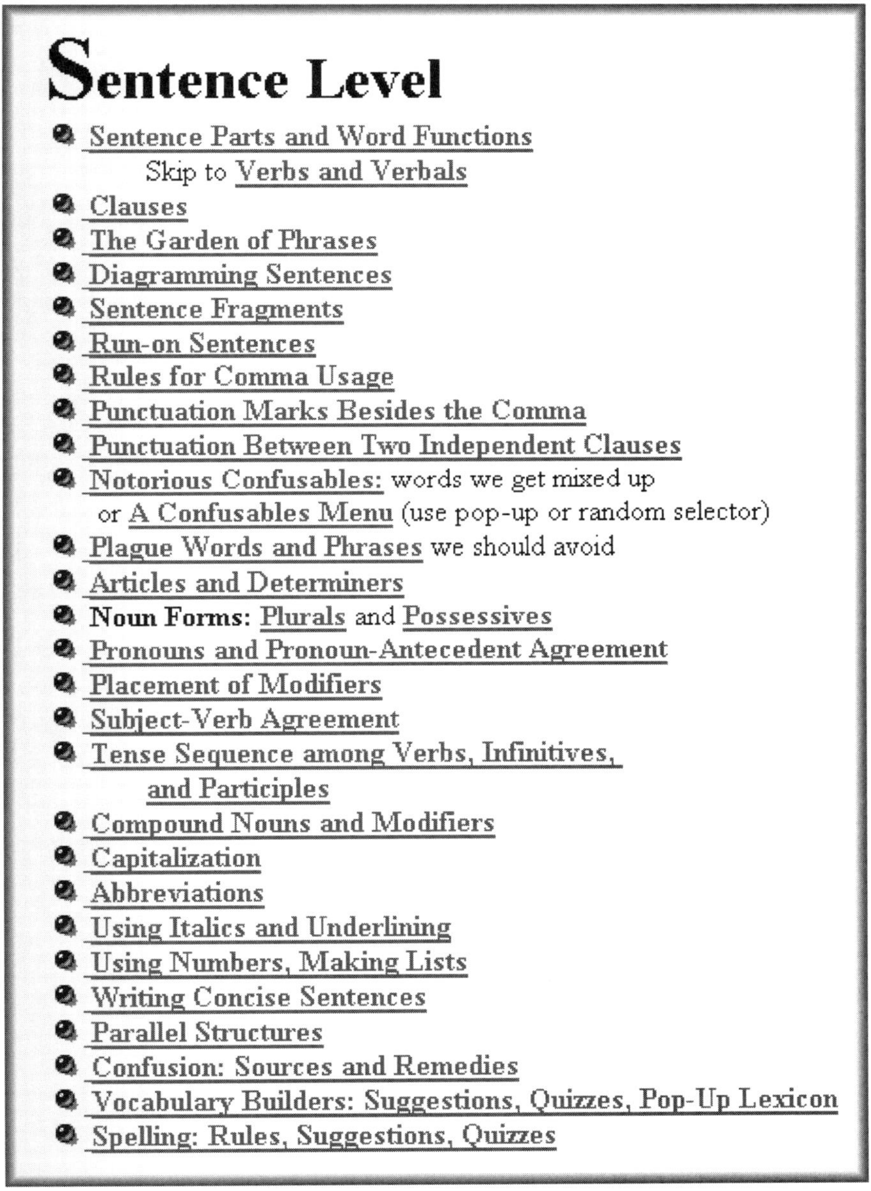

Sentence Level

- Sentence Parts and Word Functions
  Skip to Verbs and Verbals
- Clauses
- The Garden of Phrases
- Diagramming Sentences
- Sentence Fragments
- Run-on Sentences
- Rules for Comma Usage
- Punctuation Marks Besides the Comma
- Punctuation Between Two Independent Clauses
- Notorious Confusables: words we get mixed up
  or A Confusables Menu (use pop-up or random selector)
- Plague Words and Phrases we should avoid
- Articles and Determiners
- **Noun Forms:** Plurals and Possessives
- Pronouns and Pronoun-Antecedent Agreement
- Placement of Modifiers
- Subject-Verb Agreement
- Tense Sequence among Verbs, Infinitives, and Participles
- Compound Nouns and Modifiers
- Capitalization
- Abbreviations
- Using Italics and Underlining
- Using Numbers, Making Lists
- Writing Concise Sentences
- Parallel Structures
- Confusion: Sources and Remedies
- Vocabulary Builders: Suggestions, Quizzes, Pop-Up Lexicon
- Spelling: Rules, Suggestions, Quizzes

Fig. 5.8. Even more topics here. Just point and click.
Copyright 2000; Hartford, Connecticut. Used by permission

WELCOME TO HAKAN'S ENGLISH LANGUAGE PRACTICE AND FUN PAGES

Page Contents
Slang Quizzes | Confused Words Quizzes | Common Errors Quizzes | Trivia Contests For Prizes |
| Miscellaneous Quizzes | Idioms Quizzes | Riddles | Humor Pages | ESL BookStore | ESL Bookmarks

Fig. 5.9. The image indicates available exercises and quizzes plus links to other resources.
Used by permission

Kathy Schrock's Guide for Educators — Literature & Language Arts
http://discoveryschool.com/schrockguide/arts/artlit.html
Links to resources on everything from children's writing to Bullfinch's Mythology. Lots of literature lesson plans and excellent writing resources. This excellent site is part of the Discovery Channel School. All Levels. Sample topics are shown below.
Literature and Language Arts

- Aesop's Fables Online Exhibit
- Guide to grammar and writing
- Tales of Wonder : folk & fairy tales from around the world

Lesson Stop—Language Arts
www.youthline-usa.com/lessonstop/languagearts.html
Lots of lessons and ideas here at the K–12 level. A partial list of the lesson topics is shown in Figure 5.10.

All Language Arts Areas

1. Art-to-Zoo Language Arts Lessons (3-5)
2. AskERIC Language Arts Lessons (K-12)
3. CEC Language Arts Lessons (K-5)
4. CEC Language Arts Lessons (6-8)
5. CEC Language Arts Lessons (9-12)
6. Encarta Language Arts Lessons (K-12)
7. English Lessons (5-6)
8. English Lessons (9-12)
9. Exemplary Language Arts Lessons (K-12)
10. Language Arts Activities (K-12)
11. Language Arts Activities for Middle School Students (6-8)
12. Language Arts Lesson Ideas (K-12)
13. Language Arts Terminology Lesson Ideas (K-12)
14. PBS Arts and Literature Lesson Inventory (preK-12)
15. SCORE Language Arts CyberGuides (K-12)
16. Teaching Ideas: ESL (K-12)
17. Teaching Ideas: Journalism (K-12)
18. Teaching Ideas: Technology (K-12)

Fig. 5.10. Choose your lesson according to topic and grade level as shown in the image.

Lynch, Guide to Grammar and Style

http://andromeda.rutgers.edu/~jlynch/Writing/

Besides the very good guide to grammar and style that you will find here, you will find some good ideas and resources for teaching university-level literature if you click on the name "Jack Lynch" then scroll down to peruse Professor Lynch's online course materials.

High school teachers should also get some good ideas here.

OnLine English Grammar

www.edunet.com/english/grammar/toc.cfm

Here is a very good resource for providing students with rules and examples of English grammar from pronunciation of the alphabet with sound files, to adjectives, adverbs, nouns, possessives, determiners, verb usage, and so forth.

Elementary levels.

- Table of Contents: The alphabet in English, adjectives, adverbs, nouns, possessives, determiners, pronouns, verbs.
- D.E.N. Home-Page
- English Grammar Clinic
- Home-Page: OnLine English Grammar
- Subject Index (alphabetical)

Outta Ray's Head Literature

www3.sympatico.ca/ray.saitz/litera1.htm

Mainly high-school level lessons, ideas and resources. Don't miss this site (see Fig. 5.11) if you are teaching or taking a high school literature course. Click on the "Lessons" button for a good selection in popular genres of literature, poetry, and writing.

Jr.-Sr. High levels.

- *The Meaning of Literature*
- *The Meaningful Assignment*
- *Independent Novel Study-- Intermediate*
- *Another Independent Novel Study -- Intermediate*
- *Independent Study with an "exhibition" component*
- *A Board Game from a Novel*
- *Semi-Independent Novel Study -- Grade 11-- Lord of the Flies*
- *Flimibuff -- Lord of the Flies -- Senior*
- *Lord of the Flies --question sheets and answers*
- *Film or Play Review -- Intermediate*
- *Visual Assignment on Relationships -- Intermediate*
- *Growing Up Portfolio Assignment -- Intermediate*
- *Personal Choice Parallel Reading -- Gr. 10*
- *Reading Group Tasks -- Intermediate*
- *Interactive Approach to The Scarlet Letter -- Intermediate*

Fig. 5.11. A small sample of the content is shown in the image. Scroll down the page at the site for many more.

Used by permission

OWL Handouts

http://owl.english.purdue.edu/handouts/index2.html

Here is Purdue University's wonderful contribution to learning writing skills on the web. This is another "don't-miss" site filled with practical resources as shown in the list below.
High school to university level.

- Writing (Planning/Writing/Revising/Genres)
- Sentence Construction
- Punctuation
- Parts of Speech
- Professional Writing
- Writing in the Job Search
- Using the Writing Lab ESL
- Exercises/Answer Keys
- Research Papers
- Spelling

Pinchbeck—English

www.bjpinchbeck.com/frameenglish.htm

The youthful BJ Pinchbeck has once again done his homework in providing some excellent links to useful sites for teaching and learning English. There are extensive resources for Literature, Grammar, Mythology and Poetry. There are many links to online books, short stories and poems (including children's stories), as well as study guides, grammar sites, and a lot more.
All levels.

Pronouncing American English

www.jps.net/jhalbert/PronunciationSite/pronunciation.html

This will be a handy resource for teachers working with students who have foreign language backgrounds or others who need help with basic pronunciation of English. There are handy diagrams as well as guides and comprehension quizzes to assist teachers and their students.
Elementary levels.

The five categories dealt with are listed below.

- Intonation
- Linking

- Rhythm
- Speech sounds
- Word stress

Resources for Writers and Writing Instructors

http://andromeda.rutgers.edu/~jlynch/Writing/links.html

Here is another very good set of writing resources (see Fig. 5.12) for higher-level classes. Refer students to the appropriate sites for self-study, or use the resources to help prepare your own lessons for use in the classroom. There are also very good links for grammar exercises and quizzes for lower-level and ESL learners.

Elementary to advanced levels.

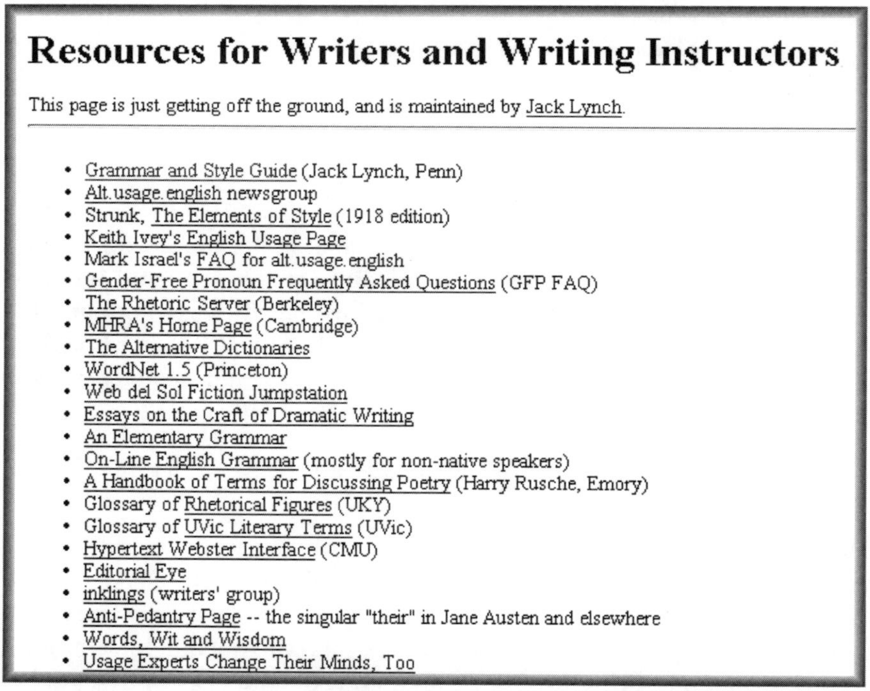

Resources for Writers and Writing Instructors

This page is just getting off the ground, and is maintained by Jack Lynch.

- Grammar and Style Guide (Jack Lynch, Penn)
- Alt.usage.english newsgroup
- Strunk, The Elements of Style (1918 edition)
- Keith Ivey's English Usage Page
- Mark Israel's FAQ for alt.usage.english
- Gender-Free Pronoun Frequently Asked Questions (GFP FAQ)
- The Rhetoric Server (Berkeley)
- MHRA's Home Page (Cambridge)
- The Alternative Dictionaries
- WordNet 1.5 (Princeton)
- Web del Sol Fiction Jumpstation
- Essays on the Craft of Dramatic Writing
- An Elementary Grammar
- On-Line English Grammar (mostly for non-native speakers)
- A Handbook of Terms for Discussing Poetry (Harry Rusche, Emory)
- Glossary of Rhetorical Figures (UKY)
- Glossary of UVic Literary Terms (UVic)
- Hypertext Webster Interface (CMU)
- Editorial Eye
- inklings (writers' group)
- Anti-Pedantry Page -- the singular "their" in Jane Austen and elsewhere
- Words, Wit and Wisdom
- Usage Experts Change Their Minds, Too

Fig. 5.12. Sample topics from the page are shown in the image above.

Spotlight
http://voyager.rtd.utk.edu/~ddoak/Schools/bedford/harrisms/spotlight.htm

Here you will find many excellent poetry exercises and lessons at elementary to high school levels. There are lessons on such things as figurative language, including similes, metaphors, personification, and so on, plus lessons on famous poems and poets, various styles of poetry including Haiku, acrostics, limericks, and much more. Try the online poetry general knowledge quiz as well.

Elementary to high school levels.

The Lesson Plans Page
www.lessonplanspage.com/javaframe.htm

There were nearly a thousand lesson plans in a variety of subject areas last time we checked, so you should find quite a few that you can use.

Pre-K to 12 levels.

The OnLine Books Page
http://digital.library.upenn.edu/books/

Search through the more than eleven thousand books online by title, author or subject. Here you will find free and complete online publications, including classics, and even banned books. (See Fig. 5.13.)

Higher levels.

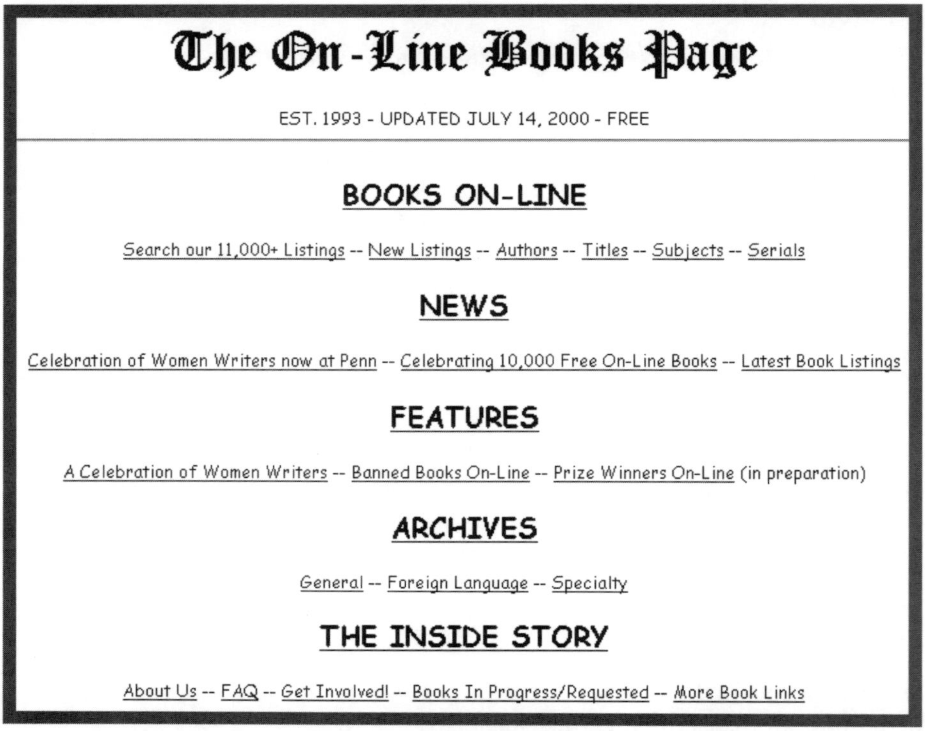

The On-Line Books Page

EST. 1993 - UPDATED JULY 14, 2000 - FREE

BOOKS ON-LINE

Search our 11,000+ Listings -- New Listings -- Authors -- Titles -- Subjects -- Serials

NEWS

Celebration of Women Writers now at Penn -- Celebrating 10,000 Free On-Line Books -- Latest Book Listings

FEATURES

A Celebration of Women Writers -- Banned Books On-Line -- Prize Winners On-Line (in preparation)

ARCHIVES

General -- Foreign Language -- Specialty

THE INSIDE STORY

About Us -- FAQ -- Get Involved! -- Books In Progress/Requested -- More Book Links

Fig. 5.13. See the many features at this excellent site.
Copyright 1993-2000 by John Mark Ockerbloom. Used by permission.

Vocabulary Activities

www.aec.ukans.edu/LEO/index.shtml

Here you will find many activities, games and quizzes designed to help learners of English develop their vocabulary. Most are appropriate for elementary English or ESL classes. Click on the "Studying English" section as shown in the image below, where you will find links to games, exercises, quizzes, and other resources for teaching or learning vocabulary. There are also sections for grammar, reading, listening, and writing.

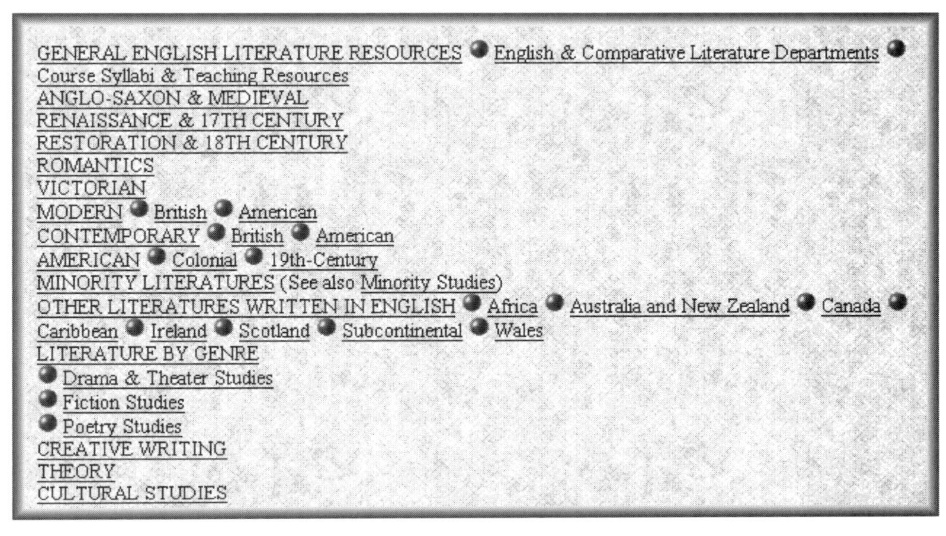

Fig. 5.14. Try the general English resources section or click on specific genres or periods.
Used by permission

VOS English Literature
http://vos.ucsb.edu/shuttle/english.html

At this site (see Fig. 5.14) you will find resources for the classics, as well as general literature. Scroll down the page to find your area of interest and click on your preference.
Advanced levels.

Welcome to K–12 World!
www.k-12world.com:80/cy_curr_res.cfm

This link will take you to K–12 World's main topics list since we can't send you directly to the English resources. You will need to click on the "Language Arts" section to access the resources listed below. Once there you will find everything from high school newspapers (Why not have your students publish their own newspaper online?), to children's classics, to mythology. All levels. Also check out the "Educator Resources" in the frame at the left of the page to find ideas for curriculum planning, and other useful resources.

Language Arts resource links to:

- Composition
- Grammar
- Journalism
- Literature
- Reading
- Speech

Chapter 6

ESL

The following sites contain many resources and lessons that will be of great help to teachers and learners of English as a Foreign Language. Many interactive sites will also be helpful for elementary-level native speakers of English who need supplementary exercises to improve their English skills particularly in grammar, reading, writing, and vocabulary building. There are also bilingual and multilingual dictionaries, quizzes, and a lot of other fun and interesting ways to help students improve English skills.

CHAPTER OVERVIEW

- ➢ Teaching ideas and links, pages 120–121, 123–124
- ➢ Verbs, pages 120, 124
- ➢ Writing, pages 121–123, 125

ESL

CLN ESL

www.cln.org/map.html#ESL

This site will link you to some very good resources and instructional materials including an ESL Teachers' Guide with lesson plans. There are many other resource links as well. Click on the selections as shown below to access the many ESL sites.

- Curricular resources in ESL
- Instructional materials in ESL
- Theme page: listening

Dave's ESL Cafe

www.pacificnet.net/~sperling/

Here is one of the best of the ESL Internet sites (see Fig. 6.1) in terms of variety of resources and ease of access.

Students can click on the Idioms, Quizzes, Phrasal Verbs or Slang sections, while teachers will find a lot of good ideas for teaching in the Idea Cookbook. You can even check out the Job Center if you are bored with your job lately.

Basic to advanced levels.

ESL Cafe News
Address Book | Announcements
Bookstore | Chat Central | Discussion Forums
FAQs | Help Center | Hint-of-the-Day | Idea Cookbook | Idioms
Job Center | Mailing List | Message Exchange | Phrasal Verbs | Photo Gallery
Quizzes | Quotes | Search the Web | Slang | Student Email | Teacher Email | Today in History | Web Guide
Links

Fig. 6.1. Click on Idea Cookbook shown in the image to access some great ideas for teaching ESL.

English as a Second Language: Lessons and Tutorials Online

http://dir.yahoo.com/Social_Science/Linguistics_and_Human_ Languages/Languages/Specific_Languages/English/English_as_a_Second_ Language/Lessons_and_Tutorials_Online/

This Yahoo site lists a lot of great resource sites for ESL, including many sites with online quizzes, and exercises in grammar and writing, reading comprehension, vocabulary, speaking, and listening.

All levels.

ESL Teacher's Guide Section II

http://humanities.byu.edu/ELC/teacher/Sectiontwo/SectionII

This site (see Fig. 6.2) contains beginning ESL lessons and ideas for teaching them. Click on the selections down the page for lessons on

- Lesson 1: Greeting and Introduction
  - Module I: Teaching the Dialog
  - Module II: Dialog Expansion, Structure Drills
  - Module III: Cloze Type Dictation Exercise
- Lesson 2: Filling Out Forms
  - Module I: Teaching the Dialog (Continued)
  - Module IV: Teaching Pronunciation
  - Module V: Teaching Numbers
  - Module VI: Teaching a Command Sequence Lesson
  - Module VII: Teaching the Alphabet
  - Module II: Dialog Expansion, Structure Drills (Continued)
  - Module VI: Teaching a Command Sequence Lesson (Continued)
- Lesson 3: Personal Information
  - Module I: Teaching the Dialog (Continued)
  - Module II: Dialog Expansion, Structure Drills (Continued)
- Lesson 4: Asking about Classroom Objects
  - Module I: Teaching the Dialog (Continued)
  - Module VI: Teaching a Command Sequence Lesson (Continued)
- Lesson 5: Telling Time
- Lesson 6: Finding a Job
- Lesson 7: Ordering Food
- Lesson 8: Calling on the Phone
- Lesson 9: Shopping for Clothes
- Lesson 10: Telling the Date
- Lesson 11: Visiting the Doctor

Fig. 6.2. Follow the lessons in order, or pick out the ones you like best and adapt them to your own classroom.
Used by permission

such things as greetings and introductions, telling time, ordering food or getting a job. There are also accompanying teacher-training modules for each section.

For intermediate level lessons, click on the words "Back to ESL Teacher's Guide" at the top of the main page and then on "Section III".

Free Education: English as a Second Language
www.free-ed.net/fr06/fr0603.htm

There are several good links here but one or two were still in the process of development at the time of this writing. We recommend that you take a look at "EnglishPractice.com" which you will find in the "Other Free Courses and Tutorials" section. There you might try the "weekly lessons" section for a wide range of lessons at the beginner, intermediate, and advanced levels as well as TOEFL level. The English Grammar Pages have some higher level interactive exercises and good advice for teachers of ESL. There is also information here about the US Immigration and some good links to other resources. Here is what the developers have to say about their own site.

Free-Ed's exclusive online guides are designed to help you get onto the right learning path and stay focused until you reach your goals.

Courses and Tutorials

- English Grammar Pages
- EnglishPractice.Com

Interactive Textbooks and References

- English Dictionary

Course Outlines, Lecture Notes, Quizzes, Etc.

- The ESL Quiz Center
- Self-Study Quizzes for ESL Students

Helpful Study Materials

- Fluency Through Fables
- The American President
- Dave's ESL Cafe

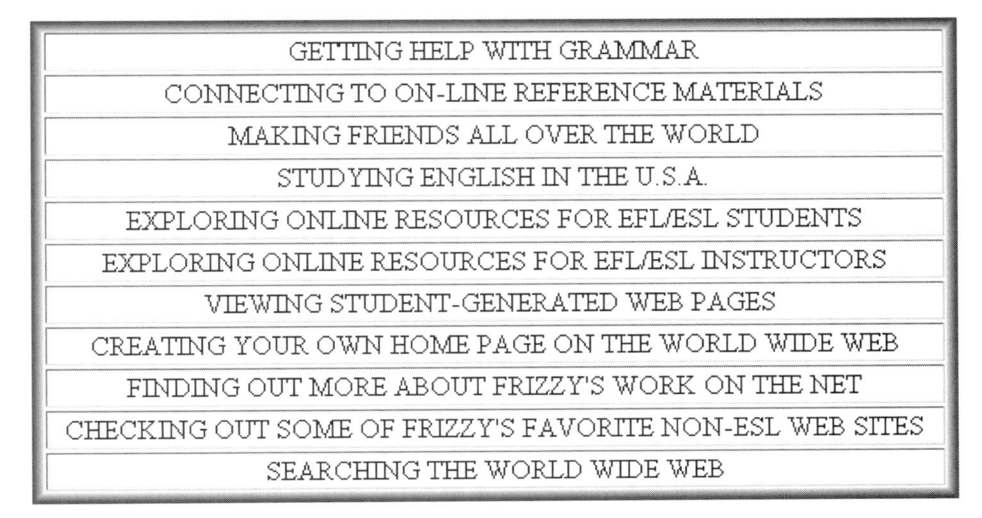

Fig. 6.3. Click on the main menu as shown in the image on the left, or scroll down the page once you get to the site to look at the complete list.
Used by permission

Frizzy University Network (FUN)
http://thecity.sfsu.edu/~funweb/
Lots of resources here (see Fig. 6.3) for ESL learners to improve their grammar, vocabulary and particularly their writing skills. Teachers will find useful ideas and resources in the Instructors' section.

Grammar Quizzes (Self-Study Quizzes for ESL Students)
www.aitech.ac.jp/~iteslj/quizzes/grammar.html
Here (see Fig. 6.4) you will find a very good selection of interactive quizzes on a variety of grammatical functions.
Quizzes are classified as easy, medium, or difficult.

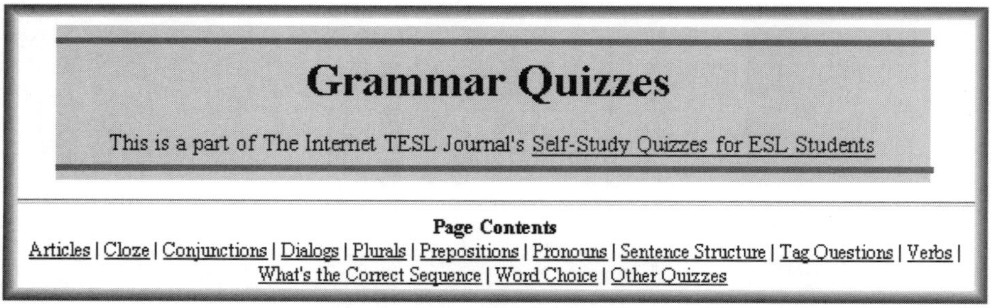
Grammar Quizzes
This is a part of The Internet TESL Journal's Self-Study Quizzes for ESL Students
Page Contents
Articles | Cloze | Conjunctions | Dialogs | Plurals | Prepositions | Pronouns | Sentence Structure | Tag Questions | Verbs |
What's the Correct Sequence | Word Choice | Other Quizzes

Fig. 6.4. Have students click on the Self-Study Quizzes as shown at the top of the image, or check out the sections in the menu under "Page Contents" for exercises, ideas, and other quizzes.
Copyright (C) 1995-1999 by The Internet TESL Journal. Used by permission

Hakan's ESL (English As a Second Language) Pages
http://members.tripod.com/~hakancan/index2.html

This site (see Fig. 6.5) has a lot of good resources such as a dictionary of slang and common idioms, and interactive quizzes.

Much of the slang is British rather than American, but likely helpful for any ESL students who want to broaden their "street vocabulary."

To get rid of the pop-up windows you get with each click, just click on the cross at the right hand corner.

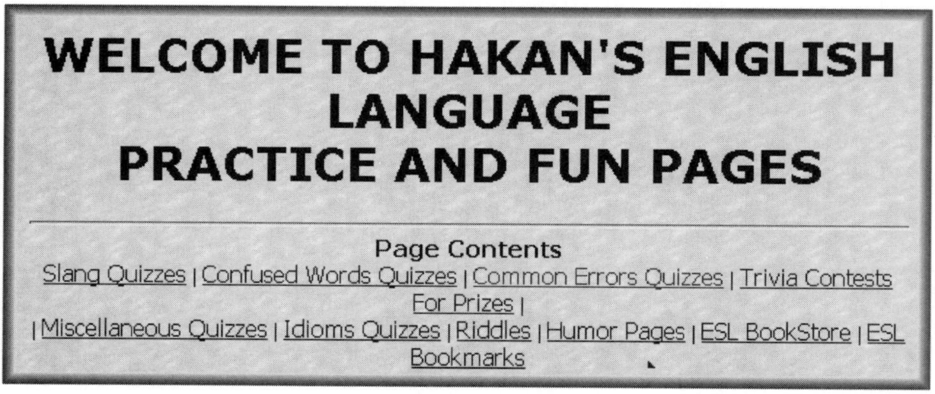
WELCOME TO HAKAN'S ENGLISH LANGUAGE
PRACTICE AND FUN PAGES
Page Contents
Slang Quizzes | Confused Words Quizzes | Common Errors Quizzes | Trivia Contests For Prizes |
| Miscellaneous Quizzes | Idioms Quizzes | Riddles | Humor Pages | ESL BookStore | ESL Bookmarks

Fig. 6.5. Try the various quizzes as shown in the illustration.
Used by permission

Index of ESLoop

www.webring.org/cgi-bin/webring?index&ring=esloop

We included this site because of its many links to excellent resources all around the web. You will find links to sites with interactive quizzes, cultural information, such as the habits of Japanese businessmen, crosswords, fun activities, resources for teacher trainers, practice for the US citizenship test (free only for residents of Minnesota), and more.

Internet TESL Journal

www.aitech.ac.jp/~iteslj/

There are good teachers' resources in this monthly journal including articles, lesson plans, handouts, quizzes, puzzles, cultural information, humor, and so forth.

Kathy Schrock's Guide for Educators—Regions of the World & World Languages

http://discoveryschool.com/schrockguide/world/worldrw.html

This site provided by The Discovery Channel School provides one of the best collections of resources for ESL on the World Wide Web. It contains links to foreign language resources and geographic and cultural information about many regions of the world in addition to ESL exercises and activities.

Lesson Plans on the Web

www.ncbe.gwu.edu/classroom/lessons.htm

This site has very good links to such resources as adult education lesson plans, tips for teachers, bilingual biographies of famous women (English/Spanish), ESL writing resources, and thematic units.

Teachers Page of Lesson Plans

www.library.ualberta.ca/library—htm/libraries/counts/lessons.html?ESL

This resource-rich site (see Fig. 6.6) provided by the University of Alberta Library links you to ESL lesson plans and other resources for teaching and learning. Scroll down the page to the ESL selection and click on it, or check out some of the other helpful resources such as Teaching Tips or elementary school English lessons which can also be helpful in teaching ESL.

ESL: English As a Second Language

- TESOL'99 Workshop: Creating Internet-based Activities
- Lesson Plans & Resources for ESL, Bilingual and Foreign Language Teachers
- ESL Web Guide: Lesson Plans
- The Internet TESL Journal: (Teachers of English as a Second Language) -- lessons, lesson plans and handouts for the ESL classroom.
- Adult Education ESL Teachers Guide
- NCBE - National Clearinghouse for Bilingual Education

Fig. 6.6. Lots of lesson plans and other great resources at this site.
Used by permission

TESL: Handouts for Classroom Use

www.aitech.ac.jp/~iteslj/links/TESL/Handouts_for_Classroom_Use/

This site is absolutely loaded with handouts which you will find very helpful for teaching ESL, including complete course outlines, teaching guides, printable worksheets, exercises, and puzzles.

Chapter 7

Foreign Languages

The following foreign-language sites contain resources and lessons which will assist teachers and learners to more easily teach or acquire foreign-language skills. The resources included range from basic to advanced levels. Even those with limited Internet skills will easily find useful and often entertaining ideas, lesson plans, multimedia, and other supplementary resources to brighten up any learning environment. Just follow the links to the world of learning.

CHAPTER OVERVIEW

DICTIONARIES

Babylon.com—Translator and Converter

www.babylon.com/

Babylon Lite (see Fig. 7.1) is a single-click translator, dictionary, and converter. An Internet tool that lives on your desktop and enables you to translate any onscreen words and expressions from English into your chosen language (English, French, Spanish, Portuguese, German, Dutch, Swedish, Italian, Hebrew Japanese, Chinese—traditional and simplified dialects). The newest version is enhanced with an instant currency, time, metric conversion tool along with the option of a calculator, plus a text to speech *Add-On* feature!

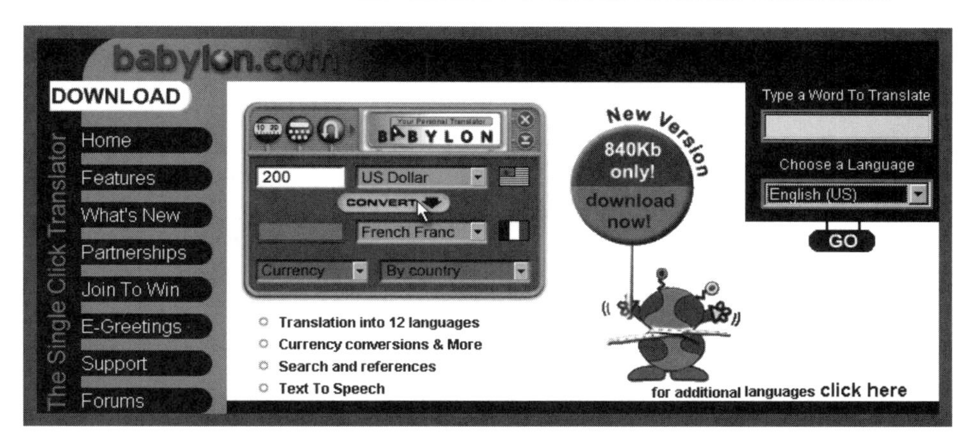

Fig. 7.1. Click on the words "Translation into 12 languages" to download the language translator.

Bilingual dictionaries list

www.issco.unige.ch/resources/Linguistics/bilingue-angl.html#espagnol

From basic travel dictionaries to specialty bilingual dictionaries and thesauruses, this site from the University of Geneva provides whatever translations you need in English, French, Spanish, German, Italian, Russian, and several other languages.

Dictionaries, glossaries and lexicons online

www.issco.unige.ch/resources/Linguistics/dictionnaires-angl.html

This is another page from the University of Geneva with a slightly broader focus. Following is a list of available resources at the site:

- Acronym dictionaries
- Monolingual dictionaries: French, English, German
- Bilingual dictionaries: From English to Danish, Dutch, Finnish, French, German, Italian, Russian, Spanish, and from Danish, Dutch, Finnish, French, German, Italian, Russian, Spanish to English
- Multilingual dictionaries: data processing, general, economy, sciences, technique: Danish, Dutch, English, Finnish, French, German, Greek, Italian, Portuguese, Spanish, Latin, Swedish, and for acronyms, abbreviations, and scientific nomenclature

- Downloadable dictionaries: Afrikaans, American, Aussie, Chinese, Computer, Croatian, Czech, Danish, Databases, Dictionaries, Dutch, Esperanto, Finnish, French, German, Indi, Hungarian, Italian, Japanese, Latin, Literature, Movie TV, Music, Names, Net, Norwegian, Places, Polish, Random, Religion, Russian, Science, Spanish, Swahili, Swedish, Turkish, Yiddish

General English-Spanish Dictionary

www.activa.arrakis.es/ind-en.htm

This is a very good dictionary containing over 25,000 translations between English and Spanish, with no downloads necessary. Click on the American or British flags for English directions and then scroll down the page to choose specific language databases such as accounting, business computing, electronics or others.

Hypertext Webster Gateway: Dictionary

http://work.ucsd.edu:5141/cgi-bin/http_webster

This is a very easy-to-use online dictionary of the English language. You can type in a word to search for an exact or approximate match.

- This hypertext Webster interface provides a point-and-click client interface (for non-linemode browsers) for accessing various dictionary services on the Internet.

OneLook Dictionaries

www.onelook.com/

This site (see Fig. 7.2) has grown to well over two million words and counting in about 600 online dictionaries. Type in the word you want and the search engine will give you a choice of online dictionaries containing the definition. Includes acronyms and technical terms.

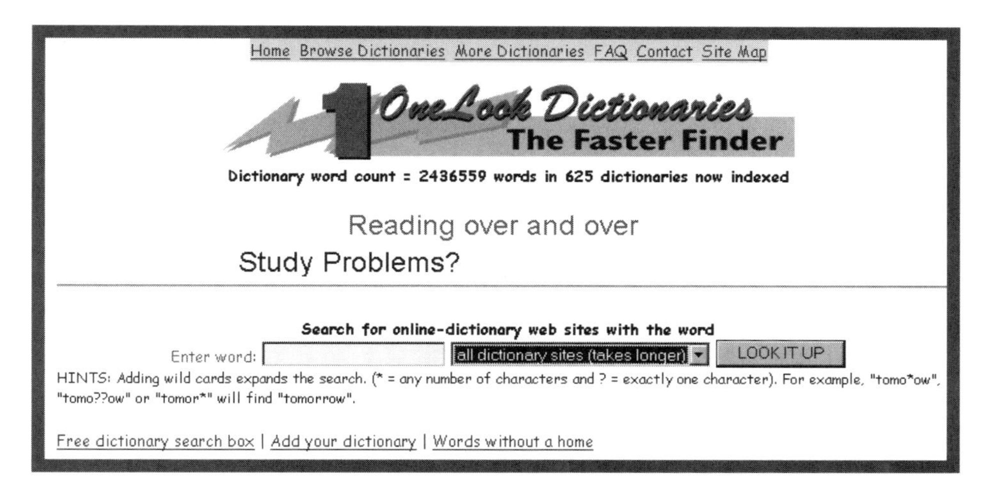

Fig. 7.2. Enter a word in the text box as shown in the illustration for rapid translation.
"OneLook" is a registered trademark owned by Robert K. Ware, Englewood, Colorado, USA. Used by permission

The Human-Languages Page

http://cgi.hardlink.com/~chambers/HLP/dict.cgi

This excellent site has dictionaries in a very wide range of languages from American Sign Language, to Cherokee, to Chinese, Hawaiian, European languages, Ethnic languages—take your pick. There is even a chess dictionary.

FRENCH

An Intermediate Guide to French

www.frenchlesson.org/

Tutorials, guides, exercises, readings and a verb conjugation test. There is a lot here (see Fig. 7.3) for intermediate learners to sharpen their skills in the French language.

- Conjugations
- French Gender
- Practice & Exercises

Rousseau
1712-1778

- What's New 5/1/00
- Recommended French Learning Materials
- Text Editor with Accents
- Corrections 5/1/00

Quick Links
Reference
- Babblefish Translator
- French WebConjugue
- Hachette Dictionnaire En Ligne

Media
- Le Monde

Welcome Login FRENCHLESSON.ORG

Le premier qui, ayant enclos un terrain, s'avisa de dire: 'Ceci est à moi' et trouva des gens assez simples pour le croire, fut le vrai fondateur de la société civile. - Discours sur l'origine et les fondements de l'inégalité parmi les hommes . (l754)

Rousseau en Cartes Postales

TUTORIALS & GUIDES

Conjugations
A complete guide to French conjugations. Interactive practice implemented through Java applets.

French Gender
- learn the gender of nouns -- the rules and the exceptions with interactive practice.
- an overview of aspects of french grammar in which gender must be kept in mind.

- Adjectives
- Participles

PRACTICE & EXERCISES

Conjugation Test
Test conjugation skills using a Java applet. If you are having trouble with a particular verb, click on that verb and be transported to a section describing how to conjugate that verb in the conjugation guide.

Miscellaneous Grammar Exercises
Practice relative pronouns, the proper use of the subjunctive, prepositions and more. The Exercises were donated by a University of Texas French professor.

Gender: Trial by Fire
Find out how good you are at noun gender.

Fig. 7.3. Click on the specific areas of study, or have students login (free registration) for automatic tracking of progress.
Used by permission

Fluent French

www.signiform.com/french/

This surprisingly good site is the product of a man who learned French in school and in Paris, and has made his experience of learning a model for an excellent series of lessons on French language and culture.

- Words and Expressions
- Comparisons with English
- Fine points

French Assistant

www.language-student.com/french/

Here is a good site to send your students for independent learning or review at the beginners to intermediate level. There are well-constructed interactive exercises that should help students more rapidly master the essentials of the French language.

French Language Course Pages

www.jump-gate.com/languages/french/

From pronunciation guides with sounds to vocabulary and idioms, this site is another good one for learning beginner-level French. There are a couple of good links as well, including to Le Monde, a French online newspaper. Other lessons include Articles and Genders, Pronouns and Verbs, Adjectives and Plurals, Sentences, The Family, Comparing, and Time.

The creators of this site state that this French course is intended to allow you to understand written French (newspapers, articles, magazines, signs on the road during your next trip in France, etc.) and to write a letter to a French friend or correspondent.

French Learning Website

www.kameleo.com/french/index.html

This developing site has some good beginner level resources with new ones being added regularly. Topics are listed below.

- Learn and Practice the French Language

- Discover the Francophone Culture
- Other Resources: Links to other French learning sites.

You'll also find an interactive map, virtual visits to Paris and Nice, and many other resources.

French Lessons from Everywhere
http://globegate.utm.edu/french/globegate_mirror/frlesson.html
Here is a site that is loaded with links to resources at all levels. You will find complete courses, tests, lessons for beginner, intermediate, and advanced levels, vocabulary, readings, tutorials, and more.

Grammar
www.koronis.com/french/html/grammar/grammar.htm
Here is a good grammar helper with sound files.
Beginners level.
Topics are shown below:

- Adjectives
- Comparatives
- Adverbs
- Pronouns
- Conjunctions
- Prepositions

Logos Multilingual Portal
www.logos.it/
Check out the dictionary here (see Fig. 7.4) for translations back and forth from French to English, or nearly any other language for that matter.

Fig. 7.4. Just click on the French flag as shown in the above image to choose that language for translation.
Copyright © 2000 Logos Group. Used by permission

STP CALL: French

http://strindberg.ling.uu.se/call/french/

This is another good site with interactive lessons for beginner to intermediate learners.

The following topics are available at the site:

- Le génitif (The genitive)
- Le verbe 'être' (The verb 'be')
- Les adjectifs et les adverbes (Adjectives and adverbs)
- Les noms (Nouns)
- Les verbes: Un exemple d'une conjugaison (Verbs: an example of a conjugation)
- Passé composé
- Text with vocabulary
- Tout/toute/tous/toutes/tout le monde

Table of Contents, French Fun

http://library.advanced.org/12447/contents.html

Beginner level interactive lessons on topics including letters and numbers, gender and articles, subject pronouns, basic verbs and conjugations, introduction to regular verbs, adjectives, all-purpose phrases, past and future tenses, and 101 nouns, verbs, and adjectives.

Tennessee Bob's Famous French Links

www.utm.edu/departments/french/french.html

Here is another site full of links to resources for learning French at all levels. A few of the many topics are listed below:

- Art, Music, Film and General Culture
- Books and Literature
- Education in French-Speaking Schools
- Finding New Francophone Sites
- French across the Curriculum and in Every-day Life
- History of France and the French-Speaking World
- Press, Radio/TV, Telephone
- The French Language
- Virtual Francophone Tourism

SPANISH

AltaVista Translations

http://babelfish.altavista.com/translate.dyn

Internet translators such as this one at Alta Vista are useful for translating single words and short phrases. Be careful with them though, since many words have several meanings and the translator can't know the one you want in any particular context. English /Spanish, Spanish/ English. Other languages.

AskERIC Lesson Plans—Foreign Language

http://ericir.syr.edu/Virtual/Lessons/Foreign_Lang/index.html

There are new lesson plans posted here periodically, so once you visit this site and use the ones that you like, you can go back for new stuff as it's posted.

Grades 1–12.

Some of the current topics are listed in the screen capture in Figure 7.5.

Foreign Language

- Chain Stories Grade: 9-12
- Concept Attainment Model "Boulangerie (Bakery)" Grade: K-12
- Comida Grade: 9-12
- Contents of My Backpack Grade: 1
- In the Big City Grade: Second Year of Spanish
- Introductions in Spanish (Grade 9)
- Foreign Language and Culture (gr. 9-12)
- Mexico - Language and Literature Grade: 3-4
- Pinyin - Learning the Chinese Language through Phonetics Grade: 9, 10, 11, 12, Higher education, Vocational education, Adult/continuing education
- Que hora es? What time is it? Grade: 3+
- ¡Tarjetas Postales! Grade: 9 - 11
- "Tasty Tidbits From Spain" Grade: 5 - 8
- ""To Know Spanish" or "To Know Spanish"" Grade: Second Year or Higher - Spanish

Fig. 7.5. Choose the lessons according to grade level and topic.
Used by permission

Bahasa

www.bahasa.com/Spanish.html

Here is an interesting way for beginner level learners to study, review, and even do self-tests of basic vocabulary in Spanish. Matching words in English and Spanish are scrolled across a frame for study, and when learners are comfortable that they know the matching words, they can scramble them and do a self-test.

You need to use a Java-enabled browser such as Netscape to view these exercises.

Topics are listed below:

- Adjectives
- Clothing
- Colors
- Communication
- Directions
- Family
- Greetings
- Months
- Parts of the Body

- The Days of the Week
- The Home
- Transportation
- Weather

Basic Spanish for the Virtual Student

www.umr.edu/~amigos/Virtual/

This excellent site, filled with easy-to-follow modularized lessons and readings, was designed by a couple of students with the cooperation of native speakers from Colombia, Costa Rica and Ecuador. There is a link to an elementary Spanish Curriculum that you may want to check out if you are designing a program.
Beginner to intermediate levels.

- Learn Spanish from 50+ modules covering pronunciation, nouns, verbs, adjectives, adverbs, pronouns, and other themes

Learn Spanish: A Free Online Tutorial

www.studyspanish.com/tutorial.htm

Here is a site learners will want to explore for its useful resources and lessons. Teachers can assign lessons to their students and the site's computer will keep track of students' progress. You have to register for this service, but it is free.

- Whether you are a student or teacher, you'll find lots of useful information here, including the FREE online tutorial, which includes written and oral exercises and currently covers 75 separate topics.

Logos Multilingual Portal

www.logos.it/

This useful site (see Fig. 7.6) has dictionary translations, and a Universal Verb Conjugator. When you get to the site, click on the word "Verba" in the menu at the left. When you get to the conjugation page, just type in the verb and click "conjugate."

Fig. 7.6. Click on the Spanish flag as shown in the above image for instructions and menus in Spanish, or click on the American or British flags for English translations.

Spanish Course For Beginners Online

www.geocities.com/Athens/Thebes/4319/

You will find a dozen well-prepared lessons (see Fig. 7.7) complete with a final test for beginner-level students. Read the developer's comments below:

The objective of this course is to get familiar with the Spanish language. It was designed for 18 hours of instruction, plus the time the student will spend practicing and following some of the exercises that are provided. It will concentrate in sounds, phrases, and building vocabulary with a little bit of grammar.

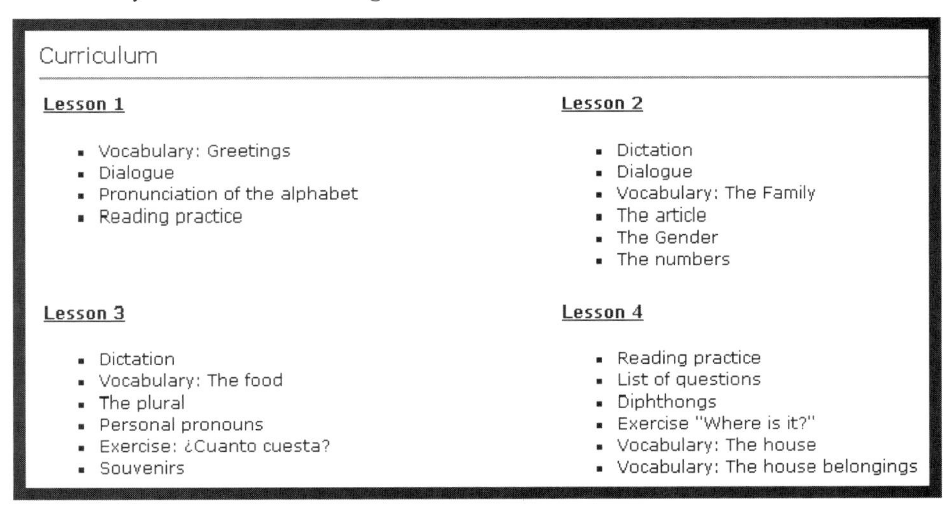

Fig. 7.7. The image shows the already well-developed curriculum.

Spanish Made Easy
www.davidreilly.com/spanish/

Here are some easy lessons for beginning students. Lessons are on topics ranging from basic greetings to numbers, short phrases, telling the time and so forth. Some of the categories are listed below:

- Lessons
- Phrases
- Vocabulary
- Conversational Dialogues

Spanish Pronto
www.spanishpronto.com

You will find some good links in the "Tools" section here as well as some good basic resources for beginner-level Spanish at this site. When you get to the site, click on any of the categories shown in the following screen capture:

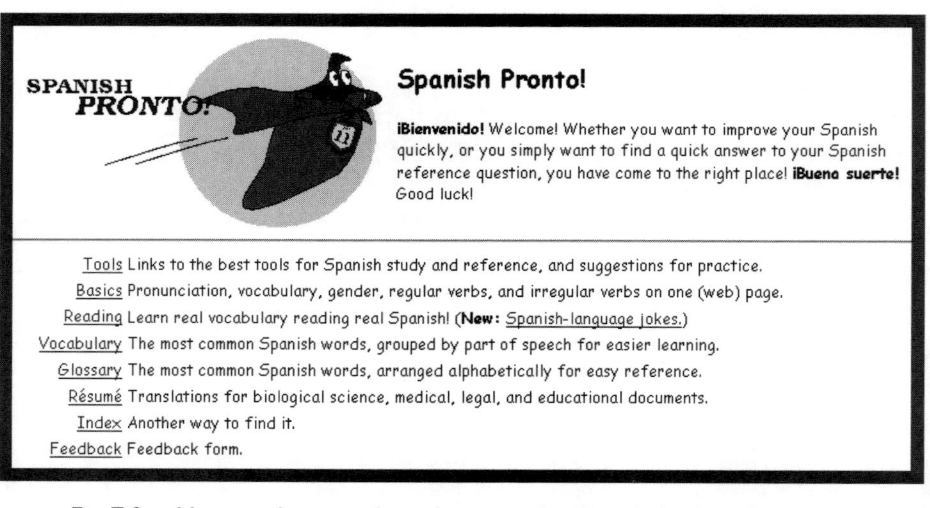

Fig. 7.8. Have students explore the areas that best help them learn.
Copyright ©1998,1999,2000. Used by permission

Web Spanish Lessons
www.june29.com/Spanish/index.html

Here you will find a good selection of basic vocabulary and grammar with easy-to-use sound files.

Webspañol—Spanish language resources online
www.geocities.com/Athens/Thebes/6177/

This site uses a wide variety of Internet resources to teach the Spanish language at all levels.

Students can begin with a pre-test, work on some interactive lessons, or access any of the other resources such as free learning software, a couple of translated Beatles' songs, chat lines, or a penpal exchange.

OTHER LANGUAGES

Free Education: Modern Languages
www.free-ed.net/fr06/fr0605.htm

This site will provide you with free online resources, courses, and tutorials for learning the following languages:
Select a language:

- Arabic
- Chinese
- Dutch
- French
- German
- Modern Greek
- Modern Hebrew
- Italian
- Japanese
- Portuguese
- Russian
- Spanish

Free Online Language Courses

http://rivendel.com/~ric/resources/course.html

Courses and resources for learning any of the 77 languages shown in Figures 7.9 and 7.10.

Ainu	Albanian	Arabic	Asturian	Basque	Bengali	Breton
Catalan	Cebuano	Chamorro	Cherokee	Chinese	Chinook	Cornish
Cree	Creole	Croatian	Czech	Dakota	Danish	Dutch
English	Esperanto	Estonian	Finnish	French	Gaelic	German
Greek	Gujarati	Hawaiian	Hebrew	Hindi	Hmong	Hungarian
Icelandic	Indonesian	Italian	Ivatan	Japanese	Kiribati	Korean
Kurdish	Latvian	Latin	Luganda	Malay	Maltese	Mandinka
Mingo	Mon	Norwegian	Pali	Persian	Polish	Portuguese
Punjabi	Quechua	Russian	Samoan	Sanskrit	Sesotho	Serbian
Spanish	Swahili	Swedish	Tagalog	Tamil	Thai	Tibetan
Tigre	Turkish	Urdu	Vietnamese	Welsh	Wollof	Xhosa

Figs. 7.9 and 7.10. Look for online language courses, dictionaries and resources or, choose a language from the extensive list shown here.
Used by permission

Kathy Schrock's Guide for Educators—Regions of the World & World Languages

http://discoveryschool.com/schrockguide/world/worldrw.html

As in all the sites at the Discovery Channel School, Kathy Schrock has put together an impressive set of links, this time to foreign language resources, plus regions of the world information and some good ESL links.

Lesson Stop | Foreign Languages

www.youthline-usa.com/lessonstop/othersubjects.html#foreignlanguage

This link lands you in the middle of the foreign language lessons section compiled for you by the Lesson Stop people.

Here you will find lesson plans developed for learners at K–12 levels.

Logos Multilingual Portal

www.logos.it/

Another truly impressive site emerges from among the estimated 50 million to one billion sites out there. Try conjugating verbs in any or all of the languages from those countries or regions shown in the following screen capture (Fig. 7.11). Or use the dictionaries for translations and even for seeing words used in context.

Fig. 7.11. The names of countries shown here under the flags will appear when you place your mouse pointer on the flags.
Copyright © 2000 Logos Group. Used by permission

The LINGUIST List: Language & Language Family Information

www.emich.edu/~linguist/languages.html

Here's another interesting place to see foreign languages in a new light. From natural languages to constructed languages and language families to written languages, you will find a lot of useful information here. And for a particularly good time you will want to check out the language novelties section where you will find the various ways that different languages express animal sounds.

WWW Foreign Language Resources

www.itp.berkeley.edu/~thorne/HumanResources.html

Here is a good mixture of dictionaries, courses, online newspapers, virtual tours, multimedia resources, and lots more. You will also find foreign-language fonts here and information on how to create many accent marks on a standard keyboard without special fonts.

The following languages are represented: Arabic, Chinese, Czech, French, German, Hebrew, Italian, Latin, Middle English, Portuguese, Russian, Scandinavian Languages, South Asian Languages, Spanish, Swahili, Tagalog, Turkish, Yiddish.

Chapter 8

Health and Physical Education

Physical educators, nutritionists, physiotherapists, and individuals just wanting to improve their physical fitness can now access a great variety of sites to assist them find the right program for themselves or their clients. Everything is here, from rules of sports and games to calorie counters. Teachers will find many ideas, exercises and lesson plans which will make teaching or coaching much easier and a lot more fun.

CHAPTER OVERVIEW

HEALTH AND PHYSICAL EDUCATION

Canadian Sport—The Centre
www.cdnsport.ca/

This site will be helpful for teachers who want the latest sports information and contacts with others in Canadian sports groups and associations who share their interests.

- Sports organizations from Archery to Wrestling

Meet Benny Goodsport and the Goodsport Gang!
www.bennygoodsport.com/

Here is a site that helps teach sportsmanship and motivate children to exercise by doing a variety of activities. Includes reading and puzzle activities related to staying healthy.
Primary school level.

PE Central: Health and Physical Education Lesson Plans
http://pe.central.vt.edu/lessonideas/pelessonplans.html

This can be an extremely useful site for physical education teachers and coaches at any level. There are enough excellent lesson plans and ideas to keep you going for years. Check out the "instant activities/ Warm Ups" menu for a wide selection of elementary school–level activities. Do not miss the Health Lesson Ideas which is full of lessons and ideas at all levels for all aspects of health including mental and emotional health, growth and development, injuries and safety, and much, much more.

- Information about contemporary developmentally appropriate physical education programs for children and youth.

Personal Trainer

www.itdc.sbcss.k12.ca.us/curriculum/personaltrainer.html

Here is a role-play exercise that can be passed on to students to help them design diet and exercise portfolios appropriate to their individual needs and resources.

Designing custom individualized diet and exercise portfolios.

Physical Education Lesson Plans for Everyone

www.sports-media.org/

Click on the "Lesson Plans" section in the frame on the left of the page to access excellent lesson plans for a wide range of activities at all fitness and age levels. Lessons range from adapted physical education, for those with disabilities, to training techniques for conventional sports and even a few less conventional ones like ultimate Frisbee or Korean martial arts. Also many drills, coaching tips, a guide to best practices in physical education . . . just about everything you are looking for.

Pinchbeck—Health and Physical Education

www.bjpinchbeck.com/framehealth.htm

As always, BJ Pinchbeck and his dad provide us with a list of good and reliable links, this time to sites focussing on health and physical education. See the categories in Figure 8.1.

Health and Physical Education

PE Central -- A must see for physical education teachers 

Health World Online -- Good information on fitness and healthy living

Prevention's Healthy Ideas -- Great fitness site...you'll want to visit this one

Health Facts Article Index -- Collection of health articles from the American Fitness Professionals Associates

Health Calc Network -- Take your fitness tests online...very interesting and helpful

Worldguide Health and Fitness Forum -- Very nice site...well worth the visit

The Fitness Files Homepage -- Another very nice fitness site

Bodies in Motion...Minds at Rest -- If you are thinking of getting into a routine you definitely want to visit this site

FitnessLink -- Excellent fitness and nutritional information...a must visit

Walking -- Many excellent links on walking to refer to here

Fast Food Finder -- Check out the number of calories in your fast food burger

Fig. 8.1. Click on your choice of topics as shown in the sample image from the B.J. Pinchbeck Web site.
Used by permission

U of A Health Information Page
www.ualberta.ca/HEALTHINFO/

Health information on a wide range of topics, many of particular interest to university-level students but useful for high school students as well. Besides health information, you will find a manual for setting up a peer health-education program, and hot health links.

Chapter 9

Math

The following Math sites contain resources for teachers and students of Mathematics from basic to advanced levels. Teachers will find many lesson plans and other resources that will make teaching and learning both easier and more interesting. Students can be directed to resources such as interactive exercises, online tutorials, calculators, and so forth in order to enhance their learning experience and free their teachers' time. Subject areas vary from basic arithmetic through to calculus, trigonometry, business math, statistics, and many other areas of mathematics.

CHAPTER OVERVIEW

MATH

Alberta Education Website

http://ednet.edc.gov.ab.ca/studentprograms/

You will need Adobe Acrobat Reader in order to access the information on this site (see Fig. 9.1).

Once you are in the Alberta Education Website and you have Acrobat Reader (which you can download for free at the site), you will need to click on the "Mathematics" link, and then you can choose your levels of interest. Download the files to your desktop and then open them with Acrobat Reader. You will find Outlines of Mathematics Programs of Study from K–12, and such helpful teaching resources as itemized specific learner expectations at all levels, as well as detailed outlines for program organization and program structure. This site was

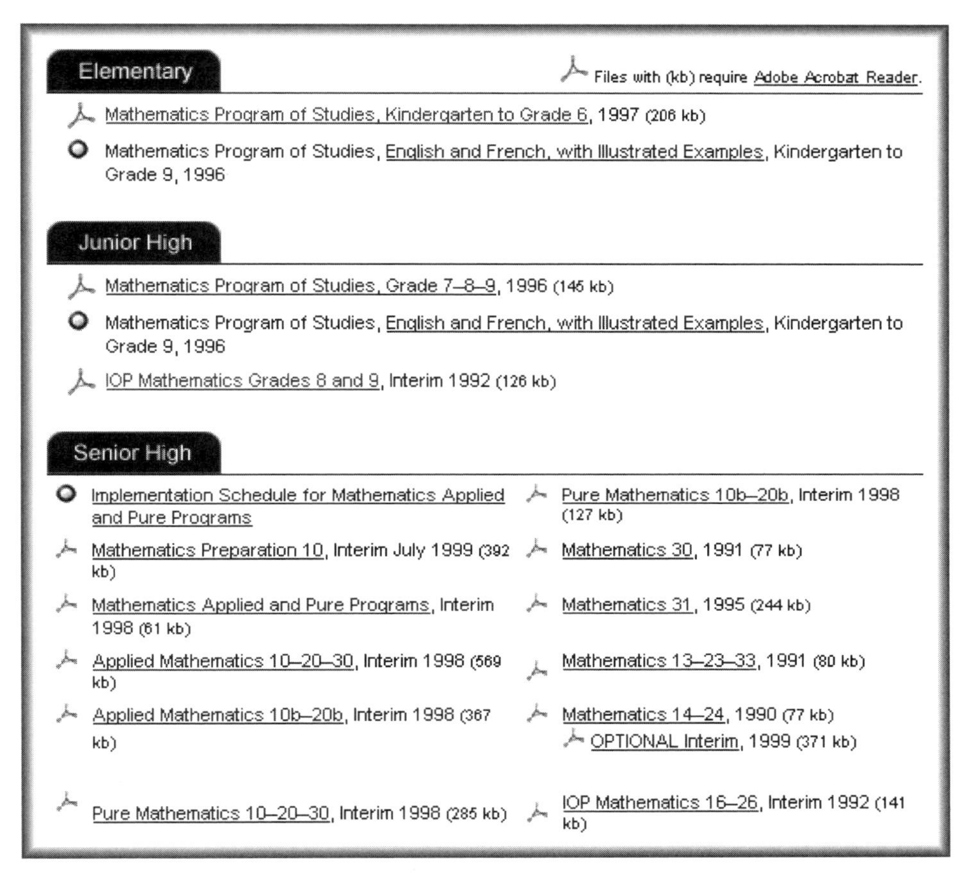

Fig. 9.1. This image from the Alberta Education Website shows available programs and other resources.
Used by permission

designed specifically for education in the Province of Alberta, Canada, as part of the Western Canadian Protocol for Collaboration in Education. However, the resources are useful in any K–12 Math Program. Bilingual, English and French.

Armadillo's Math Resources
http://riceinfo.rice.edu/armadillo/Rice/Resources/math.html
This site contains a variety of resources from Basic Mathematics to advanced level Algebra, Geometry, and Statistics. There are also links to tutorials and self-directed learning as well as biographies of famous mathematicians, a history of math, and mathematics for cartography.

- Algebra
- Geometry
- Integrated Math
- Mathematics Reform
- Projects
- Publications and Organizations
- Statistics

Ask Dr. Math

http://forum.swarthmore.edu/dr.math/

This site (see Fig. 9.2) contains an excellent archive of questions posed by students and teachers and answered by the people at the Dr. Math site. You can look in the archives for the answers to your own questions, or ask the experts directly if your questions have not been answered already.

There is also a special section called "Teacher2Teacher" for teachers with questions about teaching Mathematics.

There is a wide variety of Math topics at all levels.

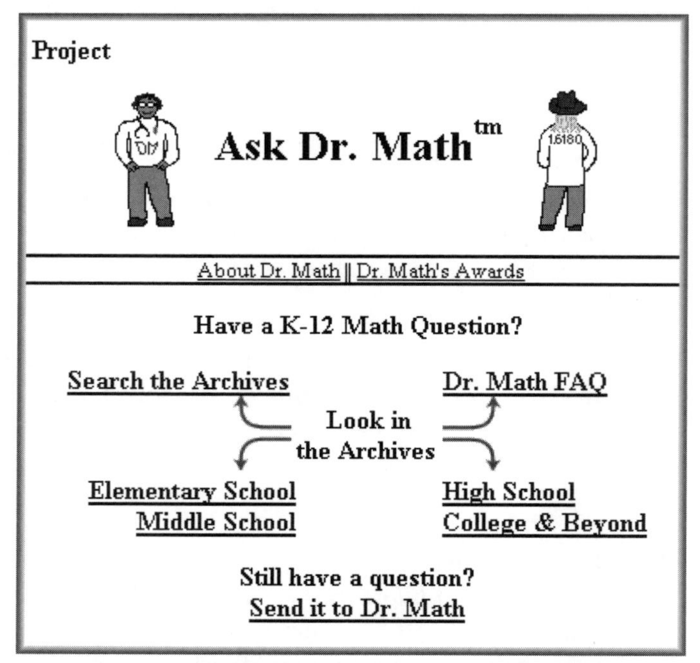

Fig. 9.2. Click on any of the links as shown in the "Ask Dr. Math" screen capture.

Used by permission

AskERIC Lesson Plans: Mathematics

http://ericir.syr.edu/Virtual/Lessons/Mathematics/

The summary below from the AskERIC Mathematics site outlines the variety of resources available here. There are many very good lesson plans at the K–12 level.

- Got an education question? If you are an educator, librarian, parent, or anyone interested in education, AskERIC's Q&A Service can help! Utilizing the diverse resources and expertise of the national ERIC System, AskERIC staff will respond to your question within 2 business days with ERIC database citations and publications, Internet resources, and referrals to other sources of information. AskERIC responds to every question with personalized resources relevant to your needs.
- Includes a SEARCH element, which allows users to search for lessons and resources on a specific topic.

Also contains lesson plans for the following topics :

- Algebra
- Applied Math
- Arithmetic
- Functions
- Geometry
- Measurement
- Probability
- Process Skills
- Statistics

Calculator City: A Web Resource for Mathematics, Algebra, Science, etc.

www.1728.com/

This site has calculators and converters that convert just about everything but cucumbers to pickles.

Convert distance, area, volume, mass, time, velocity, force, pressure, energy, power, temperature, or use the calculator to solve for two, three, or four unknowns. This is an excellent tool for students and mathematicians anywhere.

Canada's SchoolNet: Learning Resources: Mathematics
www.schoolnet.ca/home/e/resources/Links_Result_e.asp?SUBJECT=28

It takes only a couple of clicks of your mouse to get you to the resources pages where there are some excellent interactive exercises with visual and sound effects—at the elementary level—as well as Math Games at all levels. Also there are such all-time student favorites as Algebra and Calculus at more advanced levels, as well as practical Math.

K–12+ Level.

CLN WWW Navigation Map
www.cln.org/map.html#MA

Here is another great source of lesson plans and resources (see Fig. 9.3) at the K–12 level.

Click on any of the sections shown to access the easy-to-use resources. Be sure to scroll down the page to access the General Mathematics Resources as well.

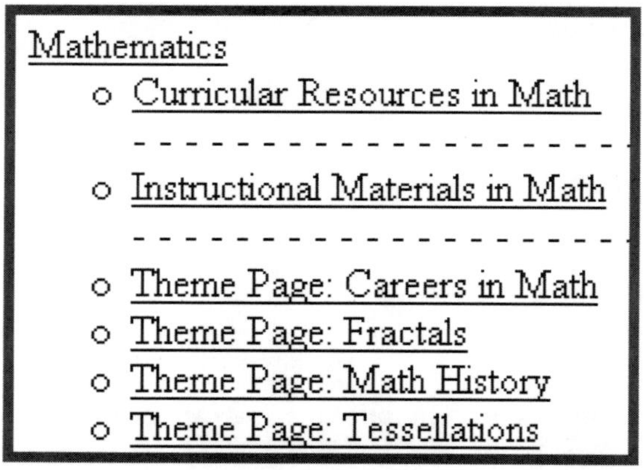

Mathematics
- Curricular Resources in Math
- Instructional Materials in Math
- Theme Page: Careers in Math
- Theme Page: Fractals
- Theme Page: Math History
- Theme Page: Tessellations

Fig. 9.3. This illustration shows the available topics in this section of the CLN site.

Over 10,000 educators view this site each week.

Let your ideas be heard - click here to submit a lesson!

Preschool	Fourth	Ninth
Kindergarten	Fifth	Tenth
First	Sixth	Eleventh
Second	Seventh	Twelfth
Third	Eighth	under-graduate

Fig. 9.4. This illustration shows the easy-to-use format at the Collaborative Lesson Archive.

Collaborative Lesson Archive
http://faldo.atmos.uiuc.edu/CLA/

Click on the appropriate grade level and join the thousands of other educators who visit this site (see Fig. 9.4) each week. You can then click on the Math button in the curriculum area or browse the many cross-curricular lesson plans and pick out the math lessons from there. There is an opportunity for you to contribute your own lesson plans as well, or to comment on the lessons available.
Preschool to undergraduate levels.

CourseServer
www.fairbanks.org/FairShare/CourseServer/courseserver.html

If you don't already have enough problems in your math class, here is the place to go to find more. Actually this site provides a wonderful tool in the form of a math problem generator.

Just choose your grade level and problem types, and presto, you'll have up to fifty problems for your students to solve in areas ranging from basic arithmetic to algebra.
All levels.

CTC Math/Science Gateway: Mathematics
www.tc.cornell.edu/Edu/MathSciGateway/math.html

Another winner as far as the variety of topics and ease of use in accessing resources. You are just a few clicks away from almost anything you need in supplementary resources and interactive exercises and games.
K–12 plus links to University level resources.

- General Topics
- Fractals
- Geometry
- History of Mathematics
- Mathematics Software
- Tables, Constants and Definitions

Curriculum
http://unite.ukans.edu/explorer-db/browse/static/Mathematics/index.html

The list below outlines the wide variety of topics available at this site. The site is easy to use and loaded with lesson plans and resources.
K–12 Level.

- General Mathematics
- Algebraic Ideas
- Geometry
- Mathematical Tools
- Measurement
- Problem Solving and Reasoning
- Statistics and Probability
- Whole Numbers and Numeration

Dave's Math Tables
www.sisweb.com/math/tables.htm

Here is an easy-to-use site filled with math reference tables for general math, algebra, geometry, trigonometry, linear algebra, discrete math, odds and ends, statistics, calculus and advanced topics. There is also a message board and a chat room with a shared drawing whiteboard to be used for math purposes only. The site is available in English or Spanish.
High school to advanced level.

Math Reference Tables

- General Math
- Algebra
- Geometry
- Trigonometry
- Linear Algebra
- Discrete Math
- Odds and Ends
- Statistics
- Calculus
- Advanced Topics

Education World ® — Lesson Planning: Math Sites to Count On!

www.education-world.com/a_lesson/lesson061.shtml

New and exciting ways to liven up your math lessons at all levels. Many games and fun activities, links to online Math tools, as well as a lot of good lesson plans.
K–12 level.

- Dozens of math-related Internet sites that will add to your lessons and multiply your effectiveness! Included: Recommended sites for teachers of K–3, 4–6, and 7–12. Also Games for Math Whizzes and More Math Resources for Teachers!

Education World®—Math: General Resources

http://db.education-world.com/perl/browse?cat_id=1515

This site is from the same folks who built the previous one and is just as good with a broader focus. Besides the topics listed in Figure 9.5, you will also find links to Math Challenge, a variety of sites offering assistance in using calculators for various functions, and much, much more.
All levels.

MATH

TOP : *Math

17 total subcategories. Displaying 1 - 17 .

*Associations & Organizations
*Directories & Indices
*Teacher Resources
Calculators
Companies
Education Programs
History
Magazines & Journals
Math Games
Math Problems
Math Projects
Mathematicians
Newsgroups & Listservs
Patterns
Primary Math
Secondary Math
Treasure Hunts

Fig. 9.5. Try the "Teacher resources" shown in the left column, or choose from amongst the many other resources.
Used by permission

Fractions
www.mathleague.com/help/fractions/fractions.htm#addingand subtractingfractions

This is an excellent place for students to review and study fractions without much assistance from a teacher. Lots of examples and clear explanations. The site is not interactive, though, so the students have to be somewhat motivated to read through the exercises, but it can free up a teacher's time to work with less motivated students while the others learn independently.

- Prime numbers
- Greatest common factor
- Least common multiple
- What is a fraction?
- Equivalent fractions
- Comparing fractions
- Converting and reducing fractions

- Lowest terms
- Improper fractions
- Mixed numbers
- Converting mixed numbers to improper fractions
- Converting improper fractions to mixed numbers
- Writing a fraction as a decimal
- Rounding a fraction to the nearest hundredth
- Adding and subtracting fractions
- Adding and subtracting mixed numbers
- Multiplying fractions and whole numbers
- Multiplying fractions and fractions
- Multiplying mixed numbers
- Reciprocals
- Dividing fractions
- Dividing mixed numbers
- Simplifying complex fractions
- Repeating decimals

Frank Potter's Science Gems—Mathematics

www.sciencegems.com/math.html

This site has just about everything a teacher or student could ever want in the field of Math, with over 11,000 links to math resources at every level and about any Math-related topic. The list below shows available topics.

- Grades K–3 Mathematics
- Grades 4–6 Mathematics
- Pre-Algebra
- Algebra I
- Euclidean Geometry
- Algebra II
- Trigonometry
- Pre-Calculus
- Calculus
- Probability and Statistics
- Advanced Geometry
- Number Theory
- Measurement
- Functions
- Discrete Mathematics

- Mathematical Structure
- Logic
- Linear Algebra & Matrices
- Group Theory
- Topology
- Algebraic Geometry
- Other Advanced Topics
- History of Mathematics

Free Education: Mathematics
www.free-ed.net/fr07/index.html

Free online courses, tutorials, and activities from basic arithmetic to advanced levels (see Fig. 9.6). Includes pre-tests to help determine which areas can be skipped and which ones need to be studied.

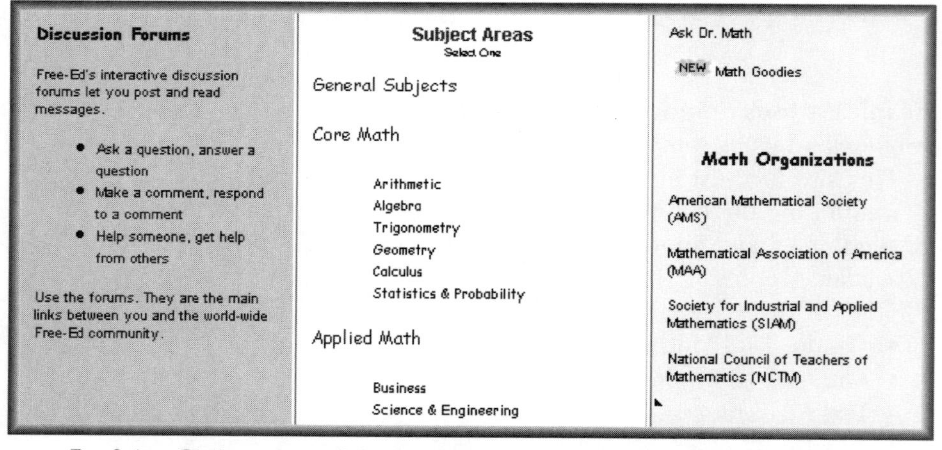

Fig. 9.6. Click on any of the topics shown in the illustration to access courses and resources at Free Education's Math site.

Gopher Menu
gopher://bvsd.k12.co.us:70/11/Educational_Resources/Lesson_Plans/Big%20Sky/math

This site is difficult to describe because of its great variety of lessons and activities at the K–12 level. Excellent site.

IB Higher Level Mathematics Syllabus
http://is7.pacific.net.hk/~cismath/IBH.htm

As the title states, you'll find all the advanced level resources you need here, with over 100 links to mathematical paradise.

Core

- Number and Algebra
- Functions and Equations
- Circular Functions and Trigonometry
- Vector Geometry
- Matrices and Transformations
- Statistics
- Probability
- Calculus

Option

- Statistics
- Sets, Relations and Groups
- Discrete Mathematics
- Analysis and Approximation
- Euclidian Geometry and Conic Sections

K–8: Math in General
http://forum.swarthmore.edu:80/ces95/k8_math.html

Lesson Plans, Activities, Games and many other resources for the K–8 levels. Below is a list of topics at the site.

- Geometry Forum
- Mathematics Education
- Mathematics
- Math/Art Amusements
- Math Lessons
- CTC Math/Sci Gate

- Chance
- Math Resources
- Popcorn Math
- Lesson Plans
- Calculator Math
- Exploring Fractals

K–12 Lesson Plans

http://teams.lacoe.edu/documentation/places/lessons.html#math

Once again, the topics listed in Figures 9.7, 9.8, and 9.9 are but a small sample of the many resources and lessons in this site.

K–12 level.

Mathematics

Appetizers and Lessons for Math and Reason

A variety of mathematics and logic lessons provided by Alan Selby, Ph.D.

Arithmetic Lesson Plans

Links to more than two dozen of the best arithmetic lessons plans on the Internet compiled by the Swarthmore College's Math Forum staff.

Big Sky Math Lessons

Lesson plans for math educators, grades K-12.

Fig. 9.7–9.9. These illustrations show examples of a few of the many available topics at the K–12 Lesson Plans site.
Used by permission

Collaborative Lesson Archive

Find math and science lessons for grades 2-12.

CRPC GirlTech Lesson Plans '96 & '95

These lesson plans were designed by teachers to take full advantage of Internet resources and teach standard concepts in mathematics and sciences in new and exciting ways.

Encarta Mathematics Lesson Plans

A collection of lessons and student activities for K-12 teachers.

ETA: Teacher Lesson Plans

Several nice lesson plans are offered here on tangrams and geometry.

Euler's Formula for Polyhedra

Students will discover Euler's formula for polyhedra, and will be able to show that it works for any convex polyhedron.

Explorer Curriculum Browser

This site offers a rich resource of mathematics and natural science lesson plans and information.

A Fractal Unit for Elementary and Middle School Students

A series of lessons on fractals by Cynthia Lanius.

Math Forum Lessons & Courses

Links to a great number and variety of math lessons and courses.

Fig. 9.8. K–12 Lesson Plans.
Used by permission

K–12: Math in General

http://forum.swarthmore.edu:80/ces95/6_12_math.html

A twin site to the one above, this one is for all levels. Topics from this site are listed below.

Math in general

- Chance
- CTC Math/Science Gate
- Fractal FAQ
- Geometry Forum
- Math Lessons
- Math Resources

Math Lesson Plans

A scrolling page of lesson plans provided by Teachers Helping Teachers.

Math Lesson Plans

A collection of lesson plans provided by California State University, Northridge.

Paso Partners

Lessons integrating math, science and language, provided in both English and Spanish.

Place Math

Internet-Based lessons and activities on math and aeronautics for children with physical disabilities funded through a cooperative agreement with NASA.

SCORE Mathematics

Schools of California Online Resource for Education provides excellent lessons for all grade levels.

Teachnet.Com Lesson Plans

Find lesson plans on geometry, maps & graphs, money, real world, terminology, and general lesson ideas.

Teaching Mathematics in the Middle and Secondary School

Lesson plans provided by students at Barry University.

Fig. 9.9. And even more of the resources available at the K–12 Lesson Plans site.
Used by permission

- Math/Art Amusements
- Mathematics
- Mathematics Education

Science: Mathematics
- Archives: Lessons
- Calculus Graphics
- Calculus Modules

Discrete Math and Graphing Calculators
- Exploring Fractals

- Lesson Plans
- Mega Math
- Newsgroup: math
- Project Mathematics!

Kathy Schrock's Guide for Educators—Math
http://discoveryschool.com/schrockguide/math.html
Besides the resource links listed below, you'll find a lot of other great links including an Encyclopaedia of Math, Roman Numeral Conversion, and a Superkids Math Worksheet Creator that really works.

- Ask Dr. Math
- Eric's Treasure Trove of Mathematics
- History of Mathematics Archive
- Totally Tessellated

Lesson Stop—Math
www.youthline-usa.com/lessonstop/math.html
There are a lot of great lesson plans and many other resources here. Some of the topics are listed below.
All levels, K–12.

- Algebra
- All Mathematics
- Applied Math
- Arithmetic
- Functions
- Geometry
- Measurement
- Probability
- Process Skills
- Statistics

Math Forum: Arithmetic Lesson Plan Sites
http://forum.swarthmore.edu/arithmetic/arith.sites.html
This site concentrates on Lesson Plans, as the title suggests. It contains quite a few of the most popular links on the web as well as some you may not see at other Math sites.
K–12 level.

K–12 Topics
- Algebra
- Arithmetic
- Calculus
- Discrete math
- Geometry
- Pre-calculus
- Prob/Stat

Advanced Topics
- Analysis
- Calculus
- Diff. Equations
- Game theory
- Discrete math
- Geometry (coll.)
- Geometry (adv.)
- Linear algebra
- Modern algebra
- Num. Analysis

Math Forum Internet Mathematics Library
http://forum.swarthmore.edu/library/

This is a very well-organized and easy-to use site, with as many resources as you will likely need in an average lifetime. It is organized both by topic and grade level. Topics are outlined in Figure 9.10.
K–12+ level.

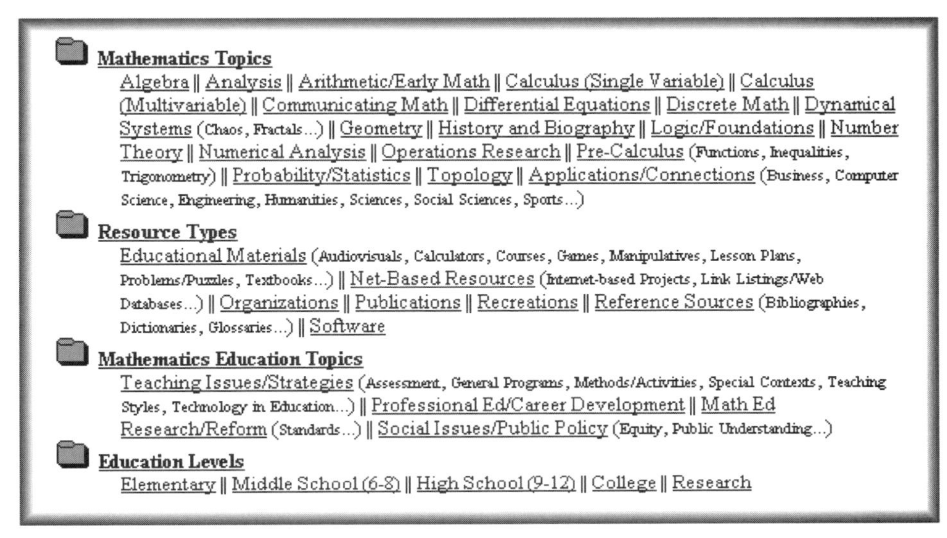

Fig. 9.10. Examples of the topics available at the Mathematics Forum site.
Used by permission

Mathematics Archives—Topics in Mathematics

http://archives.math.utk.edu/topics/

Another well-organized site (see Fig. 9.11) with resources listed by topic or accessible through a search agent on the main page. It contains some of the best sites for arithmetic lesson plans.
K–12+ level.

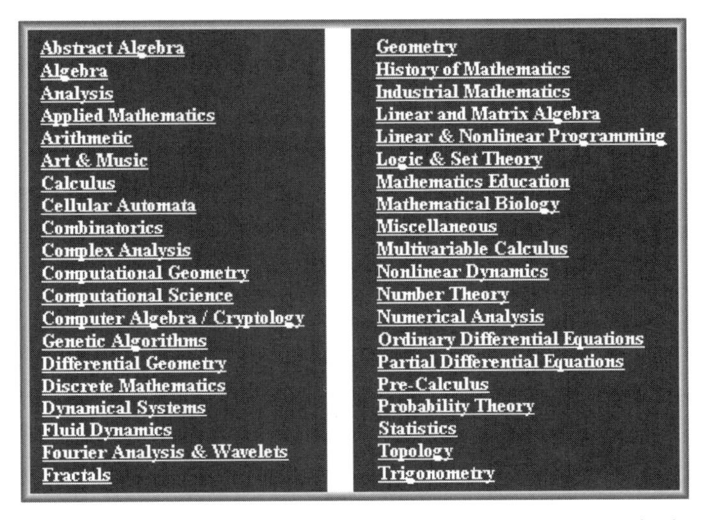

Fig. 9.11. Here is an outline of available topics at the Mathematics Archives site.
©1996-1999 Mathematics Archives. Used by permission

Mathematics Encyclopedia

www.mathacademy.com/platonic_realms/encyclop/encyhome.html

This detailed interactive encyclopedia should provide you with just about any information you need to know in the field of mathematics, including mathematical terms and definitions, biographies, history, and even a language translator. Click on "Subject" to access the list of topics covered on this site.

Online Schoolyard Math Feature

www.onlineschoolyard.com/channels/channels.asp?d=School&m=2&c=18

When you get to this site, you'll have to click on the "Math" button at the left of the page to get you to a colorfully presented list of topics and resources. You can click in the box at the top of the page to select a general topic, or scroll in the two windows on the page for specific links. Lots of games, flashcards lessons, and many other resources.

K–12 level.

Click on "Subjects" to access a drop-down menu containing the following math resources:

- Add, Subtract, Multiply and Divide
- Algebra Avenue
- Counting Corner
- General topics
- Geometry
- History of Mathematics
- Measurements
- Pre-calculus/Calculus
- Probability/Statistics
- Strain Your Brain

Pinchbeck—Math

www.bjpinchbeck.com/framemath.htm

Here is an unusual site. Begun in 1996 by a twelve-year-old boy and his dad, Pinchbeck's Homework Helper is an award-winning site with some of the best resources on the web. The Math section contains many links to Lesson Plans, Conversion Tables, Math Terms, Word Problems, and many more resources. Take a look at Figure 9.12.

K–12 level.

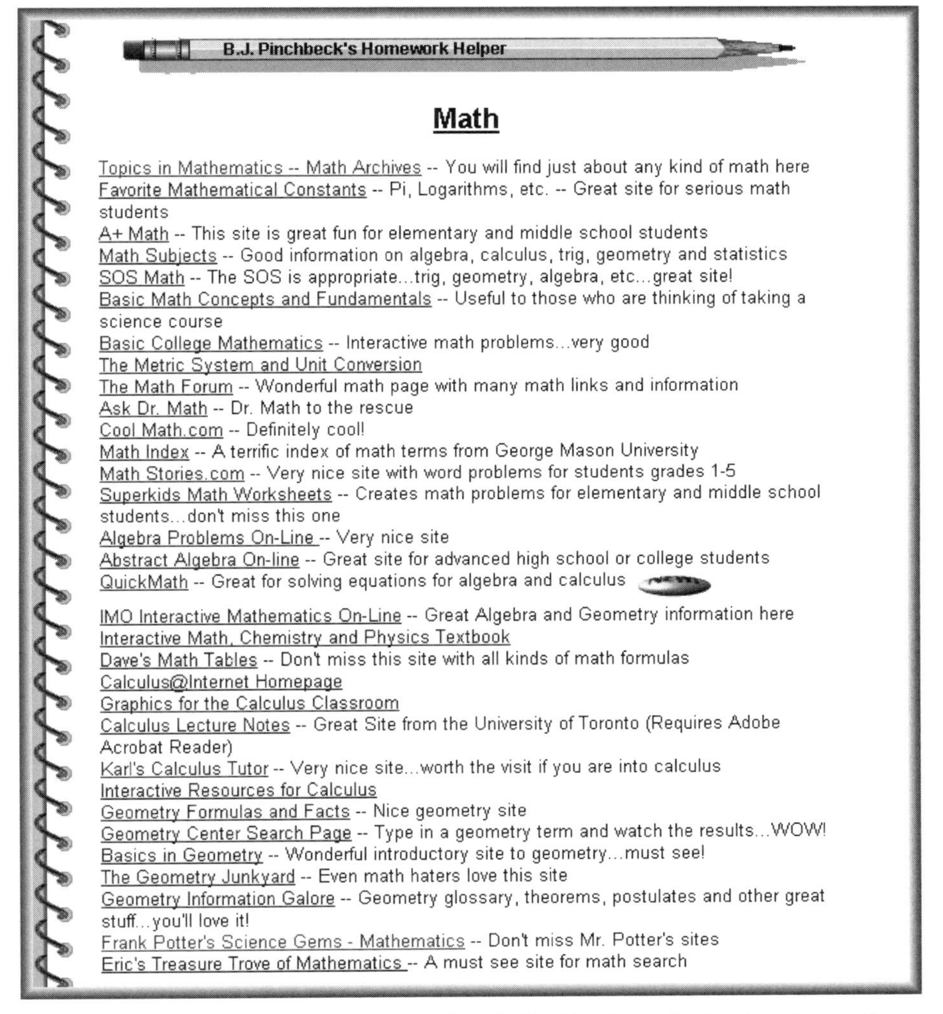

Fig. 9.12. Here is a sample page from the BJ Pinchbeck math site showing available topics.
Used by permission

Practical Uses of Math And Science

http://pumas.jpl.nasa.gov/

A collection of one-page examples of how math and science topics taught in K–12 classes can be used in interesting settings and everyday life.

Below are some of the topics, with more being added as we write.

- Automatic Windshield Wipers
- Coastal Threat: A Story in Unit Conversions
- Could a World of Swimmers Raise Sea Level?
- Dr. Smith vs. The Lawyer
- Grandpas Social Security
- How Far Can You See?
- How Many Days Are in a Year?
- How Now, Pythagoras?
- How thick is the Earth's atmosphere?
- Hypothermia in the Little House
- Ice Sheets and Sea Level Rise
- Just what is a logarithm, anyway?
- Learning from Slide Rules
- Learning to Think Globally
- Length of the Day
- Making Months
- Mixing & Stirring
- Modulus in the Real World
- Particle Man and the Photon
- Preventing Hypothermia
- Rotational Motion and Rocket Launches
- Snowmelt and Floods
- Spoon Mirror
- The Shadow of the Dog
- There's Air in There!
- Two Answers are Better than One

Scientific American: Ask the Experts: Mathematics
www.sciam.com/askexpert/math/index.html

Answers to a lot of interesting questions like "What is the origin of Pi?" or "How does a laser measure the speed of a car?" Or have students ask their own questions of the experts.

Higher levels mainly.

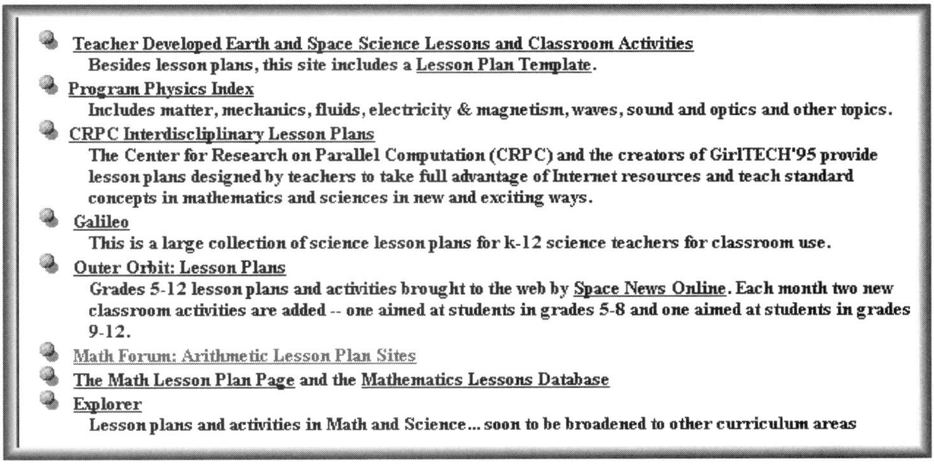

- Teacher Developed Earth and Space Science Lessons and Classroom Activities
  Besides lesson plans, this site includes a Lesson Plan Template.
- Program Physics Index
  Includes matter, mechanics, fluids, electricity & magnetism, waves, sound and optics and other topics.
- CRPC Interdisciplinary Lesson Plans
  The Center for Research on Parallel Computation (CRPC) and the creators of GirlTECH'95 provide lesson plans designed by teachers to take full advantage of Internet resources and teach standard concepts in mathematics and sciences in new and exciting ways.
- Galileo
  This is a large collection of science lesson plans for k-12 science teachers for classroom use.
- Outer Orbit: Lesson Plans
  Grades 5-12 lesson plans and activities brought to the web by Space News Online. Each month two new classroom activities are added -- one aimed at students in grades 5-8 and one aimed at students in grades 9-12.
- Math Forum: Arithmetic Lesson Plan Sites
- The Math Lesson Plan Page and the Mathematics Lessons Database
- Explorer
  Lesson plans and activities in Math and Science... soon to be broadened to other curriculum areas

Fig. 9.13. Scroll down to click on the math topics of your choice at the Teachers' Page of Lesson Plans site.
Used by permission

Teachers Page of Lesson Plans

www.library.ualberta.ca/library_html/libraries/coutts/lessons.html#science

This site (see Fig. 9.13) not only explains to new teachers what lesson plans are and why they are needed, but also has links to some of the best sites on the web for accessing lesson plans.
K–12+ level.

The Lesson Plans Page—Math Lesson Plans

www.lessonplanspage.com/Math.htm

Select the "Lesson Plans Page", then select "Math" from the topics menu. From there you will be able to select the grade level (see Fig. 9.14) and you will be whisked to the magic land of pre-made lesson plans.
K–12 level.

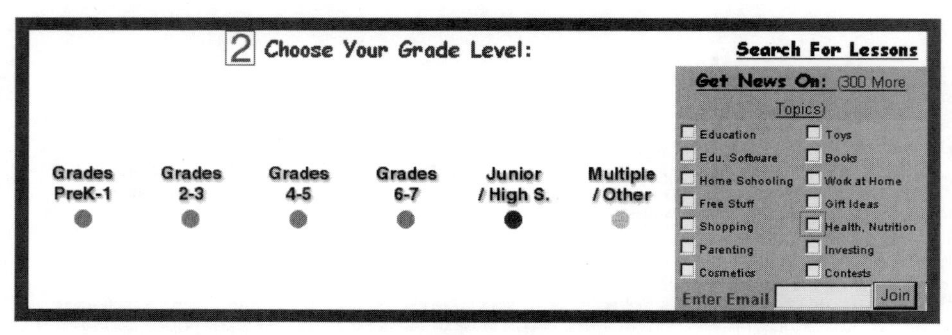

Fig. 9.14. Click on the appropriate grade level as shown in the illustration.
The Lesson Plans Page™ is owned and operated by EdScope™, L.L.C.

The Math Forum—Math Library—Math Topics

http://forum.swarthmore.edu/library/topics/

The list below is only a small sampling of what waits for you on the Math Forum pages. Lots of advanced-level Math, but also contains the basics. Overall it is a very thorough site.
All levels.

- Algebra
- Analysis
- Arithmetic Early
- Calculus (SV)
- Calculus (MV)
- Communicating Math
- Differential Equations
- Discrete Math
- Dynamical Systems
- Geometry
- History/Biography
- Logic/Foundations
- Number Theory
- Numerical Analysis
- Operations Research
- Pre-Calculus
- Prob/Stat
- Topology

Vassar's CoolSchool/Go to Class!!

www.coolschool.edu/gomath.htm

This site has most of the usual topics, but also contains a good section on "Special Topics" that all Math lovers are sure to find interesting.

K–12, but mainly higher-level resources.

- Calculus
- Geometry
- Math
- Special Topics
- Tools

Welcome to K–12 World!

www.k-12world.com:80/cy_curr_res.cfm

You will have to scroll down the page a bit to click on the math resources, but again, it's worth the effort if you are looking for resources in the areas listed below. You might also try the "Educators' Resources" page for resources on curriculum planning.

K–12, but mainly higher levels.

- Algebra
- Calculus
- Geometry
- Statistics/Probability

Chapter 10

Sciences

The following sites contain resources for teaching and learning in virtually all areas of the Sciences from elementary to the most advanced levels.

Teachers can save countless hours spent designing lesson plans by incorporating any of the hundreds of pre-made lessons available at the various sites into their own classes. Students can work independently on interactive lessons, freeing instructors' time to work with those in need of individual attention. Multimedia presentations including photographs, illustrations, graphics animations, and sounds at some sites greatly enhance learning as well.

So just click on the sites, explore a bit, play a bit, and learn how easy it is to take part in the education revolution of the new millennium. We have selected the very best sites available on the Internet for your use. Enjoy the journey.

CHAPTER OVERVIEW

General Resources, pages 180–193

Biology, pages 194–199

GENERAL RESOURCES

In the Science General Resources section, you will find sites which contain resources such as lesson plans, exercises, quizzes, science news, and so forth in more than one scientific discipline or in disciplines that do not fit specifically in any other category.

Access Excellence
www.accessexcellence.org/

This site (see Fig. 10.1) is for Health and Bioscience teachers and learners. Don't miss the "Activities Exchange" section or the "Classrooms of the 21st Century" resources.

There are ideas, lessons, and activities for all levels from middle school onwards, plus the latest information and news updates in Health and Bioscience.

Alphabet Superhighway
www.ash.udel.edu/ash/teacher/teacherframe.html

When you get to the primary site that is bookmarked here, you will have to click on the "Teacher Connections" icon on the bulletin board to access the resources shown in the menu in Figure 10.2. You can visit the solar system or breed virtual fruit flies with a few more clicks of your mouse.

All levels.

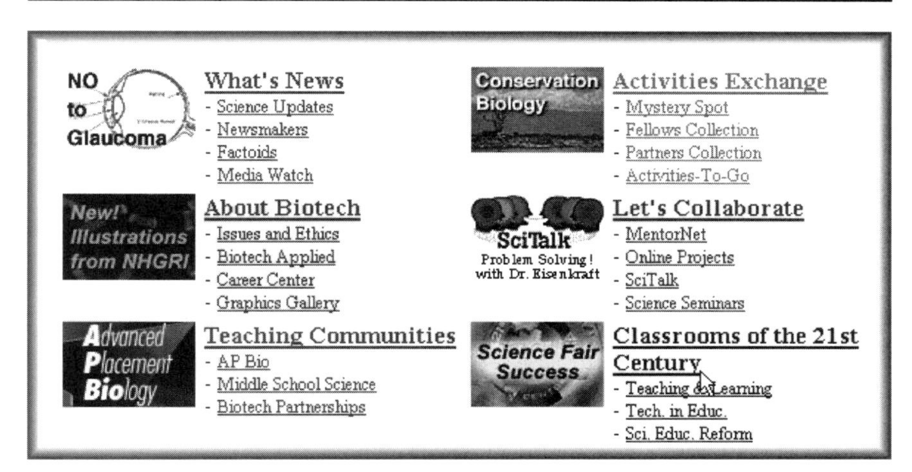

Fig. 10.1. Click on any of the areas as shown in the sample illustration to access the many excellent resources.
Used by permission

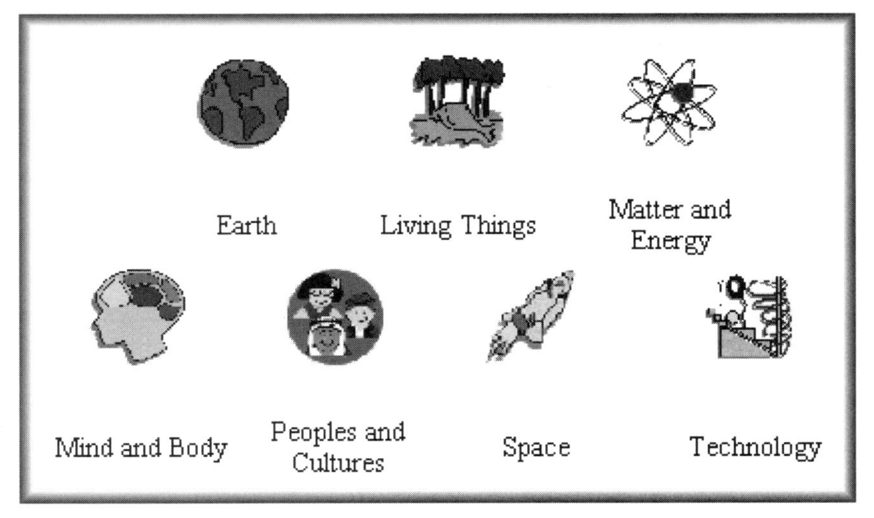

Fig. 10.2. Follow the pictured links shown in the illustration to the area of your choice.
Used by permission

AskERIC Lesson Plans: Science

http://ericir.syr.edu/Virtual/Lessons/Science/index.html

From Agricultural to Space Sciences, you can click on a wide choice of lessons and resources in the many areas of science. Or, if you are stuck on a science question you can just ask ERIC. See the list of topics below followed by the site developers' description of their free services.

All levels.

- Agriculture
- Biological and Life Sciences
- Careers
- Earth Science
- General Science
- History
- Instructional Issues
- Natural History
- Physical Sciences
- Process Skills
- Space Sciences
- Technology

Got an education question? If you are an educator, librarian, parent, or anyone interested in education, AskERIC's Q&A Service can help! Utilizing the diverse resources and expertise of the national ERIC System, AskERIC staff will respond to your question within 2 business days with ERIC database citations and publications, Internet resources, and referrals to other sources of information. AskERIC responds to every question with personalized resources relevant to your needs.

Also includes a SEARCH element, which allows users to search for lessons and resources on a specific topic.

Calculator City: A Web Resource for Mathematics, Algebra, Science, etc.

www.1728.com/

Convert units such as distance, area, volume, mass, time, velocity, force, pressure, energy, power, temperature, or use one of the calculators to solve for two, three, or four unknowns.

This is an excellent advanced level resource.

Canada's SchoolNet: Learning Resources: Sciences

www.schoolnet.ca/home/e/resources/Links_Result_e.asp?SUBJECT=33

This site (see Fig. 10.3), like most of the sites in this section, has too broad a range of science topics to classify in a particular section of the sciences. If you are willing to explore a bit, you will be rewarded with excellent resources on many topics within the areas of science, and even a site on "bad science." You can easily access the resources in the disciplines listed below with a click or two of your mouse. K–12 level.

- Biology
- Biotechnology
- Chemistry
- Earth Science and Geology
- Engineering
- Physics
- Resource Sciences
- Space and Astronomy

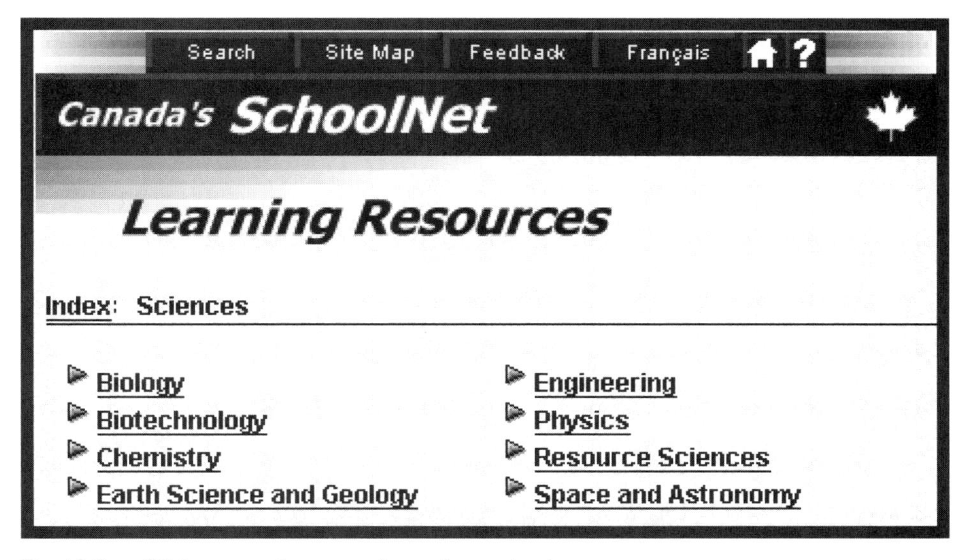

Fig. 10.3. Click on a science topic as shown in the menu.
Used by permission

CLN Science

www.cln.org/map.html#SCI

This link will direct you to the center of the Community Learning Network's science resources as outlined in the following list. A couple more clicks will get you to many lesson plans and other very useful resources.
K–12 level.

Curricular Resources in:

- Astronomy
- Chemistry
- General Science
- Geology
- Life Science
- Paleontology
- Physics
- Weather and Climate

Instructional Materials in:

- Astronomy
- Chemistry
- General Science
- Geology
- Life Science
- Paleontology
- Physics
- Weather and Climate

Cornell Theory Center Math and Science Gateway

www.tc.cornell.edu/Edu/MathSciGateway/

Here you will find a lot of science resources and lessons for teachers and students, primarily for grades 9–12. Teachers at other levels may find many of the resources useful as well with minor adaptations.

- Astronomy
- Biology
- Chemistry
- Earth & Environmental Science
- Health and Medicine
- Meteorology

- Monthly Science/Math Topic
- Physics
- Science

Curriculum
http://unite.ukans.edu/explorer-db/browse/static/Natural^Science/index.html

Here you will find easily accessible lesson plans from elementary to advanced levels on a very wide range of topics from bacteria growth to rockets. A few of the general subject areas are listed here:

- Common Themes
- Earth Science
- General Natural Science
- Life Science
- Physical Science

Doing Science
www.hpcc.astro.washington.edu/scied/dosci.html

This page is full of links to educational sites with resources to "help students become engaged in the practice of science." There are both elementary and higher level resources such as an online journal for high school science research, fun activities, science fairs, NASA online interactive projects, experiments, exercises, and a whole lot more. Resources for specific areas such as Astronomy, Biological Sciences, Chemistry, Earth Sciences, Physics and so forth are available by scrolling down to the bottom of the page and clicking on your choice of topic.

K–12 level and up.

Education World®—Science: General Resources
http://db.education-world.com/perl/browse?cat_id=1551

Here is a great site for educators at the Pre-K to grade 12 level. Click on lessons by grade level or scan the page for general topics. Scroll down the page for over one hundred more links. For a bit of fun check out the site called "On the Lighter Side: Simple Science," and be sure to go to the "Science Tips and Ideas" site for ideas, and materials for science fair projects.

- Chemistry
- Life Science
- Medical Science
- Physical Science
- Science Fair Resources
- Science History

Education World®—Science: Teacher Resources

http://db.education-world.com/perl/browse?cat_id=2887

We have included a second link to Education World because of the many other science resources that can be found here. Click on your specific subject area here for a list of Pre-K to grade 12 lessons and resources, including many experiments, lab activities, instructional aids, virtual field trips, and other lesson plans. There are even some resources for professional practitioners.

Lesson Plans and Experiments for grades:

- **Pre–K
- *K–2
- 3–5
- 6–8
- 9–12

Frank Potter's Science Gems

www.sciencegems.com/

Search from thousands of links for lessons and resources on a specific science topic, or select your particular interest from the topics below. Topics in pre-made lessons range from the physics of skateboarding to lessons on comets, oceans, viruses, volcanoes, and many more interesting, contemporary, and fun topics.
K–12 levels and up.

- Earth Science
- K–12 Science Lesson Plans—'99
- Life Science
- Physical Science

Free Education: Science
www.free-ed.net/fr08/index.html

Here you will find tutorials and materials for complete advanced level courses offered free by the free-ed.net site. The topics listed below from the site menu may not all be available since the site is continually being developed and improved, but those that are available generally are well presented and designed for easy use by independent learners. Teachers may want to refer students to specific areas for research, supplementary practice, and skill development, or adapt some of the ideas and resources to their own classrooms.
Advanced levels.

General Subjects & Core Courses
Agriculture
Astronomy
Biology

- Anatomy & Physiology
- Biochemistry
- Biophysics
- Botany
- Ecology
- Evolution
- Genetics & Cell Biology
- Microbiology
- Zoology

Chemistry

- Analytical Chemistry
- Biochemistry
- Inorganic Chemistry
- Organic Chemistry
- Physical Chemistry

Geography

- Human & Cultural Geography
- Physical Geography
- Regional Geography

Earth Sciences
Physics
American Association for the Advancement of Science (AAAS)
Science Online
Science Magazines Online

Gopher Menu
gopher://bvsd.k12.co.us:70/11/Educational_Resources/Lesson_Plans/Big%20Sky/science

This site links you to many good lessons and resources at the K–12 level. Check out the lab activities for new ideas and approaches to teaching and learning science.

Great Science Discoveries of the 1990s
www-sci.lib.uci.edu/SEP/GreatSci90.html

Review the great scientific advances of the past decade from the discoveries of extra-solar planets to mapping genes.
Mainly higher level resources.

- Extra-Solar
- Planets and Planetary Models
- Genome Mapping and Genetic Testing
- Global Ecosystem and Ecosystem Dynamics
- Great Science Discoveries of the 1990s
- New Materials / New Techniques
- Particle Physics—Top Quark and the Standard Model
- Universe Exploration

Kathy Schrock's Guide for Educators—Science and Technology
http://discoveryschool.com/schrockguide/sci-tech.html

This site from the Discovery Channel School provides educators and learners with very good links to a variety of science resources and lesson plans. When you get to the site click on any of the subject areas listed below to access the hundreds of available resources. Or scroll down further for some other interesting links to sites like "Flowerbase" where you can search for flowers by Botanical or common names and in several languages. Try "Neuroscience" for Kids if you want factual information (e.g., Do we really use only 10% of our brain?), great illustrations, along with experiments, activities, and more.

Lots of elementary as well as higher level resources at this site.

- Biological Science and Animal Sites
- Chemical Science Sites
- Earth, Geology, & Oceanography Sites
- Environmental Science Sites

- General Science Sites
- NASA Sites
- Physics & Optics Sites
- Space & Astronomy Sites

Lesson Stop—Science

www.youthline-usa.com/lessonstop/science.html

Here you will find hundreds of pre-made lesson plans and links to resources at levels K–12. Check out the many experiments and labs, and the many other activities which can enhance learning in any classroom at any level. Scroll down the page to find your particular field of science.

- All Sciences
- Earth and Space
- Life Sciences
- Physical Sciences

NASA's LTP—Feature Stories

http://learn.ivv.nasa.gov/features/features.html

Who better is there to interact with on science matters than the scientists and professionals at NASA? Check out the many excellent and practical resources they offer for educators and learners at all levels. And, the science topics are not only about space. There is everything here from rainforest exploration to volcanoes to weather resources as well. The accompanying screen capture (see Fig. 10.4–10.5) shows the many topics available.

K–12 levels.

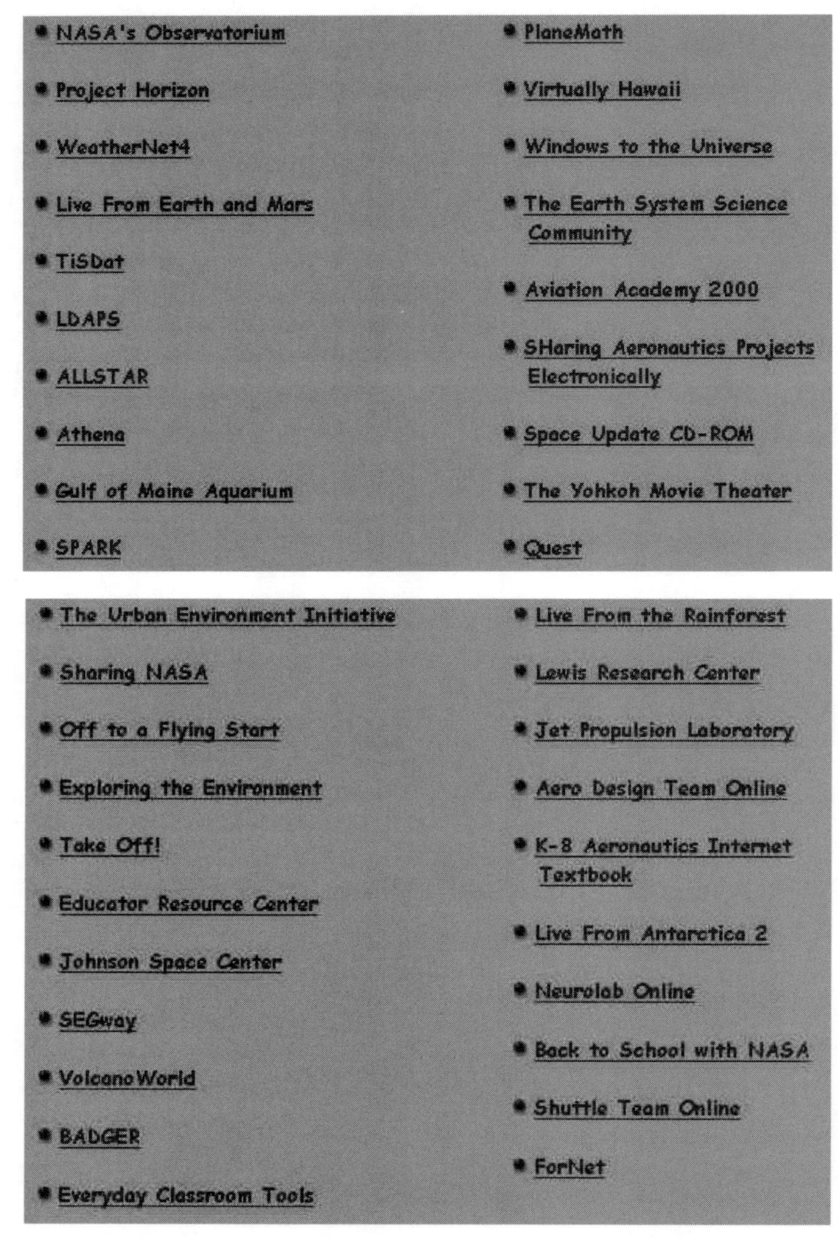

Fig. 10.4–10.5. Click on any of these topics available from the NASA site.

Pinchbeck—Science
www.bjpinchbeck.com/framescience.htm

An admirable array of direct links to very good science sites with subject matter ranging from "Bizarre Things You Can Make in your Kitchen" to amazing dinosaur sites, a heart preview gallery, and many science experiments and labs. There are sites for nearly every scientific discipline—and all grade levels, even an introduction to nuclear physics for budding Einsteins.

K–12 levels.

School for Champions
www.ronkurtus.com/science.htm#Physics

At this site (see Fig. 10.6) you will find a free online course which "combines physics and chemistry fundamentals in a way that will allow 'students' to excel in future science studies." Teachers will be able to find excellent resources which are sure to enhance any learning environment. There are wonderful experiments, labs, quizzes, audiovisual enhancements, games, tricks for good grades, and a whole lot more. This site truly makes learning science an adventure and a lot of fun. Don't miss it.

Higher levels.

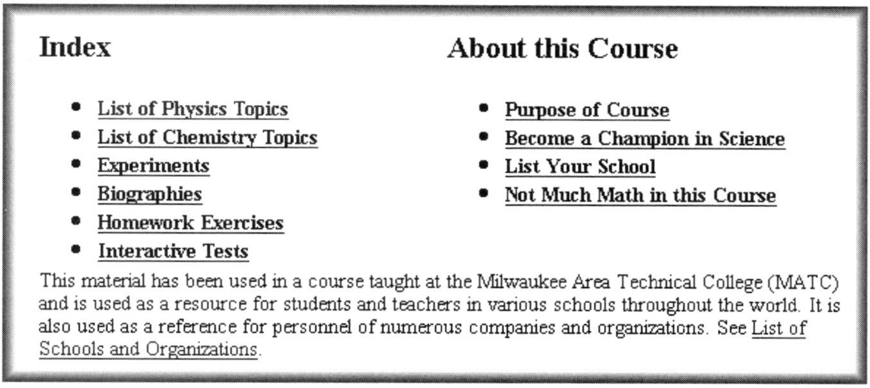

Index

- List of Physics Topics
- List of Chemistry Topics
- Experiments
- Biographies
- Homework Exercises
- Interactive Tests

About this Course

- Purpose of Course
- Become a Champion in Science
- List Your School
- Not Much Math in this Course

This material has been used in a course taught at the Milwaukee Area Technical College (MATC) and is used as a resource for students and teachers in various schools throughout the world. It is also used as a reference for personnel of numerous companies and organizations. See List of Schools and Organizations.

Fig. 10.6. The accompanying image shows the available topics and links at the School for Champions.

Teacher Resources—Educational Links

http://msgc.engin.umich.edu/cgi-bin/tour.cgi?link=/teacher_resources/html.

At this site you will find practical resources and lessons on a variety of topics in science. Try the virtual frog dissection, take an "earthquake quiz" or take a multimedia tour of the solar system. . . .
Beginner, medium and advanced levels.

Click at the top of the page to access resources by level of difficulty or just scroll down the page to find the resources in the following areas:

- Biology
- Earth Science
- Space Sciences

The Experimental Study Group

http://esg-www.mit.edu:8001/esgbio/7001main.html

This site from the Massachusetts Institute of Technology has a variety of interesting resources. There are some great practice tests, a very interesting "Biology Hypertextbook," with excellent graphics, and a search tool for science topics.
Advanced levels.

The Lesson Plans Page

www.lessonplanspage.com/javaframe.htm

When you get to the main site listed here, just scroll down the page and click on the "Science Lessons" section. From there you can choose the grade level for your class and you are well on your way to accessing many easy-to-use lesson plans. Be sure to try the multilevel lessons as well and check out the dropdown menu at the top of the page for more site options.
K–12 levels.

Units Conversion Calculator

www.thebighub.com/convertit/default.asp

Convert any measurement unit to any other one with the click of your mouse. Convert from and to such units as Celsius, Fahrenheit, and

Degrees Kelvin or from miles to meters, joules to kilowatt-hours, or even a Japanese ri to a parasang.
Higher levels.

Welcome to K–12 World!
www.k-12world.net/cy_curr_res.cfm
You will have to scroll down the page a bit to get to the science resources, but you will be well rewarded for your efforts with many lesson plans and resources links on the topics listed in the illustration below (see Fig. 10.7). Many lessons contain multimedia enhancements to facilitate and enrich the experience of learning science.
All levels K–12.

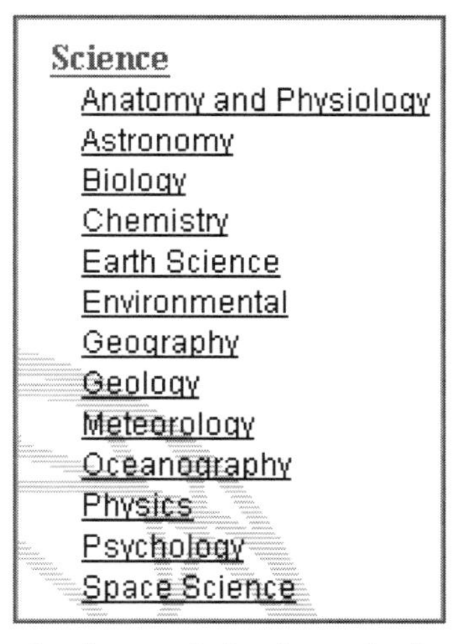

Fig. 10.7. Click on the topic of your choice from the list shown at K–12 World. *©1998 JDL Technologies, Inc. Used by permission*

BIOLOGY

BioChemNet: General Biology
http://schmidel.com/bionet/biology.htm

This site describes itself as a "Guide to the Best Biology & Chemistry Educational Resources on the Web." In it you will find many links to excellent advanced level resources. Following is a condensed list of the main topic areas, many with labs, experiments, facts, and multimedia enhancements.
High school level and up.

- Introduction to Biology
- Botany
- Cell Biology
- Ecology
- Evolution
- Human Biology
- Laboratory Experiments (Teaching Science)
- Microbiology
- Nutrition
- Zoology

BioEd: Biology Education Resources
www-hpcc.astro.washington.edu/scied/bioindex.html

Lots of advanced level biology resources here. Be sure to check out the "What's New" section at the top of the page before getting lost in the other topics shown below.

- What's New
- General Biology Topics
- Cellular/Microbiology
- Oceanography/Marine Biology
- EnviroEd: Environmental Science
- Software
- Biotechnology
- Health Education

Biology Lessons

www.biologylessons.sdsu.edu/classes/index.html

This site (see Fig. 10.8) is full of lessons, exercises, and ideas for elementary school biology teachers and their students.

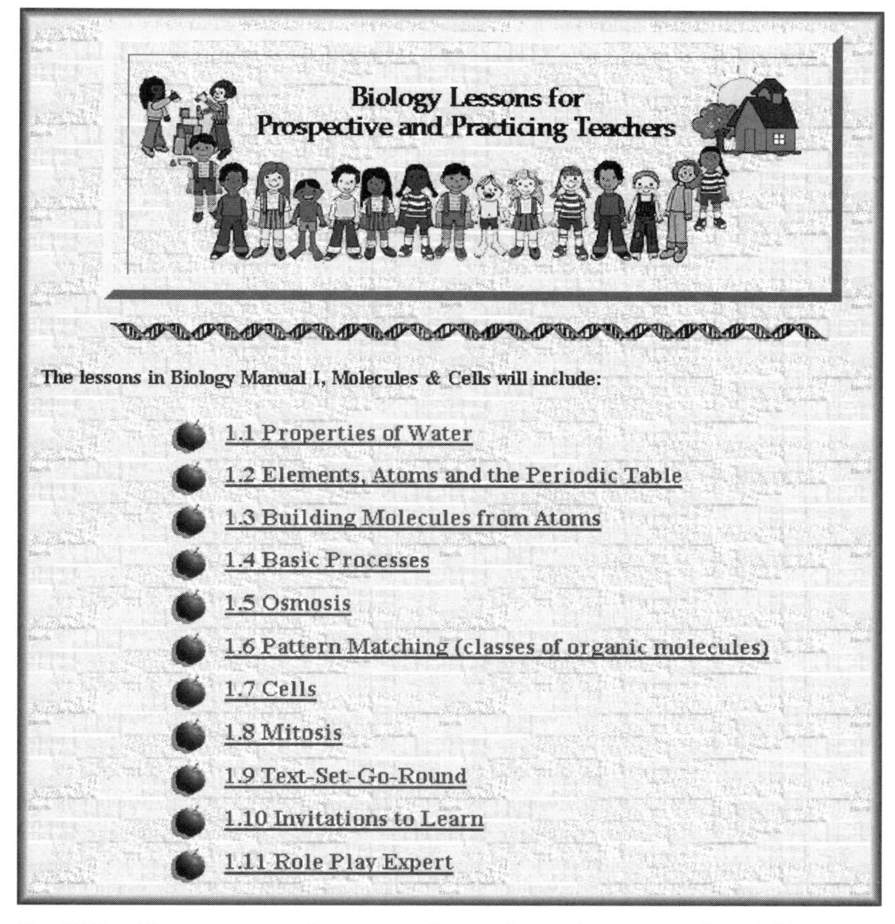

Fig. 10.8. The accompanying image shows the wide variety of available topics at the colorful Biology Lessons site.
Used by permission

Canada's SchoolNet: Learning Resources

www.schoolnet.ca/home/e/resources/Links_Result_e.asp?SUBJECT=34&SUB=Sciences&ID=33

Here is a great site for finding resources for teaching and learning at all school levels. You will find links to an impressive array of lessons, exercises, ideas, and quizzes. There are many accompanying multimedia resources, which are easy to use, so don't be afraid to try them if you are new at using computer media. You may need to download some software such as RealPlayer or Windows Media Player if you don't have them yet, and you will need a soundcard for some.
K–12 levels.

CTC Math/Science Gateway: Biology

www.tc.cornell.edu/Edu/MathSciGateway/biology.html

There are some really excellent links here provided by the Cornell Theory Center for teachers and learners at all levels. You will find lessons, experiments, games, interactive exercises, multimedia presentations, and many other tools to make teaching and learning biology easier and more fun. Below is a list of topics.

- Collections & Other Stuff
- DNA, Molecular Biology & Modeling
- Ecology
- Invertebrates
- Plants & Fungi
- Vertebrates

Education World®—Biology

http://db.education-world.com/perl/browse?cat_id=3025

At our last count there were over 70 categories of lesson plans for elementary to advanced learners. Includes interactive resources and ideas for experiments as well. Why not try the virtual dissection of a cow's eye before lunch today?
K–12 and up.

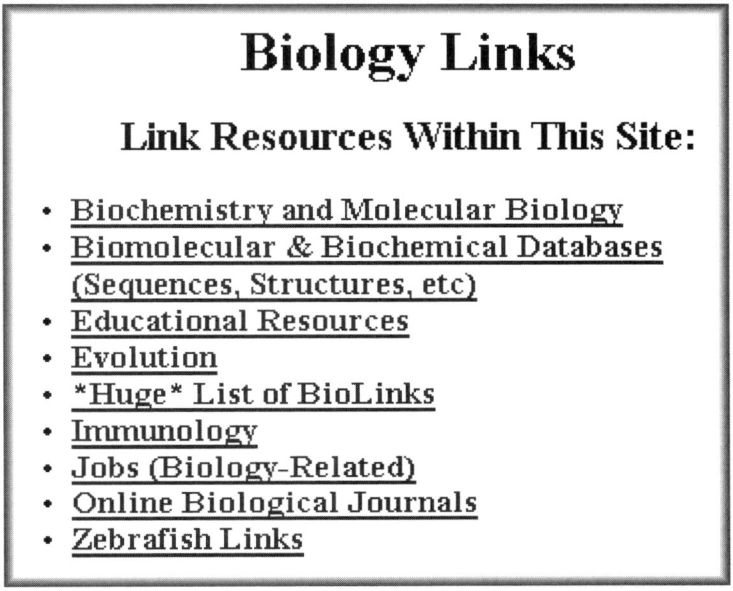

Biology Links

Link Resources Within This Site:

- Biochemistry and Molecular Biology
- Biomolecular & Biochemical Databases (Sequences, Structures, etc)
- Educational Resources
- Evolution
- *Huge* List of BioLinks
- Immunology
- Jobs (Biology-Related)
- Online Biological Journals
- Zebrafish Links

Fig. 10.9. This illustration shows some of the many available topics at the Harvard site.

Harvard Dept of MCB—Biology Links
http://mcb.harvard.edu/BioLinks.html

You will find advanced level resources at this site (see Fig. 10.9), some applicable to high school programs.

Topics range from evolutionary biology to immunology to zebrafish. This is a good way for your students to get into Harvard.

Human Anatomy Online
www.innerbody.com/htm/body.html

("Oh, the toe-bone's connected to the foot-bone . . . ")

Here is a great multimedia site for learning about the human body. Students can just click on any of the ten pictured systems then learn the names of all the body parts just by moving their mouse pointer. There are also very good animations that show various body systems in an easy-to-understand format.

Elementary to high school level.

Internet BioED Project (Biology on the Net)

www.botany.uwc.ac.za/Sci_Ed/GeneralBiology/index.htm

While some of the links here are targeted at professional biologists, there are also useful resources for high school students of biology, particularly those doing research projects. Check out the database of all amino acids, or follow the genetic trails of mutant genes. A partial list of topics is shown below.

- General Biology
- Biotechnology, Molecular Biology and Chemistry of life
- Ecology and Environment
- Essays and FAQs in Biology
- Evolution
- Expeditions and Adventures
- Human Biology and Medicine
- Online Journals and Magazines
- The Tools of Biology
- Virtual laboratory Exercises
- Viruses and Bacteria

Kathy Schrock's Guide for Educators—Biological Science & Animal Sites

http://school.discovery.com/schrockguide/sci-tech/scibs.html

Here is another page from the Discovery Channel School filled with links to many excellent resources. Take an interactive tour of the human heart, search a database of flowers, learn about genes and cloning, or take a journey with Charles Darwin and company to the Galapagos Islands.

Mainly advanced level resources but some are adaptable to elementary levels.

Science Update

www.accessexcellence.org/WN/SU/index.html

Weekly biology updates from laboratories around the world delivered to your desktop. From a fungus that kills "filth flies," to vaccines in vegetable form, here is an easy way to keep up on the latest developments in science.

Higher levels.

Scientific American: Ask the Experts: Biology

www.sciam.com/askexpert/biology/index.html

Read current and past issues of Scientific American online, or simply scan the quick article summaries to keep current. Check out the excellent archives of questions about biology, or if you can't find what you want there, just "Ask the Experts."

The Biology Project

www.biology.arizona.edu/default.html

Primarily undergraduate and graduate level resources here from the University of Arizona, but high school teachers and students as well will find many of the sites very useful if they are willing to do a little exploring. Be sure to check out the "Guided Tour" feature which gives illustrated guides to a variety of biology-related topics including cells, reproduction, genes, sexually transmitted diseases and many more. Some of the topics are listed here.

- Biochemistry
- Cell Biology (in Spanish)
- Chemicals & Human Health
- Developmental Biology
- Human Biology (in Spanish)
- Immunology
- Mendelian Genetics (in Spanish)
- Molecular Biology

CHEMISTRY

BioChemNet: General Chemistry

http://schmidel.com/bionet/chem.htm

Links for sites on many topics from "Chemistry Experiments You Can Do at Home," to "World Chemistry." Some of the many resource headings are listed below.

- High school level and up.
- Introduction to Chemistry
- Ions & Solutions
- Laboratory Experiments (Teaching Science)
- Molecules
- Periodic Tables
- Questions, Problem Sets, & Quizzes

BioChemNet: Organic Chemistry

http://schmidel.com/bionet/o-chem.htm

A sister site to the one above, this one focuses on organic chemistry, with topics ranging from, "A Beginner's Guide to Organic Synthesis," to a virtual lab on "Distribution Coefficients."
University/Advanced levels mainly but some use for high school levels.

- Laboratory Experiments (Teaching Science)
- Molecular Models & Databases
- Nomenclature
- Organic Molecules
- Problem Sets & Quizzes
- Tutorials & References

Canada's SchoolNet: Learning Resources

www.schoolnet.ca/home/e/resources/Links_Result_e.asp?SUBJECT=36&SUB=Sciences&ID=33

Here is another site filled with resource links for all levels K–12. You'll find pre-made lesson plans, experiments, quizzes, tutorials, and much more here. Some of the topics with annotations from the Canada's SchoolNet site are shown below.

BioChemNet: Biology & Chemistry Educational Resources

- This is an excellent online resource package for biology and chemistry education. Lots of resources and interesting material.

Chemical Stuff

- Chemical Calculations has a molar formula mass calculator, and a percentage composition calculator and a tutorial on atomic molecular and formula masses.

Chemistry Teacher Resources

- This site provides labs, information sheets, and other resources which teachers of chemistry in grade 9–12 can access.

Fisher Science Education

- Fisher Science Education online is an extensive compilation of science resources and information.

MathMol K–12 Activity Page

- MathMol K–12 Activity Page provides the K–12 educational community with information and materials dealing with the rapidly growing fields of molecular modeling and 3-D visualization. MathMol will provide K–12 students and teachers with basic concepts in mathematics and their connection to molecular modeling.

The Nobel Foundation

- Find out who has won the 1998 Nobel Peace Prize.

The "WWW Living-Book of Physical Chemistry: Problems and Maple-Assisted Solutions"

- This site features more than 1000 problems and Maple-assisted solutions in 6 chapters of physical chemistry: gases, thermodynamics, statistical mechanics, chemical kinetics, quantum chemistry, and spectroscopy.

ChemEd: Chemistry Education Resources

www-hpcc.astro.washington.edu/scied/chemistry.html

There are mostly advanced level resources here (see Fig. 10.10) including tutorials, lesson plans, sample exams, and more. You have to scroll down the "Courses and Topics" page a bit to get to the curriculum materials.

- What's New
- Courses and Topics
- Chemical Images and Databases
- Chemical Safety
- Periodicals and Presentations
- Software
- Educational Organizations
- History of Chemistry
- Science Reference Desk
- Material Sciences
- Other Chemistry Links

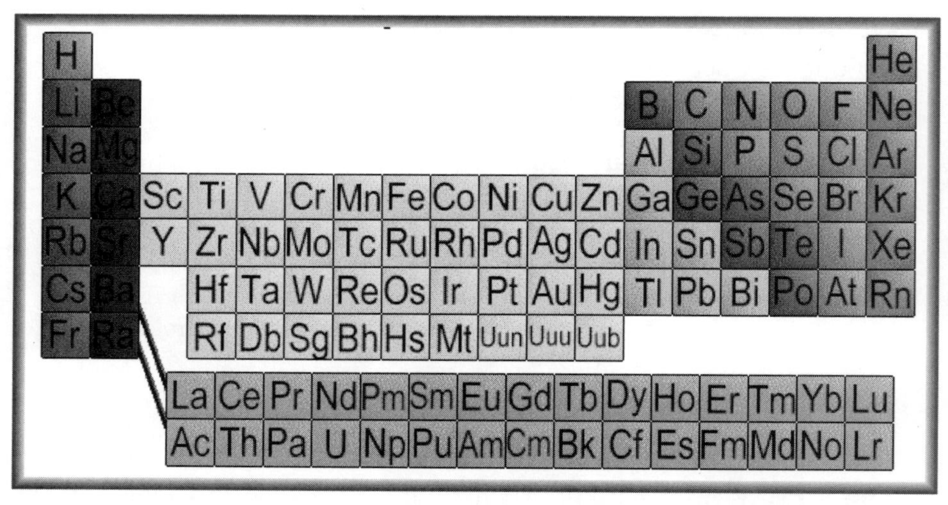

Fig. 10.10. Just click on any element for a complete account of its properties supported by such information as date of discovery, discoverer, and uses.

Chemical Elements.com—An Interactive Periodic Table of the Elements

www.chemicalelements.com/

We included this excellent interactive site (see Fig. 10.10) as an easy access to just about everything you need in a periodic table.

CTC Math/Science Gateway: Chemistry

www.tc.cornell.edu/Edu/MathSciGateway/chemistry.html

Here is another resource-rich site from Cornell Theory Center Math and Science Gateway. Topics are shown in Figure 10.11. High school teachers and students shouldn't miss the "ChemTeam" tutorial for High School Chemistry. There are links to good elementary resources at the Cornell site as well.

Elementary to advanced levels.

Chemistry

- **Links for Chemists** - free, searchable chemistry index containing more than 6000 chemistry resources in over 60 chemical categories
- **The Australian Chemistry Olympiad** - A program for talented Australian students who show outstanding ability in chemistry.
- **BioChemNet** - Educational resources in various fields including general chemistry, organic chemistry, biochemistry, and other biology topics.
- **ChemSketch** - Advanced Chemistry Development's ChemSketch 3.5 is a freeware chemical drawing and graphics program. You can draw chemical with a wide variety of atom and bond types. The package also includes many templates to get you going.
- **ChemWeb Online** - A very nice introduction to first-year chemistry, divided into about 20 topics starting with matter and its changes, atomic structure, and inorganic nomenclature, and ending up with acid-bases, redox reactions, and nuclear chemistry. This site was put together by a group of high school students as a **ThinkQuest** project.
- **ChemTeam** - A review of high school chemistry, divided into roughly two dozen topics such as atomic structure, equations and reaction types, the mole, and nomenclature.
- **Chemistry Education Resource Shelf** - This site provides high school and college-level chemistry educators with various teaching resources, including a comprehensive index to chemistry textbooks in print. Subjects covered range from Biochemistry and Computers in Chemistry to Quantum Chemistry and Writing in Science.
- **CheMystery** - A virtual chemistry textbook, to provide aninteractive guide for high school chemistry students. Lots of Java and Graphics so be prepared to wait a while!
- **The Catalyst** - This site has been developed for the high school chemistry teacher. Site can answer chemistry questions, allow teachers to post their ideas & insights, provide lesson plans and maintains links to other interesting chemistry pages.
- **Chem4Kids** - The site is designed to introduce basic chemistry ideas to younger students, but anyone can use it. Most of the content relates to the Periodic Table.
- **Food Science: Cook & Eat Chemistry** - A curriculum guide that links chemistry and food preparation. The chemical composition of food is a neat way to explore chemistry. This site has lots of information and tons of lesson plans/guides!
- **General Chemistry On-Line** - An interactive guide and Web resource for students and teachers of introductory college chemistry. This site may be useful for AP chemistry teachers trying to get students ready for the big test!
- **Molecular Modeling** - Mathematics and Molecular Modeling, from NYU. Their **Quick Tour** is particularly nice for high school students.
- **Mr. Guch's Cavalcade o' Chemistry** A resource for high school chemistry teachers and students. There are lesson plans, sample homeworks and tests for teachers. For students there is a helpdesk, tutorials, and a reference area.
- **Periodic Table** - Click on each element to find out its history and additional information.
- **RasMol: Molecular Modeling Software** - Free software for Windows, Macs, Unix and VMS which shows 3D images of molecules, especially biological macromolecules such as proteins and nucleic acids. A gallery of images is also available at this site.
- **Temperature Conversion Calculator** - Conversion to and from several temperature scales.
- **Weights and Measures** - Powers of ten, metric equivalents, and so on.

Fig. 10.11. Check out the many fine sites illustrated in the screen capture.

*Associations & Organizations	Digital Images
*Directories & Indices	Elementary School Resources
*Teachers Resources	History
Biochemistry	Magazines & Journals
Chemical Engineering	Newsgroups & Listservs
Companies	Organic Chemistry
Courses & Tutorials	Periodic Table of Elements
Crystallography	Reference
	Spectroscopy

There are 294 entries in this category.

Fig. 10.12. Click on "Teachers Resources" for many lesson plans and experiments. Try some of the other links for many more helpful chemistry resources.

Education World®—Chemistry
http://db.education-world.com/perl/browse?cat_id=1585

Be sure to click on "Teachers Resources" in the menu shown in Figure 10.12 and check out some of the links there. You will find great model labs and demonstrations along with ideas for lessons, a History of Chemistry, and much more.
Elementary to advanced levels.

General Chemistry Online
http://antoine.frostburg.edu/chem/senese/101/

Lots of excellent resources here including a pop-up periodic table, graph pad, calculators, tutorials, quizzes, glossary, a database of over 800 common compound names, formulas, structures, and properties, and much more.
All levels.

Kathy Schrock's Guide for Educators: Chemical Science Sites
http://school.discovery.com/schrockguide/sci-tech/scics.html

From the Discovery Channel School, here is another good set of links to a wealth of resources. Figure 10.13 shows recent links at this site which is updated regularly.
Resources for all levels.

- BioChemNet
  ...an extensive directory of biology and chemistry educational resources on the Net
- Biology Project: Biochemistry
  ...a content-rich site with everything you need to know about biochemistry; includes tutorials
- Catalyst
  ...lists of chemistry resources for the secondary education teacher
- ChemCenter
  ...a resource of all things chemistry for researchers and students alike
- Chemical Elements.com
  ...an easy to use, interactive periodic table site for students
- Chemistry Index
  ...a rather academic encyclopedia with chemistry articles and definitions
- Chemistry Resources
  ...an nicely chosen, annotated list of chemistry sites put together by a teacher
- Chemistry Teaching Resources
  ...an extensive, well-arranged list to all types of resources for teaching chemistry
- Chemistry Cool Tips and Ideas
  ...a nicely done chemistry support site with content and links
- Elements
  ...sites which include various aspects of the history and properties of the elements
- General Chemistry Online
  ...a great site for secondary chemistry students or a teacher who needs a bit more information
- WebElements
  ...a comprehensive site dealing with the periodic table of the elements
- WWW Links for Chemists
  ...an extensive list of links to chemistry resources on the Internet

Fig. 10.13. This image shows the many useful links that can be found at Kathy Schrock's Chemical Science Sites page.

Lesson Stop: It's ELEMENTary
www.youthline-usa.com/lessonstop/chem.html

You will find some good links here for elementary level learners including a simplified periodic table in the Chem4Kids site and many other interesting resources as shown in Figure 10.14.

Chem4Kids: Elements
Learn about elements -- what they are, how they are grouped, and some of their "rules."
The Periodic Table of Elements
This Internet version of the periodic table provides information about each element.
Chlorine Resources
Facts on Chlorine
Elemental Chlorine
Gold Resources
Facts about Gold
Uses of Gold
Calcium Resources
Calcium
About Calcium
Calcium for Life
Helium Resources
Helium
About Helium

Fig. 10.14. A click on any of the sites shows a wealth of resources.

Scientific American: Ask the Experts: Chemistry
www.sciam.com/askexpert/chemistry/index.html
This site from the well-known magazine offers answers to questions about chemistry in an easy-to-use format. Ask the experts yourself, or search the archives of previously posed questions.
All levels.

SCIMEDIA: Hypermedia Index
www.scimedia.com/chem-ed/scidex.htm#
Here is an alphabetically arranged index of advanced level scientific resources including a good chemistry selection. Find out everything that you have ever wanted to know about such things as atomic-emission gas chromatography detectors.

Spacelink—Chemistry
http://spacelink.nasa.gov/Instructional.Materials/Curriculum.Support/Physical.Science/Chemistry/.index.html
From the NASA space center, this site provides teachers and learners with many useful and interesting resources on a range of topics

including creating your own model of a periodic table, or participating in space experiments. Check out the instructional materials and curriculum resources while you are there. See some current topics in Figure 10.15.

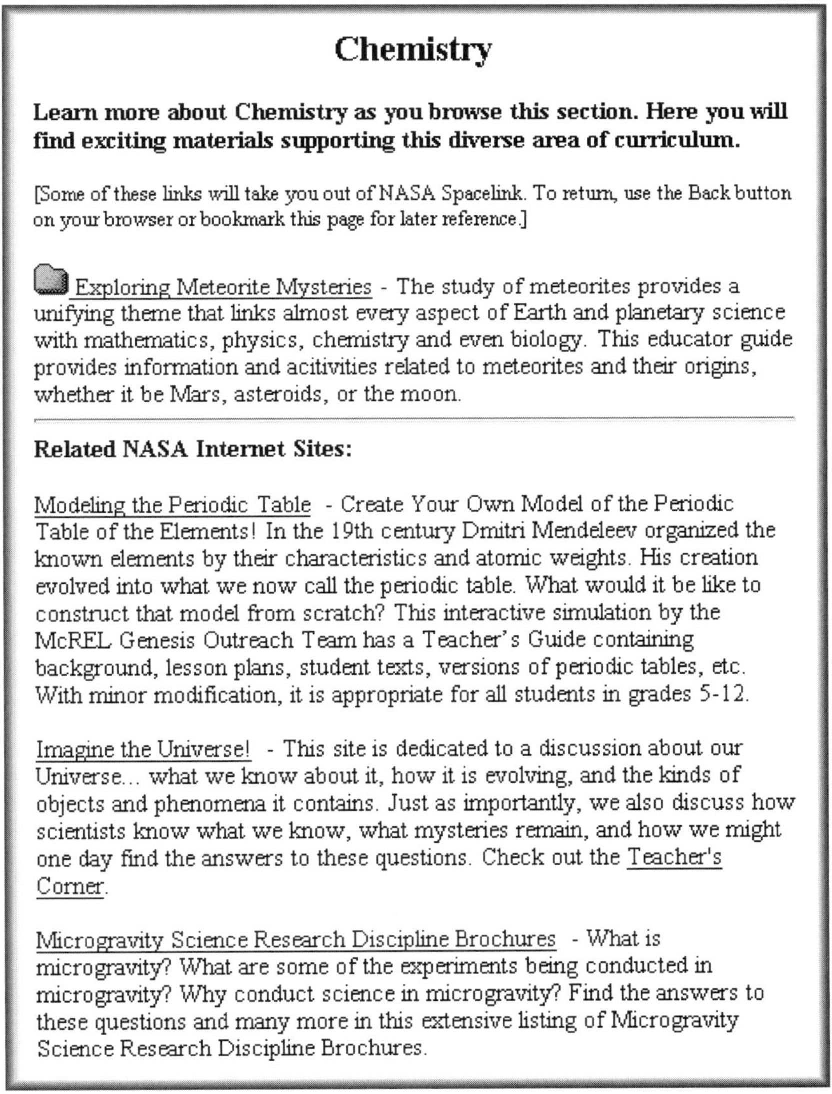

Chemistry

Learn more about Chemistry as you browse this section. Here you will find exciting materials supporting this diverse area of curriculum.

[Some of these links will take you out of NASA Spacelink. To return, use the Back button on your browser or bookmark this page for later reference.]

Exploring Meteorite Mysteries - The study of meteorites provides a unifying theme that links almost every aspect of Earth and planetary science with mathematics, physics, chemistry and even biology. This educator guide provides information and acitivities related to meteorites and their origins, whether it be Mars, asteroids, or the moon.

Related NASA Internet Sites:

Modeling the Periodic Table - Create Your Own Model of the Periodic Table of the Elements! In the 19th century Dmitri Mendeleev organized the known elements by their characteristics and atomic weights. His creation evolved into what we now call the periodic table. What would it be like to construct that model from scratch? This interactive simulation by the McREL Genesis Outreach Team has a Teacher's Guide containing background, lesson plans, student texts, versions of periodic tables, etc. With minor modification, it is appropriate for all students in grades 5-12.

Imagine the Universe! - This site is dedicated to a discussion about our Universe... what we know about it, how it is evolving, and the kinds of objects and phenomena it contains. Just as importantly, we also discuss how scientists know what we know, what mysteries remain, and how we might one day find the answers to these questions. Check out the Teacher's Corner.

Microgravity Science Research Discipline Brochures - What is microgravity? What are some of the experiments being conducted in microgravity? Why conduct science in microgravity? Find the answers to these questions and many more in this extensive listing of Microgravity Science Research Discipline Brochures.

Fig. 10.15. Click on your choice of topics as shown in the illustration. Explore the universe with NASA scientists as your guides.
Used by permission

The Catalyst: Chemistry Resources for Teachers
www.TheCatalyst.org/

This excellent site was created specifically for secondary education/ high-school teachers. Click on the Catalyst (Main) page for a variety of links to general or specific sites containing lesson plans, demonstrations, labs, periodic tables, and many other resources.
Some lower level resources as well.

EARTH AND ENVIRONMENTAL SCIENCES

Canada's SchoolNet: Learning Resources
www.schoolnet.ca/home/e/resources/Links_Result_e.asp?SUBJECT=37&SUB=Sciences&ID=33

You will find a lot of very interesting geology and environmental science resources here, some specific to Canada, but many with a broader focus as well. Check the list below for choice of topics.
Resources for all levels K–12.

- Discover Learning
- Earth Sciences Sector
- Explorezone: Animated Earth, Space and Weather Science
- Geology in the Classroom
- GeoScience: K–12 Resources
- Hooper Virtual Natural History Museum
- Mercury Project
- Michigan Technological University Volcanoes Page
- Minerals and Metals: a World to Discover
- Natural Resources Canada
- NEHP—National Earthquake Hazards Program
- Royal Ontario Museum
- Technology Tools for Today's Campuses
- The Canadian Rockhound
- The Coal Association of Canada—Classroom
- The Mining Association of Canada
- Virtual Earthquake
- Weather.ec.gc.ca
- World Data Center—Marine Geology and Geophysics

CTC Math/Science Gateway: Environment

www.tc.cornell.edu/Edu/MathSciGateway/environment.html

This site, provided by the Cornell Theory Center Math and Science Gateway, has links to resources for all levels of environmental studies. The main headings are listed below. Individual topics range from Ask a Geologist, to a Virtual Earthquake, to whale watching.

- Environmental Activism
- Geology & Soil Science
- Oceans, Lakes, Streams & Wetlands
- Other Environmental Science
- Other Environmental Science Resources
- Physical Geography & Remote Sensing

Earth Sciences

www-hpcc.astro.washington.edu/scied/earthindex.html

Each of the four main categories listed below links you to a wide range of resources and lessons. How about setting off on a virtual field trip to Antarctica or exploring the depths of the oceans courtesy of the Smithsonian Institution's National Museum of Natural History? All levels.

- EnviroEd: Environmental Science
- Geology/Earth Systems
- Meteorology
- Oceanography/Marine Biology

Frank Potter's Science Gems—Earth Science I

www-sci.lib.uci.edu/SEP/earth.html

This really is a jewel of a site containing more resources than we can list. Below are some of the topics listed in two of the frequently updated categories. Resources are for K to graduate levels, with most applicable for a minimum grade 9 level, but plenty for lower levels as well if you look around a bit.

- Measurement
- Earth in space
- Solar system
- Astronomy

- Atmosphere
- Weather
- Land/Geol
- Oceans
- Water effects
- Resources

Free-Ed Earth Sciences
www.free-ed.net/fr08/fr0806.htm

Free-Ed is a good place to look for courses, tutorials and other resources as they are developed. Right now, there is an excellent interactive glossary of geologic terms. Also, click on the "World" icon on the glossary page and scroll down the page to access practice Geology-100 exams and some good links. Advanced levels with some applicability at the high school level. Topics being developed are Geology, Meteorology, and Oceanography.

Kathy Schrock's Guide for Educators—Earth, Geology, & Oceanography Science Sites
http://school.discovery.com/schrockguide/sci-tech/scies.html

In this and the following site from the Discovery Channel School, you'll find links to K–12 and advanced resources and lessons on a great variety of Earth, Geology, and Oceanography topics from the "Birth of the Earth" to tidal waves and volcanoes.

Kathy Schrock's Guide for Educators: Environmental Science Sites
http://school.discovery.com/schrockguide/sci-tech/scien.html

A companion site to the one above, this one has a slightly different focus. Topics range from environmental ethics to mining and land management to ecology and environmental education for kids.
All levels.

Scientific American: Ask the Experts: Environment
www.sciam.com/askexpert/environment/index.html

Look through the archives of past questions to find out if there are really green flashes at sunset, or why rainbows are curved. If the answer to your question isn't there, you can "Ask the Experts" yourself.

Spacelink—Earth Science
http://spacelink.nasa.gov/Instructional.Materials/Curriculum.Support/Earth.Science/.index.html

Here is another very useful site from NASA filled with resources at the K–12 level. You will need Adobe Acrobat Reader to access some of the educators' resources, but there is a link to download it if you don't already have it. See the topics in Figure 10.16.

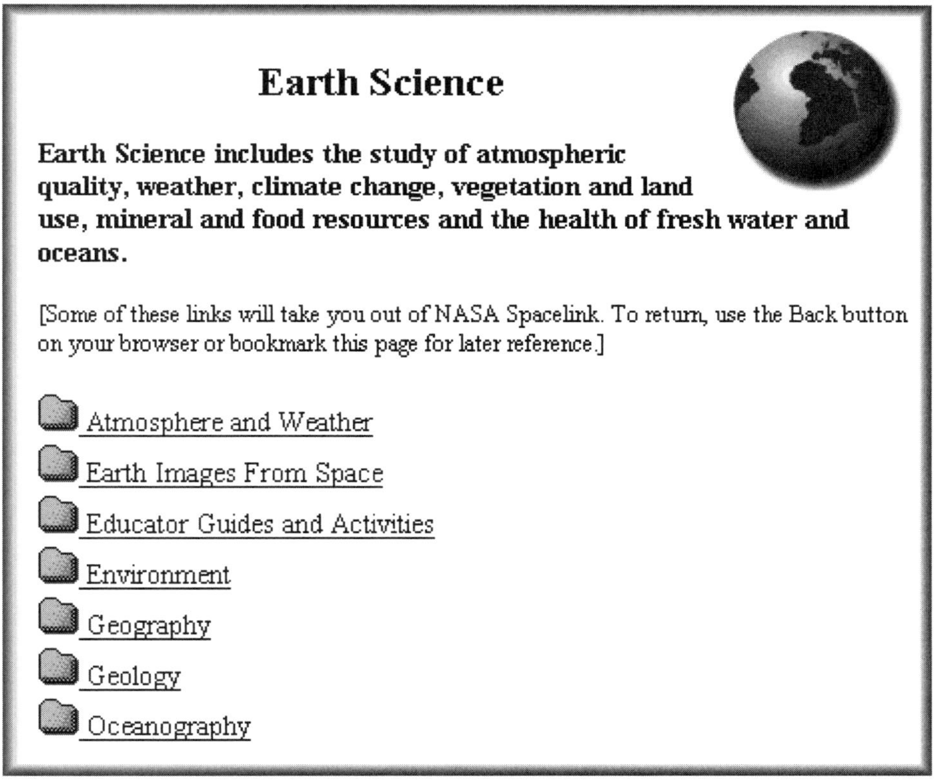

Earth Science

Earth Science includes the study of atmospheric quality, weather, climate change, vegetation and land use, mineral and food resources and the health of fresh water and oceans.

[Some of these links will take you out of NASA Spacelink. To return, use the Back button on your browser or bookmark this page for later reference.]

Atmosphere and Weather
Earth Images From Space
Educator Guides and Activities
Environment
Geography
Geology
Oceanography

Fig. 10.16. Click on your choice of topics and explore the world with NASA scientists who make it easy for you.
Used by permission

PHYSICS

Canada's SchoolNet: Learning Resources
www.schoolnet.ca/home/e/resources/Links_Result_e.asp?SUBJECT=39&SUB=Sciences&ID=33

You will find an impressive array of links in a variety of categories. Some of the many topics and links are listed below. You will find a wide range of learning resources including lesson plans, quizzes, free online courses, facts and figures, and much more.
K–12 levels.

- Canadian Nuclear Society
- Careers in Aerospace
- Fisher Science Education
- Forces in Fluids
- How Stuff Works
- National Aviation Museum
- Physics Academic Software Catalog of Programs
- Physics Around the World
- Physics On-line: information & resources for high school physics
- Science: A Curriculum Guide for the Secondary Level Physics 20/30
- Sudbury Neutrino Observatory (SNO)
- The Canadian Space Guide
- The Wonders of Physics
- Training Resources for Electronics
- Visual Physics
- Woody Finds a Rainbow in His RV
- Yuan's Scientific World: Physics, THE science

CTC Math/Science Gateway: Physics
www.tc.cornell.edu/Edu/MathSciGateway/physics.html

Advanced level resources provided by the Cornell Math and Science Gateway. As shown in Figures 10.17 and 10.18, you will find links to such handy resources as online physics tutorials filled with lessons and tests, at the high school level and up, plus physics organizations and associations, an online tour of a physics lab, and much more. There are a couple of good elementary links as well.

Physics

- **The American Association of Physics Teachers**
- **AP Physics Information** - Information and questions/answers about the AP Physics program, from the College Board.
- **Computer as Learning Partner (CLP) Project** - The Computer as Learning Partner (CLP) project provides a one-semester integrated energy curriculum teaching the physical science topics of heat, light, and sound to eighth-graders. CLP is part of an educational research effort at the University of California at Berkeley.
- **Contemporary Physics Education Project** - CPEP is a non-profit organization of teachers, educators, and physicists. CPEP materials present the current understanding of the fundamental nature of matter and energy, incorporating the major research findings of the past three decades.
- **Early Instruments** of the Institute of Physics, in Naples, Italy.
- **Fermilab** - Fermilab is a high-energy physics laboratory, home of the world's most powerful particle accelerator, the Tevatron. Scientists from across the U.S. and around the world use Fermilab's resources in experiments to explore the most fundamental particles and forces of nature. I especially recommend their **Online Tour**.

- **Harvard-Smithsonian Center for Astrophysics** - Their Education Department has a variety of projects geared to K-12 students. A few are for the elementary grades, but most are 9-12.
- **Internet Webseum of Holography** - A virtual museum where you can learn all about holography and even create your holograms.
- **The Laboratory of Atomic and Solid State Physics (LASSP)** - This page from LASSP, at Cornell University, includes a sampling of the science from their researchers. Although it's not intended for high school students, it's well written and understandable.
- **Laser Information** - A description of the lasers used in the **Laserium** show, billed as *Music For Your Eyes*.
- **Microworlds** - An interactive science magazine of current research in the materials sciences at Lawrence Berkeley Laboratory. An "ask-a-scientist" page lets students and teachers type their questions on a form and send them to LBL to be answered.
- **Particles, Atoms, and Fusion** - New features from the Contemporary Physics Education Project (CPEP) include an interactive tour of the inner workings of the atom and an online interactive "course" in fusion.
- **The Physics Classroom** - General physics information on topics such as 1-D Kinematics, Newton's Laws, Vectors - Motion and Forces in Two Dimensions, and Momentum and Its Conservation.
- **SimScience** - A website devoted to areas of science where computer simulations are at the forefront of discovery.
- **Websters World - An Online Guide to Physics** - Created by the AP Physics class at the Mississippi School for Mathematics and Science. The goal is to provide students with an online physics tutorial. The material is presented in such a way so as to cover first-year physics topics. All of the lessons were written by students in the AP Physics class. The lessons present physics concepts from the perspective of other physics students.

Fig. 10.17–10.18. These images show the great variety resources available at the CTC site.

Education World®—Physics—General Resources

http://db.education-world.com/perl/browse?cat_id=3361

Click on the "Physics" section in the top menu to find teachers' resources and lesson plans and more, or choose from the other physics topics shown in the screen capture below (see Figs. 10.19 and 10.20). Elementary to advanced level.

*Teacher Resources
Earth Science
Environment & Nature
Physics

There are 21 entries in this category.

How Things Work .

Particle Adventure .

The Wizard's Lab .

Web Pages to Help Physics Students .

DC Circuits An incredible set of tutorials on circuitry - includes self tests, example

Energy .

Energy Education Sites As compiled by the U.S. Department of Education.

Energy Quest Energy Quest(tm) is the energy education site of the California Energy Commission with games, resources, and super evironmental info for students, parents and teachers.

How Things Work Although organized poorly, this site has no equal in explaining the technological applications and connections of physics theory to everyday life. A wonderful place to send students when they ask, "Why do we have to know this"?

Illusionworks Stomach turning fun! When you need an interesting topic in optics, be sure to stop here! If your browser is Java/Shockwave savvy, you'll have even more eye-bending interactive fun!

Figs. 10.19 and 10.20. These screen captures illustrate sample topics available from "How Things Work" to tutorials, games, and illusions.

Microworlds - Exploring the Structure of Materials .

Ocean AdVENTure: From Deep Sea to Deep Space Multimedia journey to deep-sea vents, bizarre oases on the ocean's floor. Learn about fauna, formation, mysteries and more. Do fun InterActivities.

Professor Bubbles' Official Bubble Homepage Learn everything you've always wanted to know about bubbles from the expert-Professor Bubbles!

Spirit of Ford Spirit of Ford is an automotive adventure where kids and adults can experience the unique creative process behind automotive design, technology and manufacturing with hands-on exhibits, and much more.

Sunrise/Sunset/Twilight and Moonrise/Moonset/Phase You can calculate the sunrise moonset and phase times for U.S. locations at this site.

The Directorate of Time U.S. Naval Observatory is the official source of time used

The Weather Unit These full-text lesson plans center around a weather theme and also covers every subject area, including math, science, reading, writing, social studies, geography, art, music, drama, and physical education.

Thermodynamics, light and sound curriculum .

University ofOregon Web Project Topics include: Galaxy Gallery, Electronic Textbook, Weather Galaxy, Energy and the Environment, and Pictures of the Eart from the Space Shuttle.

Weather Entire units, with resources in all areas of curriculum.

Frank Potter's Science Gems—Physical Science

www.sciencegems.com/physical.html

Take a look at the extensive list of resources from this wonderful site. Lessons are classified by level of difficulty from K–12 through to university.

Physical Science Part I

- Techniques: Measurement and Scientific Investigation
- Mathematical Methods
- Mechanics of Motion
- Energy
- Linear Momentum
- Mechanics of Rotational Motion
- Solids and Fluids
- Vibrations and Wave Motion
- Thermodynamics

Physical Science Part II

- Electricity and Magnetism

- Light and Optics
- Special Theory of Relativity
- Introduction to Quantum Mechanics
- Atomic Physics
- Molecules, Fluids, and Solids
- Nuclear Structure

Physical Science Part III

- Introduction to Chemistry
- Chemical Reactions
- Intermediate Chemistry
- Organic Chemistry
- Biochemistry
- Biosphere
- Elementary Particles
- General Relativity

Kathy Schrock's Guide for Educators—Physics & Optics Sites
http://school.discovery.com/schrockguide/sci-tech/sciph.html

Here you will find nearly a dozen links to top physics sites as shown in Figure 10.21. Everything from elementary lesson plans to an excellent encyclopedia of physics and a comprehensive physics timeline.

Physical Science Activity Manual
http://192.239.146.18/resources/Science/PSAM.html

There are plenty of activities, lesson plans, and ideas here for all levels. You can download the entire manual or just the lessons and resources that you want. We have classified them here in alphabetical order, but you may have to scroll down the page at the site to find your topic.

- Introduction
- Acceleration (Free-Fall)
- Acceleration (Inclined Plane)
- Activity Series
- Air Pressure
- Baked Ice-Cream
- Bernoulli's Principle
- Center of Gravity

- Eric's Treasure Trove of Physics
  ...a comprehensive online encyclopedia of physics equations and terms
- History of Particle Physics
  ...a comprehensive particle physics timeline
- List of Physics Topics
  ...a physics course online appropriate for secondary students
- Optical Society of America
  ...OpticsNet is a site for optics and photonics resources, applications, and industry news
- Physics and Astronomy Lesson Plans
  ...over 200 elementary school lesson plans dealing with physics and astronomy
- Physics News
  ...a Canadian site which contains resources for support of secondary school physics
- Physics Around the World
  ...a classified set of links to hundreds of physics sites on the Web
- Physics Time-Line
  ...a comprehensive timeline with brief historical entries from 585 B.C. to the present
- Physlink
  ...billed as the "ulitmate physic resource", it includes links to journals, sites, history, and even physics cartoons
- Science Report Radio
  ...a series of 2-minute, RealAudio lectures (text included) on various physics topics
- Understanding: Uncertainty
  ...sites dealing with the philosophical discussion on the modern view of reality among physicists

Fig. 10.21. Samples of the resource-filled links available through the click of your mouse.

- Conservation of Mass
- Current Electricity
- Definite Proportions
- Definition of Matter
- Density
- Determination of Volume
- Electromagnetism
- Factors Affecting Rates of Reactions
- Heat
- How Fast Do Dominoes Fall
- Light

- Magnetism
- Measurement of Mass
- Measurement of pH
- Mixtures
- Newton's First Law of Motion
- Newton's Second Law of Motion
- Newton's Third Law of Motion
- Physical and Chemical Properties
- Pop Goes the Popcorn
- Pressure
- Radioactivity (Half-Life)
- Recycling
- References
- Sound
- Static Electricity
- The Learning Cycle

PhysicsEd: Physics Education Resources
www-hpcc.astro.washington.edu/scied/physics.html

Here, you'll find resources such as an introduction to problem solving, tutorials, lessons, quizzes, and much more. Many of the resources are for higher level courses, but there are also some elementary resources and lessons.

K–12 and up.

For easy access to "What's New" in Physics or courses, research tools, projects and organizations, just follow the links shown in the list below:

- What's New
- Courses and Topics
- Curriculum Development
- Resources for Demonstrations
- Software
- Physics Education Projects
- Research in Physics Education
- AAPT and Other Physics Education Organizations
- Individual Physics Education Pages
- Physics Textbooks
- Journals and Newsletters
- E-Mail Discussion Groups

- Biography/History
- Science Reference
- Suppliers of Equipment and Software
- Frequently Asked Questions
- Other Physics Links

Scientific American: Ask the Experts: Physics
www.sciam.com/askexpert/physics/index.html

The experts at this popular magazine have put together a very good archive of physics-related questions. Do you really understand "wormholes" as well as you'd like to?

Smile Program Physics Index
www.iit.edu/~smile/physinde.html

This superb site contains a collection of almost 200 single-concept lessons contributed by scientists and educators. Please note that the site developers specify that these lessons may be freely copied and used in a classroom but they remain the copyright property of the author.

The Physics lessons are divided into the following categories:

- Electricity & Magnetism
- Fluids
- Matter
- Mechanics
- Sound and Optics
- Waves
- Miscellaneous

Spacelink—Physical Science
http://spacelink.nasa.gov/Instructional.Materials/Curriculum.Support/Physical.Science/.index.html

NASA again comes through with a resource-rich site (see Fig. 10.22) to help teachers and students of physics. Students can learn all about motion, force, heat, light, sound, fluids, and much more. You will need Adobe Acrobat Reader for some resources but you can download it at the site if you don't have it.

All levels.

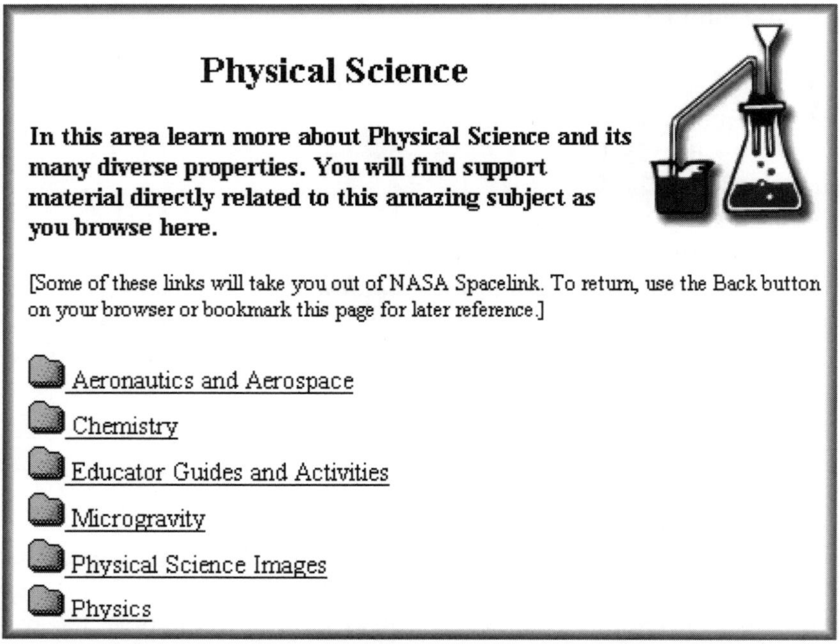

Physical Science

In this area learn more about Physical Science and its many diverse properties. You will find support material directly related to this amazing subject as you browse here.

[Some of these links will take you out of NASA Spacelink. To return, use the Back button on your browser or bookmark this page for later reference.]

Aeronautics and Aerospace

Chemistry

Educator Guides and Activities

Microgravity

Physical Science Images

Physics

Fig. 10.22. Click on the "Educator Guides and Activities" section shown in the list or go directly to the sites in your area of interest.
Used by permission

The Physics Classroom

www.glenbrook.k12.il.us/gbssci/phys/Class/BBoard.html

Here is an excellent online tutorial written especially for high-school physics students.

1-D Kinematics | Newton's Laws | Vectors—Motion and Forces in Two Dimensions | Momentum and Its Conservation | Work, Energy, and Power | Circular Motion and Satellite Motion | Einstein's Theory of Special Relativity | Static Electricity | Current Electricity | Waves | Sound Waves and Music | Light Waves and Color | Reflection and the Ray Model of Light | Refraction and the Ray Model of Light

Windows to the Universe

http://windows.engin.umich.edu/cgi-bin/tour.cgi?link=/windows3.html&sw=false&sn=0&d=&edu=mid&br=graphic&cd=false&tour=&fr=f

The Windows to the Universe site is a graphics-rich site funded by NASA dealing with Earth and Space Sciences. There are beginner, intermediate and advanced level resources, as well as a specific "kid's space." Also there are many teacher's resources with lesson plans and activities, and an "Ask a Scientist" feature.

Elementary to high school levels.

Chapter 11

Social Studies/Social Sciences

This section of the guide contains many valuable resources for teachers and learners at all levels in Social Studies/Social Sciences. Here you will find everything from excellent ready-to-use lesson plans to maps, factual information, multimedia aids, and even advanced research tools in all Social Studies disciplines. Using the Internet to assist learning can be timesaving for teachers, while being fun and interesting for students.

CHAPTER OVERVIEW

Geography, pages 244–252

Government, pages 252–255

History, pages 256–265

Psychology, pages 269–272

Sociology, pages 272–274

GENERAL RESOURCES

Alberta Education Website

http://ednet.edc.gov.ab.ca/studentprograms/

Here you will find curriculum outlines and objectives for social studies for levels K–12 (see Fig. 11.1). Teachers can use these objectives as models for writing daily objectives and lesson plans as used in most North American School settings. Adobe Acrobat Reader is necessary to access the resources. A link for downloading is available at the site.

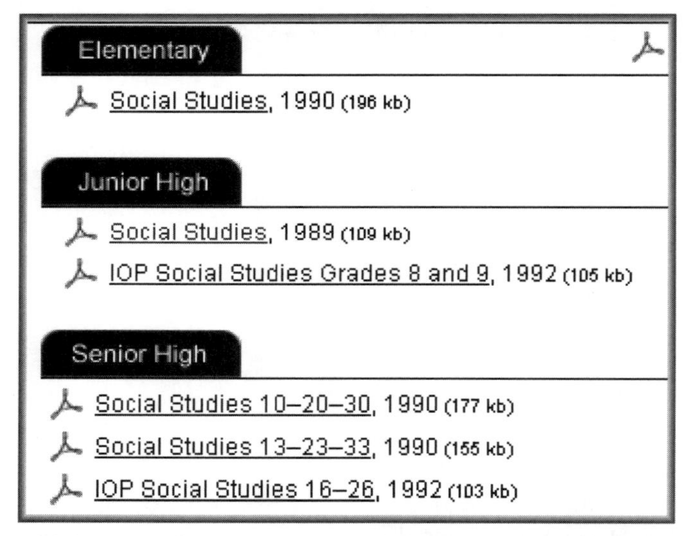

Fig. 11.1. Click on the Social Studies section at the appropriate level as shown in the image. The red icon indicates a file in Adobe Acrobat Reader format.
Used by permission

Anatomy of a Murder Home Page

http://library.thinkquest.org/2760/

Here is a great motivator for students learning about America's Legal System. Students can follow the story of a defendant in a fictitious murder case as he passes through each stage of the legal system from the investigation to the trial. The story is written like a good crime novel, but each aspect is researched and legally correct so students are entertained as they learn about what really takes place within the justice system. Students can go back and forth between the story and the accompanying factual information, such as an introduction to the legal system, They can also view actual forms that police must fill out after an arrest, or they can discuss "Rocking Supreme Court Cases" of the past. There is also a good glossary of legal terms, so what are you waiting for?

Let the investigation begin!

Jr. to Sr. high school level.

AskERIC Lesson Plans: Social Studies

http://ericir.syr.edu/Virtual/Lessons/Social_St/index.html

Lots of very good lessons here on specifically American themes in topics such as "Government and Civics," and many good lessons in other areas.

K–12 level.

The following topics are represented at this site:

- Anthropology
- Civics
- Current Events
- Economics
- Geography
- Government
- History
- Psychology
- Sociology
- State History
- US History
- World History and Cultures

Biography Find

www.biography.com/search/index.html

If your students need to know basic biographical information about just about anyone, they can easily find it here. Teachers will never again be stumped by students' questions about famous people, past or present.

Canada's SchoolNet: Learning Resources: Social Science
www.schoolnet.ca/home/e/resources/Links_Result_e.asp?SUBJECT=42

You can click on "Philosophy," "Psychology," or "Sociology" at the top of the page or scroll down to access the many other resources, and lessons as outlined in the descriptions below taken from the site. K–12 level.

Social Science Information Gateway—SOSIG

- The Social Science Information Gateway SOSIG provides researchers and social scientists with a centralized way to access relevant information over the networks. This site provides an online catalogue of high quality Internet resources, each selected and described by academic librarians and subject . . .

The Museum of Archaeology and Ethnology, Simon Fraser University

- Archaeology is the study of people in the past from physical remains found in the present. Each piece of evidence, no matter how small, can be an important chapter of a story about how people organized their day to day lives, how they developed complex ways of conducting business and politics, about their religious . . .

The Web Museum

- The SunSITE Project at UNC-CH is the primary site in a network of information services provided by key universities around the world. SunSITE operates as a library, a publishing house, a distribution center and a technology showcase. The materials available on SunSITE represent a diverse community of information . . .

Yelloweb

- If you're looking for information on any of the social sciences, chances are you'll find some useful information right here. Yelloweb provides an extensive number of links to European web sites on topics such as history, Third World development, human sciences, education, health and medicine, and . . .

CLN WWW Navigation Map
www.cln.org/map.html#SS

This Community Learning Network link (see Figs. 11.2 and 11.3) opens up a huge selection of resources, instructional materials, and theme pages for use in social studies programs in Canada. Teachers in the U.S. and elsewhere will also find many of the resources useful. K–12 level.

Social Studies

- Curricular Resources in Can. Studies: British Columbia
- Curricular Resources in Can. Studies: Canadian Geography
- Curricular Resources in Can. Studies: Canadian History
- Curricular Resources in Can. Studies: Canadian Law
- Curricular Resources in the Environment
- Curricular Resources in History
- Curricular Resources in Other Socials Studies

- - - - - - - - - - - - - - - - - - - -

- Instructional Materials in Canadian Studies
- Instructional Materials in the Environment
- Instructional Materials in History
- Instructional Materials in Other Social Studies

- - - - - - - - - - - - - - - - - - - -

- Theme Page: Air Quality
- Theme Page: Ancient Civilizations
- Theme Page: Antartic
- Theme Page: Arctic
- Theme Page: Canadian Military History
- Theme Page: Celebrating Women
- Theme Page: Countries
- Theme Page: Current Events
- Theme Page: Drylands/Deserts
- Theme Page: Endangered Species
- Theme Page: Explorers

Fig. 11.2 and 11.3. See the wide range of easy-to-access resources at CLN as shown in the site menu. Everything is here from the Arctic to tropical rainforests, and from celebrating women to learning about the Holocaust.

- Theme Page: Famous Canadians
- Theme Page: Genealogy
- Theme Page: Global Warming/Climate Change
- Theme Page: Hazardous Wastes Disposal
- Theme Page: Holocaust
- Theme Page: Hunger
- Theme Page: Immigration
- Theme Page: Mapping
- Theme Page: Medieval Studies
- Theme Page: Mythology
- Theme Page: Oceanography
- Theme Page: Overpopulation
- Theme Page: Ozone Depletion
- Theme Page: Pirates, Privateers, and Buccaneers
- Theme Page: Privacy and Technology
- Theme Page: Reduce, Reuse, Recycle
- Theme Page: Renaissance
- Theme Page: Sustainable Development
- Theme Page: Temperate Forests
- Theme Page: Tropical Rainforests
- Theme Page: Water Quality
- Theme Page: Wetlands

Fig. 11.3.
© 2000 Open School. Used by permission

Education World®—Social Sciences: General Resources
http://db.education-world.com/perl/browse?cat_id=1703

Check out any of the 23 categories shown in Figure 11.4 for a wide range of resources. Check out the "Teacher's Resources" page for some great lesson plans and activities.

All levels.

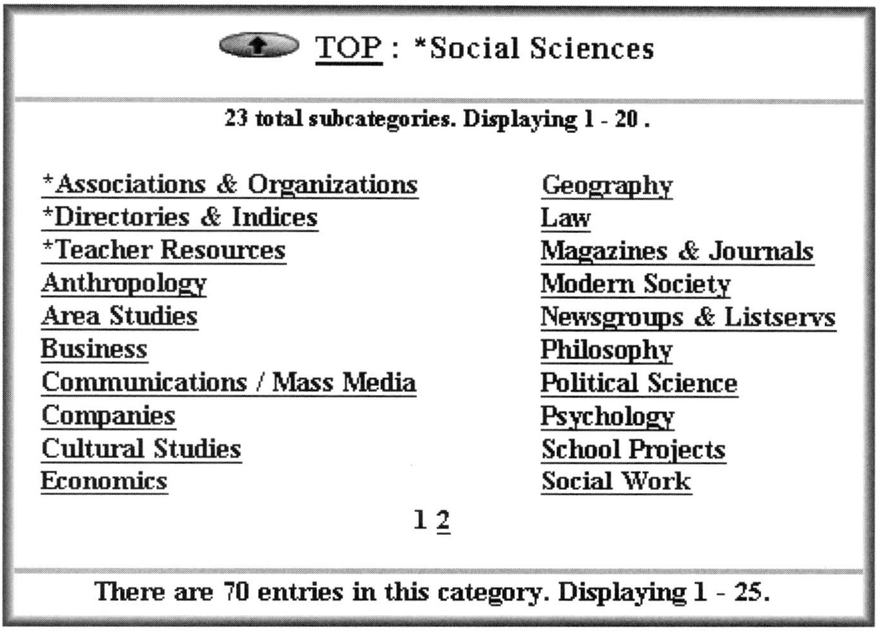

TOP : *Social Sciences

23 total subcategories. Displaying 1 - 20 .

*Associations & Organizations
*Directories & Indices
*Teacher Resources
Anthropology
Area Studies
Business
Communications / Mass Media
Companies
Cultural Studies
Economics
Geography
Law
Magazines & Journals
Modern Society
Newsgroups & Listservs
Philosophy
Political Science
Psychology
School Projects
Social Work

1 2

There are 70 entries in this category. Displaying 1 - 25.

Fig. 11.4. Resources for many disciplines are available as shown in this image. Click on page 2 for even more topics.
Copyright © Education World. Used by permission

Gopher Menu
gopher://bvsd.k12.co.us:70/11/Educational_Resources/Lesson_Plans/Big%20Sky/social_studies

Here is a good list of lessons on subjects ranging from Culture and History to Geography, Civil Rights, and Politics. Lessons at all levels, K–12.

Lesson Stop—Social Studies
www.youthline-usa.com/lessonstop/socialstudies.html

Another site filled with lessons on a wide variety of topics in social studies (see Fig. 11.5). Scroll down the page to find more resources on economics, geography, government, civics, U.S. and World History, and more.

All Social Studies

1. Art-to-Zoo Social Studies Lessons (3-5)
2. AskERIC Social Studies Lessons (K-12)
3. CEC Social Studies Lessons (K-5)
4. CEC Social Studies Lessons (6-8)
5. CEC Social Studies Lessons (9-12)
6. History Lesson Ideas (K-12)
7. Lesson Plans from TeacherLINK (K-5)
8. PBS Social Studies Lesson Inventory (preK-12)
9. SCORE History/Social Studies Lessons (K-12)
10. Social Studies Activities (K-12)
11. Social Studies Web Activities (1-7)

Fig. 11.5. The screen capture shows the topics classified by grade level. Click on your choice when you get to the site.

Schoolhouse
http://encarta.msn.com/schoolhouse/default.asp
This site contains the Encarta Lesson Collection and other educational resources.

Social Studies Lesson Plans and Resources
www.csun.edu:80/~hcedu013/
There is a very impressive array of lessons and resources at this site on a variety of Social Studies topics at all levels from K–12. Try the "Online Activities" section as well as the Lesson Plans page for more good ideas and resources.

- Lesson Plans and Teaching Strategies
- Online Activities
- Teaching Current Events
- Other Social Studies Resources
- National Council for the Social Studies
- Newsgroups and Mailing Lists
- Social Studies School Service
- Educational Standards and Curriculum Frameworks

Teachers Page of Lesson Plans

www.library.ualberta.ca/library_html/libraries/coutts/lessons.html#social

This page, provided by the University of Alberta, a prominent Canadian University, takes you directly to the menu of Social Studies resources that the webmasters there have generously provided for educators and learners at the K–12 level. Teachers will find the many ready-to-use lesson plans useful and timesaving. Below is a list of available topics at the site.

- Adventure Online
- AskAsia Lesson Plans
- Educational Enhancements
- Finding Your Way with Map and Compass
- Lesson Plans and Resources for Social Studies Teachers
- National Council for the Social Studies
- What do Maps Show?

The Lesson Plans Page—Social Studies Lesson Plans

www.lessonplanspage.com/SS.htm

When you get to the main page (see Fig. 11.6), click on the social studies section to find the wide variety of lesson plans classified by grade level.

K–12 and multilevel.

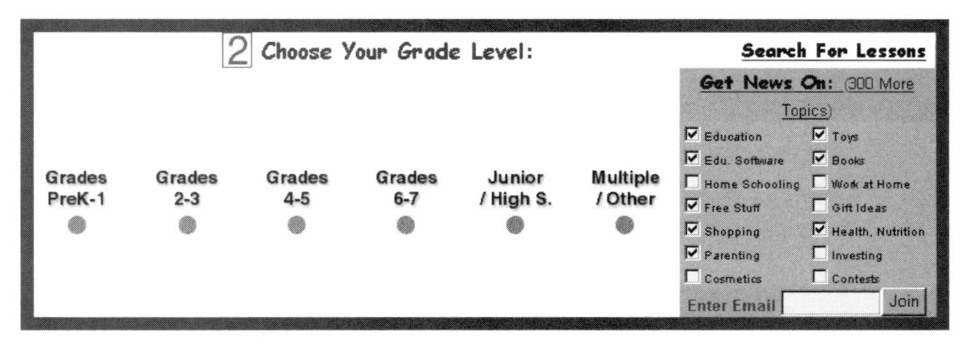

Fig. 11.6. Click on your level as indicated in this screen capture taken from the site to access the many lesson plans.

Social Studies
- Anthropology
- Civics
- Economics
- Government
- History
- Political Science
- Sociology

Fig. 11.7. Choose your subject area from the list shown here and follow the links to the many timesaving resources.

Welcome to K–12WORLD!

www.k-12world.net:80/cy_curr_res.cfm

Once again, you have to scroll down the page a bit to the social studies section then you can click on the specific topics listed or just on "Social Studies" to access lessons, maps, and other resources (see Fig. 11.7).

K–12 level.

Welcome to the Learning Page

http://memory.loc.gov/ammem/ndlpedu/welcome.html

Although this page looks quite bare of resources at first glance, don't be deceived. It is loaded with great resources and lessons for educators and students of American History and Culture.

Elementary to high school levels.

Below is a description taken from the site:

The Learning Page is a web site designed to help teachers, students, and life-long learners use the American Memory digital collections from the Library of Congress.

ABORIGINAL STUDIES

Index of Native American Indigenous Knowledge Resources on the Internet

www.hanksville.org/NAresources/indices/NAknowledge.html

The creators of this site state that it is constructed primarily for the Native American Community, but they have organized their information to make it useful to the education community as well.

You will find a lot of good traditional knowledge resources in astronomy, math, and physical and life sciences if you click around a bit.

Mostly higher-level resources.

Index of Native American Resources on the Internet—WWWVL American Indians

www.hanksville.org/NAresources/

A sister site to the one above, this one gives you a good variety of resources in the topics listed below.

Higher levels.

- Cultural Resources
- Indigenous Languages
- History Resources
- Archaeology Resources
- Educational Resources
- Indigenous Knowledge
- Legal Resources
- Health Resources
- Non-Profit Organizations
- Art Resources
- Museums
- Music Resources
- Book Sources
- Electronic Texts by and about Native Americans
- Bibliographies of Material Relevant to Native Americans
- Video & Film Resources
- Organizations
- Activist Sites
- Tribal Gaming

- Native American Media
- Genealogy Resources
- Government Resources especially for Native Americans
- Commercial Resources
- Home pages for Native Americans
- Announcements with Native American Related Content
- Job Notices
- Other Native American Related Resources
- Resources for Other Nations on the Internet
- Movie Stars
- WWW Virtual Libraries

Introduction to American Indian and Native Studies Classroom Materials

http://twist.lib.uiowa.edu/amerind/49materials.html

You'll find a great set of lectures and other materials and resources here. Look at the lecture topics in Figure 11.8 at the time of this writing. More are likely to follow.

University level mainly but definitely some applicability to high school programs.

Main Menu: Native American Indian Resources

http://indy4.fdl.cc.mn.us/~isk/mainmenu.html

There are over 300 web pages to peruse at this wonderfully colorful site including learning and teaching resources, Indian art, traditional stories, legends and myths, language resources, tutorials, and much more.

All levels elementary to advanced.

Maps of Native American Nations, History, Info

http://indy4.fdl.cc.mn.us/~isk/maps/mapmenu.html

If you are looking for a site full of colorful maps of Native North American Nations, you need look no further. This is full of historical, cultural, and political maps of pre- and post-contact periods. There are also interesting scholarly articles, and lots of resources on Canadian Native Nations as well as American.

Lecture Notes

Lecture 1: What's in a Name?
Lecture 2: Race, Ethnicity and American Indians
Lecture 3: Some Comments on Indian Sports Mascots and In Whose Honor?
Lecture 4: Some Concerns and History about Studying Indian People
Lecture 5: Recognizing and Understanding Diversity: Culture Areas, Diffusion, and Change Through Time
Lecture 6: Archaeology's Story of American Indian Origins, Part 1
Lecture 7: Archaeology's Story of American Indian Origins, Part 2
Lecture 8: Culture Change and Reservation Life
Lecture 9: Western Tribal Responses to Colonial Subjugation: Religious Salvation and Ideological Syncretism
Lecture 10: Effects of Assimilation: Northern Cheyenne and Lakota
Lecture 11: Traditional and Contemporary Music
Lecture 12: American Indian Activism and the Resurgence of Tribal Governments
Lecture 13: Native American Concerns About Education

Video Guides

In Search of the Noble Savage
In Whose Honor?
White Shamans and Plastic Medicine Men
Myths and the Moundbuilders
The Ancients of North America
Cannibals!
Contrary Warriors: A Story of the Crow
The People of the Great Plains, Parts 1 & 2
Make Prayers to the Raven
The Navajo Code Talkers
Dances for the New Generation
The Return of the Sacred Pole
Bones of Contention
Lighting the Seventh Fire

Fig. 11.8. Just look at the huge list of practical resources available at this site!

Native American

http://info.pitt.edu/~lmitten/indians.html

There are lots of links to excellent American and Canadian resources here on the topics shown as listed here. We were especially impressed with the wealth of information about individual Native Nations in the U.S. and Canada.

Higher levels mainly.

- Actors, Actresses, Storytellers, Authors, Activists
- General Indian-Oriented Home Pages
- Information on Individual Native Nations
- Languages
- Native Businesses
- Native Media—Organizations, Journals and Newspapers, Radio and Television
- Native Music and Arts Organizations and Individuals—Singers, Drums, Artists, Performers, Celebrities
- Native Organizations and Urban Indian Centers
- Powwows and Festivals
- The Mascot Issue
- Tribal Colleges, Native Studies Programs, and Indian Education

Native Studies—Art, Language and Literature

http://libits.library.ualberta.ca/library_html/subjects/native_studies/art.html

More great links here from the University of Alberta library. A couple of clicks will land you in some very interesting sites (see Fig. 11.9) to help you teach or learn about Native art, languages, and literature.

Higher levels.

Native Studies—Guides to Internet Resources

http://libits.library.ualberta.ca/library_html/subjects/native_studies/guide_native.html

There are a lot of good Canadian resources in this second site (see Fig. 11.10) from the University of Calgary Library showing the history of native groups and their interaction with Europeans from the Royal proclamation of 1763, to modern day treaties. There are links to many other resources as well for information about American and world indigenous peoples.

Higher levels mainly.

Fig. 11.9. View this colorful image for a list of some of the topics at this resource-filled site.
Used by permission

Fig. 11.10. Click on your choice of topics as illustrated in the above screen capture.
Used by permission

PCC Libraries: Native American Studies

www.library.pima.edu/native.htm

You can see the great variety of resources available from the list of topics below taken from this very good site. Click on your particular areas of interest, and follow the links to historical and geographical information, maps, organizations, articles, art and literature resources, and much more.

Higher levels mainly.

General Information

- Native American sites on various subjects, including maps, official tribal sites
- Site searchable by subject, geographic regions, or Nations
- Index of Native American Resources on the Internet; including cultural, legal, educational, governmental, and art resources
- Comprehensive general links to all sorts of information about Native Americans

Native Nations, Organizations, Events

- Alphabetic list of resources about various Native Nations
- Alphabetic list of Native organizations
- Links to sites that maintain listings of upcoming powwows

Native Literature Online

- Information about authors, their books, and in some cases, links to full text
- Historical & contemporary full-text articles, poems, books

Educational Resources

- A Guide to Native American Studies Programs in the U.S. and Canada
- A Guide to Financial Aid for NA Students
- Links to colleges, programs, schools, and educational organizations
- National Museum of the American Indian

Listservs

- Discussion group for indigenous peoples
- General information exchange about the indigenous peoples of the world
- Discussion group about Native American literature

Usenet News Groups

- General discussion concerning indigenous peoples worldwide

School Tools—Dene

www.gov.nt.ca/kids/school/school.htm

Here is a great place to visit if you are looking for information about the Dene people of Canada's North. There is also information about the Inuit people (formerly called Eskimos), and about "other" groups such as explorers and missionaries.

Check out the "Animal" and "Plant" sections or read some legends and myths while you are there. Useful elementary to high-school resources.

Spirit of Aboriginal Enterprise

http://strategis.ic.gc.ca/engdoc/sitemap.html

As the site title suggests, this site is provided to assist people in learning about the Aboriginal economy and to help Aboriginal people develop their businesses. You will also find some elementary-level lessons and other resources on some of the links such as the Aboriginal Digital Collections site.

StudyWeb

www.studyweb.com/

It will take a couple of clicks here since we can't send you directly to the Native American resources section. When you get to the Studyweb main page, scroll down to click on "Teaching Resources" then go to "Lesson Plans." There you will find lessons mostly for grades 12 and up and a few for lower levels.

To access the topics below, scroll down the screen on the main page of Studyweb and find "Full Table of Contents" near the bottom of the page. Click on it and then on the letter "N" in the index. (Quit complaining; it's worth the effort.)

The list below from the site indicates available topics at the time of this writing.

- Native American Languages
- Native American Literature
- Native American Religion

- Native Americans, Genealogy
- Native Americans, Social Studies & Culture Index
- Native Americans, Teaching
- Native Mythology

Tribal Websites
www.cradleboard.org/2000/tribal_w.html
This site contains historical, cultural, and linguistic resources for many American Native groups and tribes.
Higher levels mainly.

GEOGRAPHY

Canada's SchoolNet: Learning Resources: Social Studies: Geography
www.schoolnet.ca/home/e/resources/Links_Result_e.asp?SUBJECT=50&ID=46&SUB=Social+Studies
Here you will find many good links to a lot of different geography resources as outlined below in the list taken from the site. Check out the many Canadian resources, and don't miss the Adventure Online site if you want to add some excitement to any K–12 geography class.

- Adventure Online
- Alfred Wegner Institute for Polar and Marine Research
- Atlapedia Online
- Cam World
- Canadian Geographical Names
- Canadian Heritage Rivers
- City Net
- Class Afloat Live '99 Spring
- Community Access Program
- E-Conflict World Encyclopedia
- Global Heroes
- Government Information Finder Technology
- Institut de la statistique du Quebec
- International Trade Division
- National Atlas on SchoolNet
- Si, Spain

- Sustainable Development on Campus
- The Canadian Arctic—the Travels of Jerry Riley
- The Canadian Communities Atlas
- The Global Change Game
- The Lonely Planet
- The Old Port of Montreal
- The Statistics Canada 1996 Census Results Teacher's Kit
- The World Wide Biome Project
- Welcome to Canada's North!
- Xerox PARC Map Viewer
- Your Window on the Weather

Country Listing
www.odci.gov/cia/publications/factbook/country.html
This listing provided by the CIA gives recent detailed geographic and demographic information about all countries of the world. It's a good place for students to find basic information about different countries for their research papers and projects.

Country Studies: Area Handbook Series
http://lcweb2.loc.gov/frd/cs/cshome.html#toc
This is a continuing series of books prepared by the Federal Research Division of the Library of Congress under the Country Studies/Area Handbook Program sponsored by the Department of the Army. This online series presently contains studies of 100 countries. The following description is taken from the site:

Most books in the series deal with a particular foreign country, describing and analyzing its political, economic, social, and national security systems and institutions, and examining the interrelationships of those systems and the ways they are shaped by cultural factors.

CurriculumWeb
www.curriculumweb.org/ercntr/spiceislands/sivgeog/parc/parclcontent.html
Explore the world with interactive maps, or go to the Heritage Map Museum to see the world from an historical perspective. Take a few seconds to look over the "How to use these lessons" page and move on down to the maps and lessons.
Elementary to high school levels.

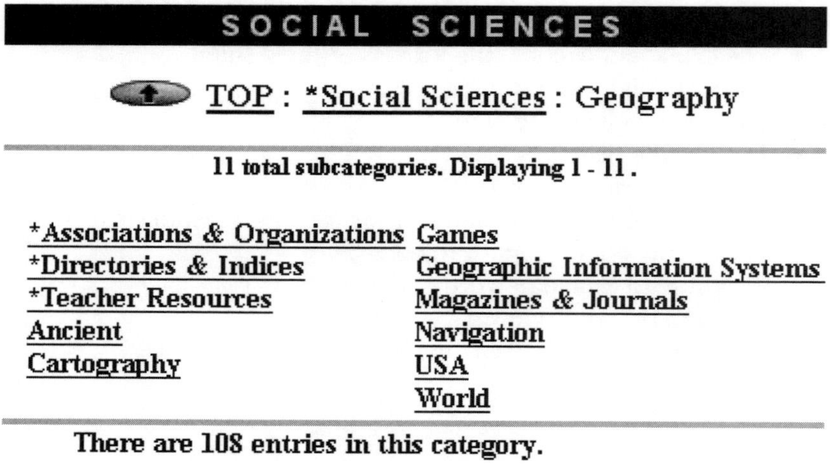
SOCIAL SCIENCES
TOP : *Social Sciences : Geography
11 total subcategories. Displaying 1 - 11.
*Associations & Organizations
*Directories & Indices
*Teacher Resources
Ancient
Cartography
Games
Geographic Information Systems
Magazines & Journals
Navigation
USA
World
There are 108 entries in this category.

Fig. 11.11. This shows some of the many available topics in the geography section.
Copyright © Education World. Used by permission

Education World®—Geography
http://db.education-world.com/perl/browse?cat_id=1812
You will find many helpful and practical resources for teaching here (see Fig. 11.11) including games, quizzes, interactive maps of watersheds throughout the U.S., and a whole lot more. For other teachers' resources you can use the next link too.
K–12 level.

Education World®—Geography: Teacher Resources
http://db.education-world.com/perl/browse?cat_id=4051
This site takes you directly to the teachers' resources page of Education World. Here you will find lesson plans, online projects, games and more.
K–12 level.
This site contains 39 entries in this category.

Free Education: Geography
www.free-ed.net/fr08/fr0805.htm
You will find some good advanced level resources here, but don't give up if a few of the links don't work, as the site is still being developed. Try the Introduction to Physical Geography resources from Okanagan

University College for a really excellent online course. At the main site click on "Physical Geography" and then on the introductory course section.

Geographia Homepage
www.geographia.com/
This interesting and colorful site gives you lots of country information on various regions of the world in a travel guide format. Click on the "destinations" in the frame at the left or the main page or scroll down to peruse the current features.

Geography Education @ nationalgeographic.com
www.nationalgeographic.com/resources/ngo/education/ideas.html
Who are better equipped to bring geography to life than the people at National Geographic? They have produced some very interesting lessons for all school levels (see Fig. 11.12).

Getty Thesaurus of Geographic Names
http://shiva.pub.getty.edu/tgn_browser/
Locate just about any place on earth including geographic features such as mountains, lakes, and rivers with this easy-to-use thesaurus. You will also find variations on spellings of place names.

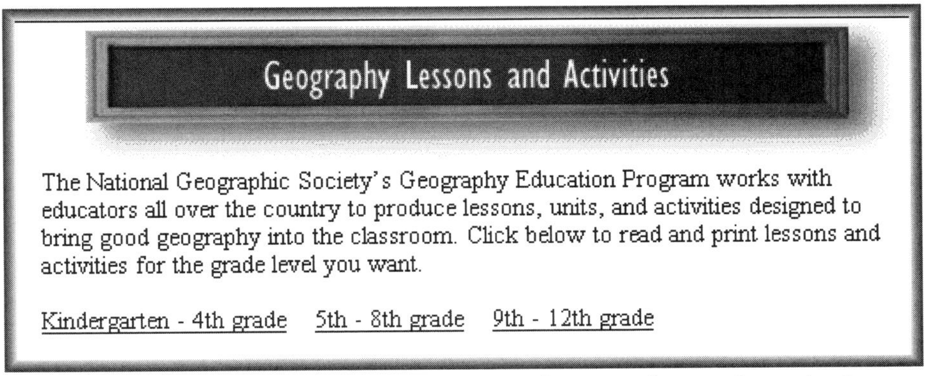

Geography Lessons and Activities

The National Geographic Society's Geography Education Program works with educators all over the country to produce lessons, units, and activities designed to bring good geography into the classroom. Click below to read and print lessons and activities for the grade level you want.

Kindergarten - 4th grade   5th - 8th grade   9th - 12th grade

Fig. 11.12. Click on the appropriate grade level for your class as shown in the image.

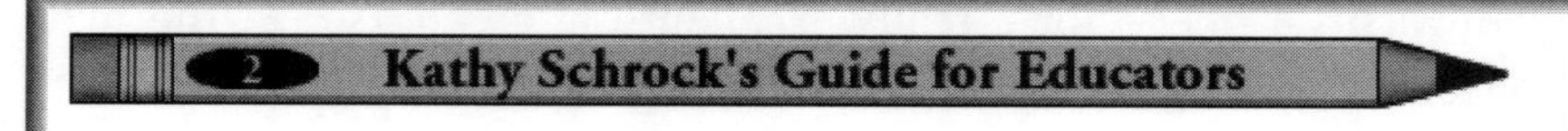

World Geography, Languages, and Regional Information

- Current World Information
- Regions of the World & Foreign Languages
- World Geography and Cartography

Fig. 11.13. The illustration shows the easy to access topics at the site. Follow the links to lesson plans and many more resources.

Kathy Schrock's Guide for Educators—World and Regional Information
http://discoveryschool.com/schrockguide/world.html
There are only a few links here (see Fig. 11.13) but they lead to some interesting places for students doing geography projects. Some of the sites have conventional information and maps while others show more unusual features of different regions of the world. You will find links that lead you to current facts, flags, national anthems and even the license plates from around the world. Great for the added touches that make geography come to life.
All levels.

Lesson Stop—Geography
www.youthline-usa.com/lessonstop/socialstudies.html#geography
Scroll down to the middle of the page to find the links shown in Figure 11.14 and follow them to lots and lots of K–12 lessons on many different topics.

Geography

1. Academy - Florida Geographic Alliance Lesson Plans (K-12)
2. Geography Lesson Ideas (K-12)
3. Geography Lessons (K-12)
4. GeoNet Game (4-12)
5. Introduction to Geography - Learning the Compass (4-6)
6. Mapping Activities (K-12)
7. National Geographic Society Lessons and Activities w/Assessments (K-12)
8. What do maps show? (5-8)

Fig. 11.14. Choose your topics and grade level as shown in the image.

Let's Go Around the World

www.ccph.com/

Here is a bright and cheerful looking site (see Fig. 11.15) where you can take elementary students for a look at some great photographs, children's art, and lesson plans. For a fee, you can also get your class involved in The Amazon River Elementary School project along with over 140 other classrooms in the US and Canada.

Fig. 11.15. Check out the sample topics as shown above in one of the site's colorful illustrations.

Make a map/The National Atlas of Canada
http://atlas.gc.ca/

In this Canadian Government site, you can select the information that you wish to see displayed on a map of Canada or its regions. At the main site click on the English or French version and then choose the National Atlas, teachers resources, or try the online quiz.

StudyWeb
www.studyweb.com/

When you get to the main page of this resource-rich site, click on the "Geography" section near the top of the page to access the many maps and themes or scroll down to find the Geography Site of the Month. A couple of clicks more will get you to some great lessons and other geography resources.
Mostly grades 5 and up.

Below are topics listed at the site:

- Interactive Maps
- Land & Ocean
- Mailing Lists
- Natural & Human-Made Disasters

Units URLS
http://oeonline.oeonline.com/~gvp/units/

There are some interesting commercial programs and lessons near the top of the page, but you can ignore them if you are on a tight budget. The good free resources are a bit down the page in a section titled "Country Rep." If you are planning a field trip to a foreign land you and the students may want to brush up on foreign language skills. African studies can be enhanced with a few words of Swahili to impress the students. Check out the United Nations site. Did you know they proudly display an ivory statue made from eight elephant tusks that was a gift from China in 1974? How the world changes! Click on the "General Assembly" section to find outlines of the many worthwhile UN activities. (See Fig. 11.16)
All levels.

Foreign Languages for Travelers
Virtual Tourist Pre-Home Page
United States Information Service
The Online Intelligence Project
The Embassy Page
Resources
Information on Africa
UNITED NATIONS ON-LINE TOUR
The Alive! Global Network
My Virtual Reference Desk - My Weather Sites
Weather Center
International Newspapers Online
Ecola's Newsstand: Get Links EZ
CNN - World News
Welcome To Pathfinder
My Virtual Reference Desk - My Weather Sites
International newspapers
Country Profiles Menu
UNICEF Home Page
United Nations Headquarters Homepage
The World Factbook 1995
Internet Resources--Countries
City.Net World Map
MapQuest FreeConnect! Service
THE WEB OF CULTURE
Afrikaners
The Alive! Global Network
Africanet
Afrikaans words and phrases
Main Street South Africa

Fig. 11.16. As the image shows, you can find links to important international agencies plus current news and information. The World Factbook link is old but you can use it to find the latest edition.
Used by permission

Xpeditions @ nationalgeographic.com
www.nationalgeographic.com/xpeditions/main.html

This is another excellent site (see Fig. 11.17) from the National Geographic Society, with nearly 600 maps, along with many other resources for learning or teaching geography. For activities and lesson ideas for all levels, check out the Family Xpeditions section.

Educators will want to check out the National Geographic homepage for educators at:
www.hanksville.org/NAresources/indices/NAknowledge.html
www.nationalgeographic.com/education

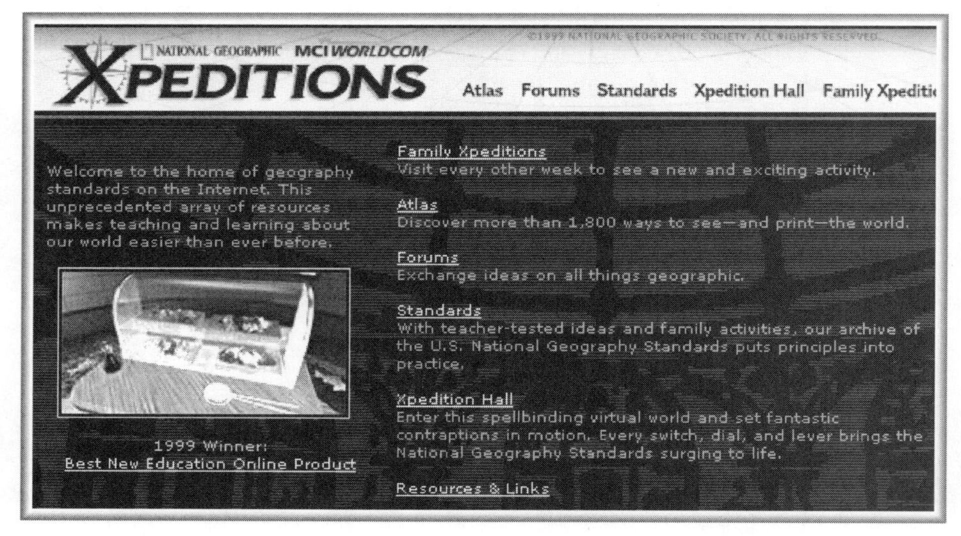

Fig. 11.17. Once you get to the page shown here, click on the "Family Xpeditions" or "Resources and Links" sections for many great lessons and ideas. *© 2000 National Geographic Society. All rights reserved. Used by permission*

GOVERNMENT

Canadian Social Trends

www.statcan.ca/english/kits/social.htm

Here is a good place for students of Canadian government to determine how demography affects decision making. The following description is taken from the site:

One of Statistics Canada's most popular periodicals, Canadian Social Trends transforms data from more than 50 national surveys into practical yet detailed information your students can use in a variety of research projects and assignments.

CIA World Factbook 1999

www.odci.gov/cia/publications/factbook/

Here you can spy on the CIA by seeing how they define and classify the nations and governments of the world. You knew, of course, that Afghanistan had a "transitional government," but were you absolutely sure that Bosnia was an "emerging democracy" or that Liechtenstein was a "hereditary constitutional monarchy"? You'll find detailed statistical information about every country in the world at this site (see Fig. 11.18).

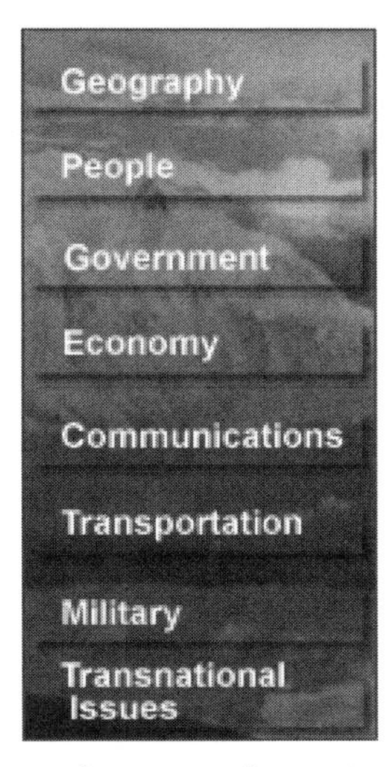

Fig. 11.18. Click on your area of interest shown in the image for quick access to world facts.

Government of Canada Primary Internet Site

http://canada.gc.ca/main_e.html

All you need to know about Canadian government structure and services is here.

Government of Canada Primary Internet Site (Canada Site) is an Internet access point through which Internet users around the world can obtain information about Canada, particularly the Government of Canada and its programs and services. Great for Canadian studies at all levels.

Intergovernmental On-Line Information Centre

www.intergov.gc.ca/

Besides the excellent Canadian Government resources, a nice surprise here is the Nations of the World section. This site links you to official and non-official sites of countries around the world.

Access Your Government :

- Canadian Municipalities
- Government of Canada
- Nations of the World
- Provinces & Territories
- Universities & Colleges

Learning Page of the Library of Congress: Lesson Ideas
http://lcweb2.loc.gov/ammem/ndlpedu/lesson.html

Lessons on American Government past and present. Examine such issues as continuity and change in the governing of the United States. Lessons for grades 4–12.

Lesson Ideas offer strategies and lesson plans developed by education professionals to help integrate primary sources, especially those in American Memory, into the classroom.

United Nations CyberSchoolBus
www.un.org/Pubs/CyberSchoolBus/

Find lessons, get involved in worthwhile school projects, learn about global trends, or easily compare country information. (See Fig. 11.19).

Fig. 11.19. The illustration shows the many resources available at the colorful CyberSchoolBus site.
Copyright © 1999 United Nations. Used by permission

- U.S. Government
- International Governments
- Museums
- Archives
- World History
- U.S. History
- 20th Century History
- Special Topics

Fig. 11.20. Follow the easy links to many interesting and timesaving resources.
© 1997 Vassar College. Used by permission

Vassar's CoolSchool/Go to Class!!
www.coolschool.edu/gosoc.htm

A very complete listing of American and International Government resources (see Fig. 11.20) including some unusual links to such things as the inaugural addresses of every American president from George Washington to Bill Clinton. Read what Abraham Lincoln really said about the abolition of slavery. Search the archives for historical documents including records, newspapers, maps, and drawings.

Welcome to the White House
www.whitehouse.gov/

Go directly to the source for government information and services, or even write the new president a letter to congratulate him on his early successes or to complain about high taxes. The White House for Kids section will be useful for elementary school teachers and students.

- Commonly Requested Federal Services
- Interactive Citizens' Handbook
- Site News
- The Briefing Room
- The President & Vice President
- The Virtual Library
- What's New
- White House for Kids
- White House Help Desk
- White House History and Tours

HISTORY

Canada's SchoolNet: Learning Resources: Social Studies: History
www.schoolnet.ca/home/e/resources/Links_Result_e.asp?SUBJECT=47&ID=46&SUB=Social+Studies

From Ancient History to Twentieth Century World History, and Canadian History, you will find a wide range of interesting topics and sites which make History come alive. There are mostly Canadian resources but there are many American and international resources as well. Look around a bit for some excellent lesson plans, historic photographic collections, multimedia presentations, and other resources which will enhance learning in any classroom.

Education World®—History
http://db.education-world.com/perl/browse?cat_id=1333

There are a remarkable number and variety of resources here (see Fig. 11.21) for studies of ancient and modern civilizations. Besides the excellent teachers' resources, you will find many other conventional and unusual resources such as a History of First Nations, History of Women, Calendars and Their History, and so much more. Lesson plans K–12.

Free-Ed History
www.free-ed.net/fr09/fr0903.htm

Free-Ed provides courses and tutorials for advanced-level learners, but high school teachers and students will find some of the resources and lessons useful. Topics include American, European, and world histories.

Courses and Tutorials

- World History 1101
- Lectures on 20th Century Europe
- Lectures on Modern European Intellectual History

Course Outlines, Lecture Notes, Quizzes, Etc.

- A Student's Guide to the Study of History

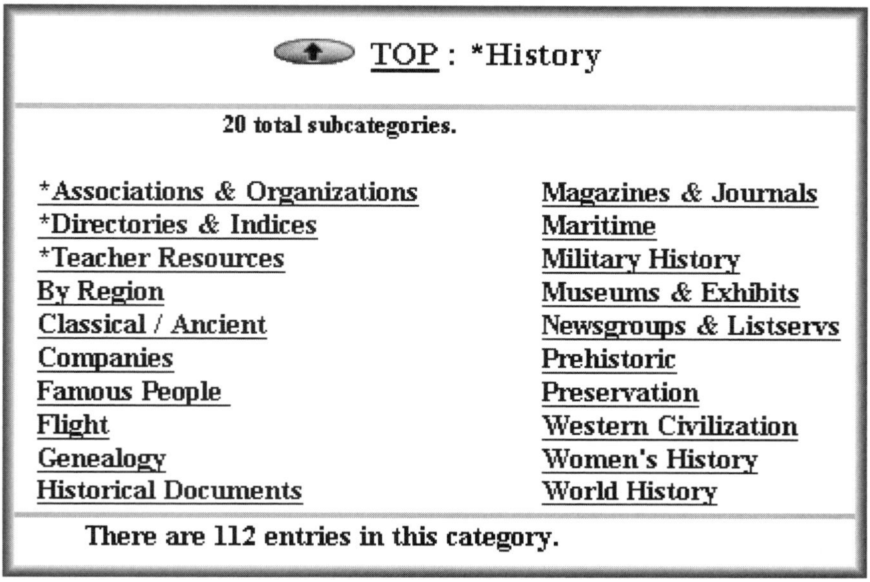
TOP : *History
20 total subcategories.
*Associations & Organizations
*Directories & Indices
*Teacher Resources
By Region
Classical / Ancient
Companies
Famous People
Flight
Genealogy
Historical Documents
Magazines & Journals
Maritime
Military History
Museums & Exhibits
Newsgroups & Listservs
Prehistoric
Preservation
Western Civilization
Women's History
World History
There are 112 entries in this category.

Fig. 11.21. Click on "Teacher Resources" as shown in the image, or go directly to some of the other great sites.
Copyright © Education World. Used by permission

Helpful Study Materials

- The History Channel
- History Channel Traveler
- B.C. to A.D. Timeline
- Style Guide for the Preparation of Footnotes and Bibliographies
- Seriously Whimsical, or Whimsically Serious, Suggestions on Writing History Research Papers

Advanced Placement (AP) Study Room

Advanced Placement (AP) course outlines and study guides can be aids to setting your study goals and keeping yourself on track.

- AP European History
- AP U.S. History
- AP Studies at free-ed.net

Timely News and Events

E-Zines: Original online magazines or online versions of print magazine.

- America's Civil War
- British Heritage

- Canadian Journal of History
- The Historical Gazette
- History Today
- Medieval Life
- Old News

Hammurabi Title Page

http://members.xoom.com/PMartin/hammurabicodeoflaw.htm

Compare laws and customs of modern civilizations to the codes of the priest-king Hammurabi who lived nearly 4,000 yeas ago (see Fig. 11.22). What *should* be done about a wife who neglects her duties and belittles her husband?

Lessons and ideas for grades 4-8 with applications for higher levels. Lots of fun.

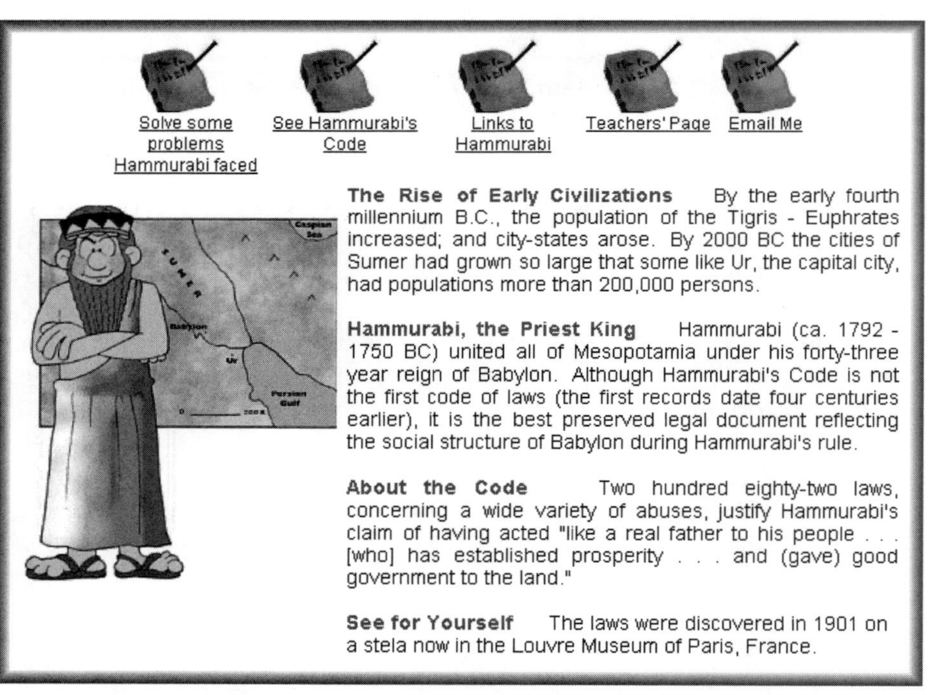

Fig. 11.22. Click on the teacher's page as shown here or have your class debate solutions to the problems faced by Hammurabi.

Copyright 1998 Phillip Martin. Used by permission

K–12 Lessons Plans

http://teams.lacoe.edu/documentation/places/lessons.html#social

Look through the lessons in the areas shown below for American and World History resources, or check out the many other resources in such sites as "Japan Lessons," "Searching for China," or any of the many others areas for lesson plans, ideas, and projects at K–12 levels. You will also find many online activities such as quizzes and games to spice up your classes.

Center for Civic Education Lesson Plans

- Designed to help social studies teachers educate their Civics students about the foundations of democracy and the content of the U.S. Constitution and Bill of Rights.

Dear Mrs. Roosevelt Lesson Plans

- Lesson plans to accompany the Dear Mrs. Roosevelt Home Page.

Encarta Social Science Lesson Plans

- Lessons and student activities for K–12 educators.

Kathy Schrock's Guide for Educators—History and Social Studies

http://discoveryschool.com/schrockguide/history.html

Like all the sites from the Discovery School Channel, this one has excellent links to lessons and resources as outlined in the list below. You will find such topics as Africans in America, a Civil War site, and even accounts of the building of the Alaska Highway. In the world section, you will discover resources and lessons on everything from Napoleon's conquests and defeats to Vietnam War sites.

K–12 levels.

- American History Sites
- General History and Social Studies Sites
- World and Ancient History Sites
- American Memory Collection from the Library of Congress
- Castles on the Web
- FDR Cartoon Collection
- Great Chicago Fire and Web of Memories
- Lower East Side Tenement Museum
- Middle Ages

U.S. History

1. Abraham Lincoln Primary Activities (K-5)
2. Black History (4-12)
3. Civil War Gazette (6-12)
4. Colonial America and Children's Literature (4-12)
5. Crossroads - A K-16 American History Curriculum (K-16)
6. A Curriculum of U.S. Labor History (9-12)
7. The History Channel Classroom Guides (K-12)
8. In Search of the Oregon Trail (PBS) (6-12)
9. John Muir Day Study Guide (K-12)
10. Lessons about Benjamin Franklin (4-8)
11. Living History Museum (3-8)
12. National Archives Learning Curve (6-12)
13. National Archives Primary Sources and Activities for the Classroom (6-8)
14. New Deal Lessons (6-12)
15. Teaching *The Crucible* (9-12)
16. Using the Multimedia Tools of the Internet for Teaching History in K-12 Schools (K-12)

Fig. 11.23. Easily choose your topic and grade level at Lesson Stop as shown in the illustration.

Lesson Stop—Social Studies—U.S. History

www.youthline-usa.com/lessonstop/socialstudies.html#ushistory

Here is a wonderful selection of U.S. History resources and lessons (see Fig. 11.23). Travel along the Oregon Trail with the pioneers or view the issues from the Native American perspective. Follow the many links to guide you through the paths of Black History, and do not miss the Crossroads K–16 American History curriculum for hundreds of lesson plans and ideas.

K–university level.

Lesson Stop—Social Studies—World History

www.youthline-usa.com/lessonstop/socialstudies.html#worldhistory

Like the site above, this one (see Fig. 11.24) is rich in resources, this time on World History and ancient civilizations. There are great lessons at all levels on a very wide array of topics from Aztecs to Egyptians, including lessons and resources for teaching and learning about European, Asian, and African civilizations. Check out also the link to using the multimedia tools of the Internet for teaching history in K–12 schools.

K–12 and up.

World History

1. Ancient History Lesson Plans, Units, and Activities (K-12)
2. Mr. Donn's World History Lesson Plans (K-12)
3. NOVA Online - Pyramids--The Inside Story (K-12)
4. Using the Multimedia Tools of the Internet for Teaching History in K-12 Schools (K-12)

Fig. 11.24. Follow the links to lessons and resources at all levels.

Pinchbeck—History

www.bjpinchbeck.com/framehistory.htm

BJ Pinchbeck, the young lad who put together this site (with his dad's help), really did his homework once again. The sites listed below (see Fig. 11.25), and many others not shown, are absolutely loaded with lessons and resources on just about any historic topic you can imagine, and maybe some you can't.

All levels.

History

The History Net -- A wonderful site to find good information on World/American history
Hyper History Online -- A terrific site with history timelines...they keep expanding this site
Exploring Ancient World Culture -- This is the kind of site you can get lost in...give it a try
Byzantine and Medieval Studies -- An unbelievable collection of sites...a must see!!
Renassiance History on the Web -- Excellent source for finding information on the Renassiance
Labyrinth -- A tremendous site for Medieval studies...from the University of Georgetown...Great!!
Ancient Egypt - A History of Art and Culture -- Very nicely written information on ancient Egypt...very interesting
Perseus Project -- An unbelievable site about Roman and Greek history... fun to roam this one.
Ancient Greek (Hellenic) Sites on the WWW -- Every Greek site you can think of...Fantastic!!

Fig. 11.25. Check out the annotated list of resources shown here for some excellent lessons and ideas.

- 20th Century History (Modern)
- American History
- Ancient/Medieval/Middle Civilizations
- Africa
- Asian History
- Canadian History
- Caribbean Islands History
- Central American History
- Celtic History
- European History
- Middle East History
- Oceania History
- South American History
- World History
- *WAR!*
- General History Discussion Groups

Fig. 11.26. Direct students to the menu shown for research projects and online learning at StudyWeb.

StudyWeb

www.studyweb.com/

Once on the main StudyWeb site you will have to scroll down a bit to find the "History" section, where you will be rewarded with the many resources listed in Figure 11.26. Each site is again loaded with information and many lessons for use at most academic levels.
Mainly levels 6–12+.

The WWW-VL History Index

http://history.cc.ukans.edu/history/VL/index.html

This site has so many excellent resources, it is difficult to begin to describe them. Take a look at the extensive list of topics and resources in the image in Figure 11.27. Select specific countries for historical information or go directly to the teacher's resources section for lessons and ideas.
Mostly higher level resources.

US History Frameworks Schedule

http://people.ne.mediaone.net/nikos/2000us.htm

Witness the Salem Witch Trials or heed the call to arms to fight in the Revolutionary War. You may find a couple of dead links here, but don't let that discourage you from using the excellent resources that are still live. We particularly liked "US History Links 2 and 3."
Mostly advanced level resources.

Consult the WWW-VL Central Catalogue
Use the WWW-VL Search Facility

Research: Methods and Materials
Finding Aids: Bibliography - Guides - Indexes - Libraries - Archives - Manuscripts - Museums - Booksellers **Materials:** Electronic Texts - Historical Journals - Data Bases - General Reference Works - On-Line Images - Maps for Historians **Methods and Auxiliary Disciplines:** - Methodologies - Archaeology - Demography - Genealogy - Language - Timelines **Instruction:** Instructional Resources - Distance Education - Employment - Grants - Information Quality **Network Information:** Net Guide - Search Engines - Software **Scholarly Exchange:** - Scholarly Societies and Associations - Centers and Institutes - On-Line Discussion Lists

By Countries and Regions
Africa: African Studies - Algeria - Djibouti - Egypt - Libya - Morocco - Somalia - South Africa - Sudan - Tunisia **Europe:** Austria - Belgium - Bosnia - Bulgaria - Croatia - Denmark - Estonia - Finland - France - Germany - Greece - Iceland - Ireland - Italy - Luxembourg - Netherlands - Norway - Poland - Portugal - Romania - Russia - Scotland - Slovakia - Spain - Sweden - Switzerland - United Kingdom - Wales **Near East:** Armenia - Bahrain - Comoros Iran - Iraq - Israel - Jordan - Kuwait - Lebanon - Mauretania - Oman - Palestine - Qatar - Saudi_Arabia - Syria - Turkey - Tunisia - United Arab Emirates - Yemen

Countries Continued
Middle East: Central Asia - India **East Asia:** East Asia Studies China - Japan - Tibet **Oceania:** Australia - Brunei - New_Zealand - Pacific Islands **Americas:** - Argentina - Bolivia - Brazil - Canada - Chile Cuba - Ecuador - Peru - United States

Eras and Epochs:
General Prehistory - Celtic Europe - Ancient Near East - Ancient Egypt - Ancient Greece - Ancient Rome - Medieval Europe - Modern Europe

Historical Topics:
Architecture - Art - Climatology - Costume - Holocaust - Indigenous Peoples - Islam - Labor History - Maritime History - Military History - Science and Medicine - Slavery - Urban History - Women's History

Additional Information
About This Network
To Send Comments and Suggestions

Fig. 11.27. This image shows the wide range of topics from which to select at the VL History Index.
© 1999 The University of Kansas. Used by permission

Vassar's CoolSchool/Go to Class!!

www.coolschool.edu/gosoc.htm#world

Lots of choices for historical topics as outlined in Figures 11.28–11.30. Stroll through the Seven Wonders of the World, view the Civil War photograph collection, or follow the progress of the Great War on an interactive timeline.

Advanced levels.

World History

Country Studies

Exploring Ancient World Cultures

Discovery of a Palaeolithic Painted Cave at Vallon--Pont-d` Arc

Pyramids: The Inside Story

The Seven Wonders of the Ancient World

Chronology of Russian History

20th Century History

World War I Document Archive

The Great War

WWII Resources

Remembering the Holocaust

Cybrary of the Holocaust

Survivors of the Shoah

The U-Boat War 1939-1945

The Wars for Viet Nam

Revelations from the Russian Archives

U.S. History

American Memory from the Library of Congress

Black Facts

1492: An Ongoing Voyage

African-American History, Selections from the Library of Congress

Colonial America Resources

PBS: Thomas Jefferson

Democracy in America, by Alexis de Tocqueville

Civil War Photograph Collection

The American Civil War

Photographic Collection, USA 1939-1945

Fig. 11.28–11.29–11.30. The above images show the easy availability of the many topics and fascinating resources for use in history classrooms throughout the world.

WebChron

http://campus.northpark.edu/history/WebChron/

Our reaction to this site was an unqualified "Wow" when we found it. Here you will find a series of hyperlinked chronologies and historical articles on World History, Regional Chronologies, and Cross-cultural Chronologies complete with dates, events, and accompanying graphics. It's a nice way to involve your students in history. Applicable for elementary to high school levels.

Welcome to K–12WORLD!

www.k-12world.net:80/cy_curr_res.cfm

At the main site you will have to scroll down to the Social Studies section then click on "History" where you will find around 100 history resource links on a variety of topics. You can easily access the many lesson plans and ideas classified by grade-level appropriateness. Some of the topics you may be interested in include American Memory, Current Events, and Around the World Countries, plus there are maps and atlases, critical thinking strategies, and a lot more.
K–12 levels.

PHILOSOPHY

Classroom Philosophy Resources

www.epistemelinks.com/Main/MainClas.asp

This is a good place for students of philosophy to find what is going on in online courses, or to find tips and guidelines for writing the term paper that's due next week. Teachers can compare lecture notes or search other resources such as an online encyclopedia, dictionaries or glossaries for clarification of philosophical concepts, or review the works of the great philosophers. You'll likely find many ideas or materials from other courses that you can adapt and include in your own lessons.

Greek Philosophy Archive

http://graduate.gradsch.uga.edu/archive/Greek.html

Pontificate with Plato, argue with Aristotle, or challenge and cheer other classical philosophers of Ancient Greece (and even a Roman thrown in for good measure) as you peruse their dialogues and writings.

- Dialogues of Plato
- Works of Aristotle
- Visit our Sculpture Garden: enjoy images of Ancient Greek sculpture, ceramics, mosaics and architecture.
- Works by other Greek Philosophers
- Meditations of Marcus Aurelius

Miniature Library of Philosophy

www.marxists.org/reference/subject/philosophy/index.htm

Here is a very good place to catch up on your reading if your interests lie in philosophical writings. Read the works of such greats as Bacon, Comte, Hegel, Kierkegaard, Nietzsche, and many others.

Noesis Philosophical Research On-line

http://noesis.evansville.edu/bin/topic.cgi

This site, which recently merged with the Hippias site (including their Guide to Philosophy on the Internet), is an excellent research site for philosophy resources, allowing searches by topic or authors, as well as having links to journals, reference works, weekly reports, and to other Websites which focus on philosophy.

Philosophical Dictionary

http://people.delphi.com/gkemerling/dy/index.htm

This dictionary may take a few moments to get used to because of its slightly unusual format, but it is certainly worth the small effort. Once you have clicked on a letter of the alphabet, it will take you to a list of words or philosophers whose names begin with the letter. You just click on the person or term and you will find a wealth of information and links to sites on your topic. It also includes links to a Study Guide, History, Timeline, Philosophers, Logic, and other Philosophy pages.

Philosophy

http://english-www.hss.cmu.edu/philosophy/

This is the philosophy section of a site called "The English Server" which was created ten years ago by graduate students at Carnegie Mellon University to facilitate humanities research. It is a truly excellent site containing a multitude of philosophical references from early classic to modern. Besides the Canonical texts and links to scholarly philosophical organizations, you will find collections in critical theory, history, and eighteenth century studies, which also address philosophical interests and concerns.

Philosophy 12 Home Page

www3.bc.sympatico.ca/mwebster/phil/

Here is an excellent resource for the high school teacher attempting to involve students in the pursuit of wisdom through philosophy. Read the biographies and philosophical works of such thinkers as Confucius, Descartes, Kant, Marx, Rousseau, and many others.

Content:

- Philosophies of Western, East Indian, Chinese, Native, and Latin American thinkers.

Topics:
- The nature of consciousness, knowledge, and right action.

StudyWeb
www.studyweb.com/

At the main StudyWeb page, click on the "Philosophy " section to get to the wide range of topics outlined here. This site is frequently updated so there will likely be even more resources on successive visits. Some resources can be used as early as grade 9, but most are for grades 12 and up, naturally.

Aesthetics and Creativity
- Articles, Problem Solving, Research . . .

Biographies of Philosophers
- Abelard, Aquinas, Camus, Kant, Ockham, Plato . . .

Critical Thinking
- Forums, Journals, Organizations . . .

Ethics
- Explanations, Journals, Research . . .

Existentialism
- Explanations, Introductions, Journals, Survey . . .

Formal Logic
- Articles, Human Problem Solving, Meanings, Overviews . . .

Organizations & Associations
- Aesthetics, Ethics, Objectivism, Societies, Visitor's Centers . . .

Philosophy Schools
- Courses, Degree Information, General Information, Programs, Requirements . . .

Writings of Great Philosophers
- The Sermons of Augustine, The Thoughts and Theories of George Berkeley, The Analects of Confucius . . .

The Internet Encyclopedia of Philosophy

www.utm.edu/research/iep/

Here is a great research tool to help you find all you need to know about most philosophy topics and philosophers. Click on the appropriate letter of the alphabet, or on the Timeline, Philosophy Text Collection, or Key Words.

Advanced levels.

Undergraduate Philosophical Writing

http://eee.uci.edu/programs/philoswr/

This is a realistic and practical site for students who wish to learn the fundamentals of philosophical writing.

It contains a short version for quick tips and reference and a long version with more details for students who are really serious about learning. Learn about mastering a topic, about the things not to do when you write, and how to get help with your writing at universities.

"No matter how long you spend polishing a paper, even the most elegant expression of ignorance is only worth an F."

PSYCHOLOGY

Education World®—Psychology

http://db.education-world.com/perl/browse?cat_id=2254

You will find some very innovative lessons here (see Fig. 11.31) to implement in Psychology classes, plus some sample quizzes and ideas such as variations on the classical conditioning experiment.

Grades 4–12.

Class Reunion Grades 9-12

Classical Conditioning Experiment Grades 11-12

Conflict Management Techniques Grades 4-12

Functional Relationships/Dynamics of Relationships Grades 9-12

Research Design Explained a resource for teaching the research design or research methods course.

Room 304 Psychology sites for high school teachers and students to use as a resource.

The Psychology of Color and Sound (Middle,other) posted by Kristen Kohli

misc01.txt Psychology - Classical Conditioning Experiment (11-12)

Fig. 11.31. Try the sites shown here from Education World for many great lessons and ideas.
Copyright © Education World. Used by permission

Encyclopedia of Psychology
www.psychology.org/links/Resources/
Look here to find advanced-level resources for research, news, and legal issues related to Psychology, as well as statistics, study tips, and advice for writing psychology papers.

Psychology of Religion Pages
www.psywww.com/psyrelig/index.htm
This site is more for research than for lesson plans, but teachers may also find some good resources to implement in high school classes, such as condensed biographies of some prominent psychologists, and historical and cultural perspectives on religion and society from a psychological perspective.
Advanced levels.

PsychREF: Resources in Psychology on the Internet
http://maple.lemoyne.edu/~hevern/index2.html

Click on "General Resources" at the left of the page, and then on "General Megalists of Psychology-related Links" in order to access a variety of Psychology-related topics. There are also links to many other resources for psychologists and educators. Besides the research functions, students of psychology will find resources for writing psychology papers using APA style.
Advanced levels.

PsychWeb Resources
www.psywww.com/

At this site you are in for a treat. You will find the following resources: APA-style resources, self-quizzes, brochures, mind tools (thinking and performance enhancing resources), psychological journals, online books, information on careers in Psychology, scholarly resources, and more.

School Psychology Resources Online
www.schoolpsychology.net/

School Psychology Resources for Psychologists, Parents and Educators. Research learning disabilities, ADHD, functional behavioral assessment, autism, adolescence, parenting, psychological assessment, special education, mental retardation, mental health, and more.

Social Psychology Links by Subtopic
www.socialpsychology.org/social.htm

This site contains a very impressive collection of links to a huge list of topics. Links related to prejudice and discrimination, gender, culture, social influence, interpersonal relations, group behavior, aggression, and more.
Advanced levels.

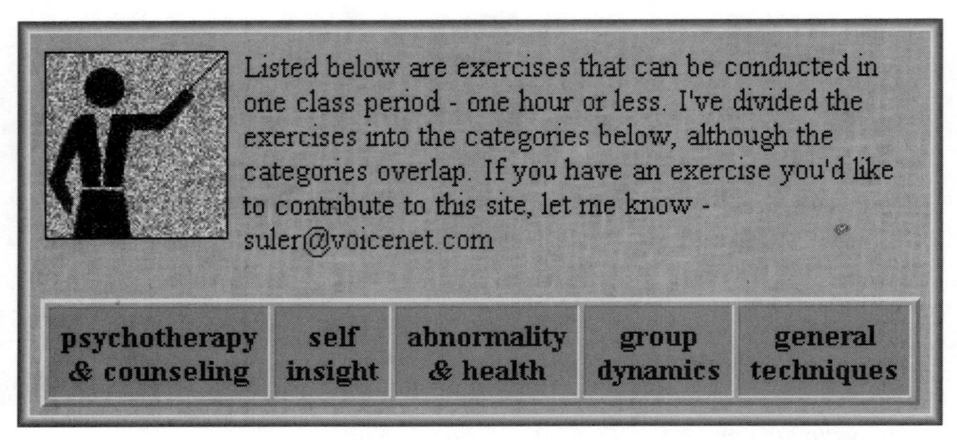

Fig. 11.32. Use the links shown in the image above to access the pre-made lesson plans.
© Suler, J. Used by permission

Teaching Clinical Psychology—In-Class Exercises
www.rider.edu/users/suler/inclassex.html

This site (see Fig. 11.32) is an excellent place to go for nearly 50 well-developed psychology lessons.

Appropriate to high school and up, but some are adaptable for lower levels as well.

SOCIOLOGY

Education World®—Sociology
http://db.education-world.com/perl/browse?cat_id=2255

This site contains a variety of interesting lessons and activities for teaching and learning about sociological issues such as cultural diversity, discrimination, family, religious tolerance, society and aging, civil rights, propaganda, and more.

Methods, Statistics and the Research Paper
www.trinity.edu/~mkearl/methods.html#rp

Here is a good place to direct students to get information on how to write a great research paper, including methodology, statistics, and style.

Sociological Subject Areas
www.pscw.uva.nl/sociosite/TOPICS/index.html

This site contains a list of all kinds of sociology topics from activism and aging to poverty, religion, and men's and women's issues. Many more topics primarily for advanced levels. Schoolteachers are cautioned to note the sexuality topics at this site before directing high school students here for research or study, as some topics may not be appropriate for all levels.

Sociology Cafe Teaching Resources
www.sociologycafe.com/

Here is a good place to start for links to teaching resources from such sites as the American Sociological Association, University of Alberta, Canada, and others. You will find resources for teaching Statistics as well as online texts, an interactive glossary and much more.

Note: To get rid of the annoying pop-up window at the main site, just click on the x at the right corner of the pop-up box.

Sociology Dictionary
www.iversonsoftware.com/sociology/index.htm

This site sometimes takes a while to load, but contains a very good, alphabetically indexed dictionary of sociology terms.

Sociology of Knowledge
www.cudenver.edu/~mryder/itc_data/soc_knowledge.html

Here is a mixed bag of articles, books, links, and other resources of interest to higher level students and researchers.

Sociology Resources
www.lib.lsu.edu/soc/sociology/sociology.html

This site from Louisiana State University offers great resources both from within their institution and from many other sites. Scroll down the page for the complete list of resources on such topics as crime, gay and lesbian studies, teenage street gangs, treatment modalities, welfare reform, women's studies, and more.

Advanced level resources.

StudyWeb

www.studyweb.com/

On the main StudyWeb page, click on the "Social Studies" section, and once there, click on "Sociology" to get to some excellent resources (see Fig. 11.33). Grades 9–12 plus advanced level resources, links, and lessons.

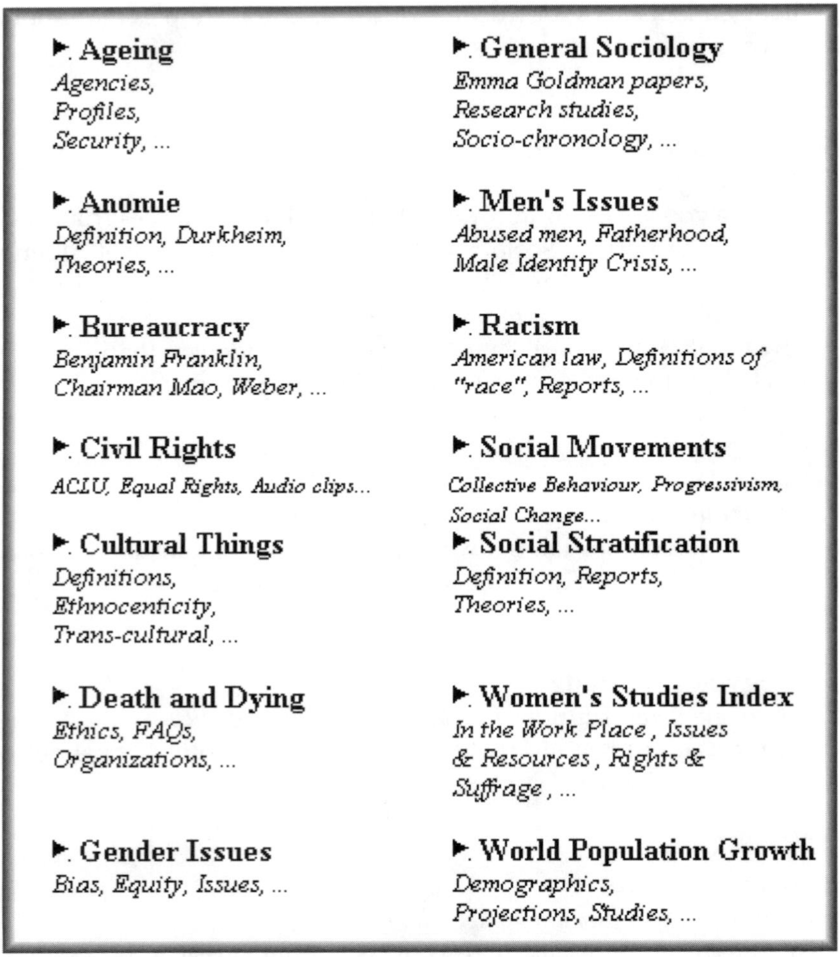

Ageing
Agencies, Profiles, Security, ...

Anomie
Definition, Durkheim, Theories, ...

Bureaucracy
Benjamin Franklin, Chairman Mao, Weber, ...

Civil Rights
ACLU, Equal Rights, Audio clips...

Cultural Things
Definitions, Ethnocenticity, Trans-cultural, ...

Death and Dying
Ethics, FAQs, Organizations, ...

Gender Issues
Bias, Equity, Issues, ...

General Sociology
Emma Goldman papers, Research studies, Socio-chronology, ...

Men's Issues
Abused men, Fatherhood, Male Identity Crisis, ...

Racism
American law, Definitions of "race", Reports, ...

Social Movements
Collective Behaviour, Progressivism, Social Change...

Social Stratification
Definition, Reports, Theories, ...

Women's Studies Index
In the Work Place , Issues & Resources , Rights & Suffrage , ...

World Population Growth
Demographics, Projections, Studies, ...

Fig. 11.33. Each topic shown in the image contains many resources and lessons classified by grade level.

Index

G

H

I

J

K

L

T

U

V

W

X

Y

Z

About the Authors

MARVIN DIGEORGIO was a teacher for over twenty years in public schools and community colleges primarily in western Canada. Until recently, he was an instructor in adult basic education and ESL at Arctic and Aurora Colleges in Canada's northwest territories. He also spent two years teaching English at I.A.I.N. University in Sumatra, Indonesia. Marvin was involved for many years delivering Instructional Skills workshops to new instructors at the community college level and has previously written a manual for training correctional officers. He now writes educational guides on a full-time basis.

SYLVIA LESAGE is a computer expert with a B.T.S. Reseaux degree in Computer Networking from A.F.P.A. de CAEN University in France. She is largely responsible for the layout and presentation elements of this guide. Sylvia speaks six languages fluently. Her vast and varied work experience throughout Europe includes a position as a library services manager for the French government. She has lived in New York, Egypt, Israel, and Mexico, and is currently visiting in Canada.

CD-ROM INSTRUCTIONS

1. Insert the CD-ROM into your CD-drive.
2. Go to your "Start" menu and select the "run" feature.
3. Type in the letter for your CD-drive (normally "D" followed by a colon, (D:), then click "OK."
4. Click on the "INDEX" icon. (This will launch your Internet Explorer or Netscape offline to read the index.)
5. Click on the academic section you want.
6. Click on the specific bookmark of the site you want. (This will signal your Internet Explorer or Netscape browser to go online and take you directly to the selected site on the Internet.)

Please read "How to Use This CD-ROM" for the complete instruction guide.